TWO GERMANIES

MIRROR OF AN AGE

Two Germanies

PETER LUST

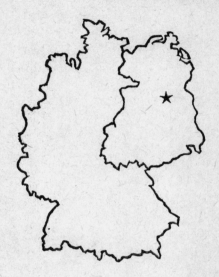

HARVEST HOUSE, MONTREAL

TWO GERMANIES: MIRROR OF AN AGE

First Harvest House edition — June 1966
Printed by Court House Printing Reg'd, Montreal.

Stand on free soil among a people free . . . .

GOETHE

If I think of Germany in the dead of night,
My erstwhile rest is put to flight.

HEINE

CANADIANA

CONTENTS

THE EAST

FOREWORD

During the past century world reaction toward Germany has been based on emotionalism and fear. Most NATO country citizens think of West Germany as a democracy and of East Germany as a dictatorship bent on conquest. In "East block" countries public opinion sees East Germany as a democracy and West Germany as a neo-Nazi state ready once again to send its legions eastward. What is the truth?

I had the unique experience of visiting both countries as a guest of both governments. I divided my time equally between the two states and was given complete freedom to go where I wanted and to interview whom I pleased. After I had completed my trip I disagreed with both Western and Eastern public opinion. Both states are still basically German with all the good and bad qualities associated with the German character. Each government fears the allegedly aggressive intent of the other and these fears are real; the two parts of a once united country have started a cold war of their own. Had the American Civil War never erupted into military action, had the South's secession been allowed to become permanent, conditions on the North American continent would be similar to those of present-day Germany.

We should judge the two states not with emotion, but with reason. The existence of more than one state on German soil is not unusual. German unity has been a brief experience by historical standards. During the seventy-five years of its existence, a unified Germany started two world wars. The German people have contributed much to man's progress — whenever the country was divided. The golden age of German letters, the era of her greatest philosophers and composers reigned before 1870, the year of German unification. German unity has indeed been an unhappy experience for mankind. This is the reason why the two German states may not be reunited in our lifetime.

This book tries to contribute some understanding of the true conditions existing in both German states today.

AN INVITATION TO BOTH GERMANIES

Two world wars have made Germany the centre of world attention. The public at large agrees that the Nazi state bears sole responsibility for World War II and its 50 million dead. But a number of historians deny the sole German war guilt of World War I. The Imperial Government of the Kaiser cannot be charged with the entire responsibility for that holocaust; but little doubt remains that at least a major share of the guilt rests with Berlin.

Since the turn of the century German governments have paid careful attention to Germans living abroad. A sizeable share of the Kaiser's budget was spent on keeping contact with the *Auslandsdeutsche*. An Imperial law made certain that no German lost his citizenship while living abroad. Naturalization procedures of foreign courts were not recognized by German law.

The Imperial Government registered but limited success. Most Americans and Canadians of German descent identified themselves with the allied cause. "The treason of our fellow-Germans living abroad helped to ensure our defeat in the great war"; this statement by Erich von Ludendorf, made in 1922, reflected the point of view of the German nationalists at home. It became the basis for Adolf Hitler's major effort to organize the *Auslandsdeutsche* during the first six years of Nazi rule. The Nazi organization *Verein für das Deutschtum im Ausland* (Federation for Germans Abroad) became one of the Nazi hierarchy's most powerful organizations. Hitler succeeded where the Kaiser had failed. The major part of Germans abroad were organized into powerful "fifth columns". In most European countries about to be overrun by the Nazi war machine they often seized power days before the Wehrmacht's arrival. In the United States and Canada Hitler's success remained limited. But from the Nazi viewpoint the achievements were nevertheless impressive.

After 1945 contact between Germans abroad and at home became less frequent. For a time, they were practically non-existent. During the early 1950's the Federal Republic began paying attention to Germans abroad. From the political standpoint it was a sensitive field, for the world remembered Hitler's ties with the *Auslandsdeutsche* only too well. Direct official contacts remained limited. The tasks left open by the collapse of the Federation for Germans Abroad were slowly taken over by cultural organizations, travel bureaus, and —eventually— by the West German foreign service. The old country exercised its influence with tact and care. But the attempts to direct thought and influence Germans abroad could once again be felt — and the people feeling them most strongly were United States and Canadian German-language journalists.

Contact between the ethnic press and the West German Government was handled by the press attachés of the German consulates. No political pressure was used — formally. The ethnic press operated under the jurisdiction of the country in which it was published. Foreign influence could rarely be pinpointed — it existed beneath the surface of everyday events. A sudden telephone call by a local German-owned business firm to a recalcitrant German-language newspaper: "Sorry, we may have to cancel our ad — you printed an editorial criticizing certain actions of the Bonn Government; would you please be so kind and retract in a follow-up article? You would? Excellent! In that case, we will of course continue our ad."

The *Montrealer Nachrichten* is the largest German-language newspaper to appear in the eastern half of Canada. By American standards it is small, but it wields considerable influence among its readers. Because the newspaper had steadfastly refused to endorse West German Government policies, it had become a veritable thorn in the side of the Bonn authorities. I had been in the front-line of this editorial war ever since I had joined the paper in 1963.

The *Nachrichten*'s editor-in-chief, mercurial, unpredictable Mario von Brentani, had been brought up in the old German social-democratic tradition. He objected to the proposition advanced by Bonn, that only the Federal Republic had the right to speak for the German people. He was the only German-language editor who had for many years printed news stories from both East and West Germany. He had accepted advertising for the Leipzig Fair, East Germany's largest annual trade exhibition. His editorial policy had caused raised eyebrows in West German Government circles. It started many heated telephone calls from the West German consulate to the *Nachrichten* editorial desk. Business concerns controlled or influenced by the West German Government would dangle lucrative contracts before Brentani's eyes, then abruptly withdraw them. But the *Nachrichten* editorial policy remained unchanged. Reports from both states; refusal to join the fashionable one-sided lament about the Berlin wall; rejection of the Federal Republic's claim of sole German representation.

During all these years I had kept friendly contacts with several West German Government employees. I had many discussions with Wolfgang Scheur, Press Attaché of the West German Consulate in Montreal. Scheur was an unusual German civil servant. As a boy he had so strongly disagreed with Nazi policies, that he had run away from home, crossed the border into Jugoslavia and eventually ended up working in a Palestinian Kibbutz — one of the few non-Jews to enjoy this experience. After 1945 he returned to West Germany and joined the civil service. By West German standards he was a liberal, a man who shared many of his political views with newspapers like *Der Spiegel*. He disagreed with many of the Federal Government's more conservative ideas. But he endorsed West German non-recognition of East Germany. The fact that my articles described conditions in both countries, irritated him. During my years as a German-language journalist, I had never been approached by members of the East German Government. This was understandable. East Germany maintains no diplomatic or consular staff in Canada. No East German commercial establishment exists in the western hemisphere. I had become reasonably certain that our newspaper was unknown in the German Democratic Republic, the formal name of East Germany. I was therefore greatly surprised when on June 6, 1965 I received a short letter from an East German association calling itself the *Bund Neue Heimat*. Under an East Berlin dateline it contained the following message: "We read your articles with great interest. The *Bund Neue Heimat* would like to invite you for a three-week visit to the GDR. This invitation is issued under the auspices of our Department for Foreign Affairs. You will be notified further."

Four days later my doorbell rang and a clean-cut young man in a sport-jacket and crew-cut introduced himself: "I represent the *Bund Neue Heimat* and have come to bring you your tickets".

"Not quite so fast, young man. I haven't accepted your invitation yet. You understand that our readers might type me pro-GDR, if I accepted?"

"I understand. We won't mind if you combine your visit to our country with a similar visit to the German Federal Republic."

My visitor explained his position at length. He was a native of Leipzig, East Germany's second-largest city. In order to immigrate to Canada he required a West German passport (Canada neither recognizes East German travel documents nor admits their holders). With the assistance of several highly placed East German officials he had "fled" to West Germany where he established residence long enough to qualify for a West German passport. From the Federal Republic he proceeded to Canada where he established contact with his home government. "Don't get me wrong", he explained. "I am no spy. I do not deal in confidential information; I simply do a public relations job for my country. I send reports home about Canadian public opinion. I visit travel bureaus and try to get Canadian tourists to visit East Germany. All this is very complicated — for as you know our country does not officially exist. No, I am not exactly an undercover man. The Mounties might call me a 'borderline case' — just barely this side of legality."

My editor-in-chief was interested. "Go by all means", he advised, "but try to get a West German invitation as well. Otherwise you'd have a limited one-sided report. That might be very bad for circulation! See what you can do."

The shortest distance between two points is a straight line. I called up the West German Press Attaché at the Consulate and told him what had happened. "Do you think I should go? Will the West German Government cooperate with me even though I am going East?"

"You will get no cooperation from my government whatever", he replied. "In fact, I even hesitate to advise them of your plans. Only if you insist will I inquire. As your friend, I will tell you that this is the craziest idea I have heard a German-language newspaperman propose!"

Four days later he called me back. "I am flabbergasted. Bonn did not object; they like the idea. You will go to East Germany with their knowledge. Perhaps there has been a little thaw in our special cold war. There are a few conditions: first, you stay the same length of time in both countries; second, you don't engage in political polemics in either country; third, you report truthfully what you see — let the chips fall where they may. Finally,

you start your trip in the Federal Republic. *Lufthansa* will fly
you over. You travel in style — first class all the way. We'll get you
all the interviews you want. Name them, we'll prepare them. At
the end of your West German trip we'll deliver you to the East
German authorities at Checkpoint Charlie in Berlin. You take it
from there. The East Germans will fly you back home."

I was surprised. "You mean, Wolfgang Scheur, that your West
German Government will actually cooperate with their hated East
German competitors in arranging my trip? This sort of thing has
never happened before!"

"I know it never happened before. It is the first time the two
governments ever worked together in planning a journalist's trip.
It is a good sign. Make the best of it!"

The next two weeks were spent in hurried preparations for a
trip which I felt would be a "first" in several ways. I had been
promised access to the hitherto classified files describing the exact
damage of the great Dresden air raid, documents which not even
British author David Irving * had seen. The East German Government assured me that I could move freely without escort wherever
and whenever I felt like it. I was promised interviews with Walter
Ulbricht and many of his top aides. The West Germans promised
me an interview with chief war crimes prosecutor Erwin Schuele,
whose hidden Nazi past had recently been discovered. I was
promised access to all Nazi war crime files and discussions with the
policy-making members of the Federal Republic's Parliament.
Looking back at the results of my trip, I have to admit that both
governments kept their word.

My trip started July 4, 1965. It ended six weeks later. The
following is the record of my visit to two Germanies.

---

* Author of a best-selling book on the Dresden raid, which was published
in England. See *The Destruction of Dresden*, London, 3rd Ed., 1964.

THE WEST

CHAPTER I

FRANKFURT, WEST GERMANY'S PORT OF ENTRY

I left Montreal International Airport on a hot summer evening. I travelled light — without hat or coat. "You won't need it", my wife had assured me. "Germany is a warm and dry country!"

An icy rainstorm welcomed me on arrival in Frankfurt. The temperature had dropped to a chilly 40 degrees. I learned very soon that the world's weather is changing for the worse! North America's climate is getting warmer — Europe is getting colder. But bad weather barely manages to spoil the impression made by Frankfurt, the first German city seen by our jet-age tourists.

I had last visited the capital of Hesse-Nassau during the drab years of the Great Depression. Even then this city of half a million had somehow maintained its *joie de vivre*. Frankfurt never fully accepted the doctrines of Hitler, an honour the city shares with Hamburg and Stuttgart. The war had damaged it badly. The ancient town centre had been gutted. The Roemer, the huge hall where the emperors of the Holy Roman Empire were crowned, the house where the poet Goethe, Frankfurt's greatest son, was born, and many other historic buildings had been destroyed or damaged. They have all been rebuilt since in their original splendour. Frankfurt also is the home town of the Rothschild family. The old Rothschild house has been repaired — but the family is gone forever. The allied bombers goofed a few times. While managing to destroy most of Frankfurt's historic sights, they failed to place a hit on Nazi Germany's most important war plant, the notorious I.G. Farben whose headquarters were located at Hoechst, a Frankfurt suburb. The undamaged Farben building served the US military authorities as their first headquarters when occupation started in 1945. Between 1945

and 1948, Frankfurt actually was the capital of the American occupation zone. The importance the city gained during these years
has never been completely lost. Frankfurt had been slated to
become the Federal Republic's capital. Because other towns
objected, Bonn was finally selected.

Since Frankfurt is the first stop of most German-bound
tourists, the civic authorities try their best to please the public. The
results are impressive. Neon signs of unusual size illuminate huge
buildings reminiscent of New York. Frankfurt no longer appears to
be a German city. Barring a few side alleys, the cobblestoned
streets are gone. Wide boulevards and modern buildings charac-
terize the town. Sidewalk cafés borrowed from Paris, department stores fashioned after Manhattan's 34th Street, and crowds
reminiscent of American rush-hour traffic. Before the war the Germans had been a nation of cyclists. Today most of them drive
cars. The city's largest department store, Neckermann, is a post-war
creation. It is more efficient and more Americanized than most New
York department stores. Its mail order sales compare to those of
Montgomery Ward or Sears. At first glance Frankfurt appears to be
the most Americanized of all German cities. Later I learned that
Düsseldorf surpasses Frankfurt in this respect.

It took me two days to reevaluate my first impressions. Beneath
its glittering surface Frankfurt has remained German. It contains
more neo-Nazis than Jews — former German Jews who decided to
return to the old country prefer to settle in Berlin or Düsseldorf.
Frankfurt's Jews remain part of its past history — all travel firms
advertise tours through the old Jewish centre. "Yes, we would like
to have our Jews back", explained one of Frankfurt's leading politicians. "Can you help us convince them to come back? We would
even pay them handsomely to return — for reasons of public relations, of course!" When he noticed my expression he hastened to
add: "I did not mean this as an insult — please promise me not
to mention my name in your stories". I promised the local bigwig
that I would keep his name confidential.

It was the first incident of my trip dealing with the complex
relationship between former persecutors and their victims. Similar
incidents kept cropping up at frequent intervals during my West
German trip. Officially West German gentiles and Jews get along
well. Beneath the surface their relations remain strained. The
government has introduced legislation making anti-Semitic
statements a criminal offence. "We can distinguish three types of

Germans", a leader of Frankfurt's small Jewish community confided to me. "Former Nazis — there are not too many left. True friends of our people — their number is still smaller. And finally those who screamed *Heil Hitler* and today treat us with cool courtesy. Some of them even treat us with respect. They shake hands a bit too obviously; they bow too formally; their smiles appear forced. But it makes them feel good to practise democratic tolerance. They usually do it in public so that everybody will admire them for it. Could there ever be another Hitler? Look around you! Just give them a few nuclear bombs and see what will happen!"

In Frankfurt I ran into a group of Soviet visitors attending an international convention. "We are Soviet business men", one explained. "We work on a salary plus commission basis. Yes, there are some businessmen left in our country. Anyway, call us managers for the public welfare." During the past decade communism has started to compromise with the free enterprise system.

US service men still dominate the streets of Frankfurt. It is one of the few German cities where large numbers of American soldiers can be seen. Their relations with the German public are not always good. Of allied personnel I found British soldiers getting along best with the German public. Several nasty incidents involving American soldiers and German civilians have poisoned the atmosphere. Press and television usually ignore such incidents.

"Frankfurt's largest industry is its international commerce. Its second largest is the memory of its great son, Johann Wolfgang Goethe." Although Heinrich Heine's bon mot no longer holds true, Goethe's house of birth is a "must" for all Frankfurt visitors. But it was four weeks later in the East-German town of Weimar, the place where Goethe spent most of his adult life, that I found Heine's statement still valid.

Frankfurt was the first German city I visited. It also was the only place in West Germany where I was able to stroll without escort. The West German Government takes care of its visitors in a most efficient manner. In each town a young man, usually a student, awaits the visitor, takes him to a hotel, sees to it that he gets his meals, and arranges and accompanies him to all interviews. The organization running this show is called *Inter Nationes,* a government-owned travel bureau which specializes in taking care of the physical (and sometimes spiritual) needs of the Federal Republic's guests. Some of the young men and women have achieved an amazing aptitude in the business of shadowing visitors. Whenever I felt the urge to be alone I would send my escort home. More often than not I would spot him later on following me at a respectful distance. "No, I don't do this for political reasons", one of the young students protested, when I cornered him by backtracking two blocks. "We are paid by the hour and mileage. When you send me home I lose income. I hate to lose my pay. So I follow. There is always the chance that you might need me later." I could not help but smile at this rather mercenary argument.

But I did not yet know all this during my stay in Frankfurt. My first *Inter Nationes* guide awaited me at the Bonn airport.

CHAPTER II

BONN, UNIVERSITY TOWN
TURNED CAPITAL

It takes half an hour's flying time to reach Bonn from Frankfurt — my first experience with German planes. West Germany uses old-fashioned propeller craft for domestic runs. Distances are so short that jets would be uneconomical. Propeller planes cover the longest flight distances in less than three hours — it would hardly warrant a multi-million dollar investment to further shorten this flying time. The German national airline *Lufthansa* owns a fleet of reliable planes and boasts that none of them ever crashed. The machines may be safe, but to travel in them is sometimes an unusual experience. They fly at levels between 5,000 and 8,000 feet and rarely fly around bad weather. They hit it head on. During the thirty minutes between Frankfurt and Bonn I suffered more than during the seven-hour jet flight between Montreal and Frankfurt. Most German air travellers seem to treat air sickness as a matter of little concern. Most flights end with a stereotyped announcement over the plane's loudspeaker: "We deeply regret that we encountered such bad weather and could not serve any refreshments. We sincerely hope your next trip will be more pleasant." A smiling *Lufthansa* official told me in Bonn that the airline saves between ten and fifteen million marks in annual food bills thanks to rough weather.

Bonn and Cologne share the same airport, situated halfway between the two cities. A young *Inter Nationes* guide and a black government limousine awaited me. "Your schedule for today is crowded", the young man remarked. "I suggest we check it on our way to town."

The guide, an honour student at Bonn University, was right. The schedule was crowded. One quick interview with Chancellor Erhard or his top aide. A visit to the Presidential Palace.

"President Luebke is absent. You will meet the Chief of Protocol
there; but the visit should prove interesting. The rest of the
morning is reserved for the Foreign Office. You spend the afternoon
at the Press Office. Your luncheon and dinner appointments are
set. After dinner..."

"Is there a chance that I can at least see the Beethoven
monument and some of the sights?"

"We might try that immediately after lunch. You haven't much
time. After all, Bonn is the capital!"

It is Europe's most unusual capital. Bonn never wanted to become the seat of the West German Government. It still gives the impression of a sleepy semi-medieval university town of great beauty.
Its geographic and social centre is the great market place. The
town square resembles that of Brussels.

The Presidential Palace, the Chancellery and the Ministerial
departments are built along avenues utterly unable to cope with
the traffic suddenly thrust upon them. Many elderly residents
resent the intrusion their ancient city suffers. A definite barrier
exists between old and new citizens. The most interesting aspect
of Germany's new capital is the apparent absence of the military
services. Berlin's daily life was determined by its officer corps and
army personnel, not only during the days of the Kaiser and the
Nazis but even during the years of the Weimar Republic. From this
point of view Bonn appears to be non-German. Government
business is carried on by civilians and — considering Germany's
past history — with a minimum of pomp. The Army influence
remains and is strongly entrenched behind the scenes, but tourists
rarely see it.

I found my Frankfurt impressions reconfirmed. I had left Germany in 1933. Since then there has been not only a political but a
complete social change. Factory workers drive small automobiles,
own refrigerators and TV's and dress, look and act like members
of the middle class. Germany's aristocracy has all but disappeared,
and the profiteers of the *Wirtschaftswunder*, the economic miracle,
cannot be distinguished from their less fortunate fellow citizens
except by their huge Mercedes cars; the workers usually stick to the
Volkswagen.

Bonn's Presidential Palace is comparatively simple compared to
structures like the White House or Ottawa's Rideau Hall. Its staff
wear the cutaway and striped pants associated with their trade.
My first few appointments with Secretaries and Chiefs of Protocol

were rather nondescript. They could have happened in any other country. It took me one full day to line up my first vitally important appointment. West Germany's foreign policy is determined by the Chancellor and the Foreign Minister. Its day-to-day business is conducted by legation counsellors guided by instructions from the cabinet. The *Legationsrat* handling German relations with the USA and Canada is a diminutive Bavarian named Alois Schlegl. I had never heard his name before and am certain very few members of the North American public are familiar with it. But Schlegl is in complete charge of the day-to-day contacts between Washington and Ottawa on the one hand, and Bonn on the other.

Schlegl is a hand-picked follower of Foreign Minister Gerhard Schroeder, a man who has identified himself with the United States-West German alliance. Schroeder and Erhard favour this alliance policy as against Konrad Adenauer's theory of a strongly united Europe under the guidance of France and Germany. Schlegl — formerly German ambassador to the African State of Mali — had never been a Nazi and has no sympathy for German nationalism. He is one of the members of the West German diplomatic corps whose name has never been mentioned by the East German Government or other critics of Bonn. I asked Schlegl two questions: "Is there any chance of a final Berlin settlement?" and "Does West Germany agree with the present United States policy in Viet Nam?" He answered as I had expected he would. "There is always a chance of a final Berlin settlement provided East Germany will compromise and accept some of our demands", and "West Germany and the USA are allies. We will endorse United States policy anywhere in the world." During the latter part of my West German trip I found that the Viet Nam war was very unpopular in Germany. But the Bonn Government's line is firmly pro-United States in this respect. I did not hear a single word of anti-United States criticism on government level, with one notable exception: "Don't quote me", I was advised by a Press Department official. "How can I possibly agree with air attacks against unarmed civilians? I worked for the government during the Spanish Civil War. Remember Guernica? Remember the helpless Ethiopians being burned by Mussolini's planes? I saw horrible things on the Russian front. I don't like what goes on in Viet Nam; but please promise you won't quote me." I promised.

After lunch my young guide kept his word and took me to the **Beethoven house. The great composer could not possibly have**

remembered the building, for his parents moved to another Bonn
residence when he was only four years old. But to most Germans
Beethoven's birthplace has become a place of pilgrimage and
worship (no other expression fits). By eighteenth century standards
the Beethovens were a prosperous family. The house is well-built
and comfortable. A great number of memorabilia of Beethoven's
later life were brought here and have changed the character of the
house into a museum. The displays include some unusual items. I
had always thought of Beethoven as a tall, muscular man. Actually
he was short — almost dwarfish; this is borne out by his coat, his
trousers and his walking sticks, kept under glass. Several years
ago a mentally unbalanced East German expellee set fire to the
building. It was partly destroyed — later rebuilt.

Before 1945 Bonn had two major industries: its university and
the sale of Beethoven souvenirs. Today its major industry is government, with Beethoven still running a close second. It is hard to
gain entrance to the Beethoven house. Long lines of waiting
tourists queue up outside. The ancient wooden floors bend under
the weight of thousands of visitors, and special hours have been
set aside to accommodate visiting VIP's and their entourage. Beethoven, whose misanthropy and hatred of crowds was proverbial,
would shudder were he to revisit the place of his birth.

During the evening I managed to escape my friendly *Inter
Nationes* guide. I visited two beauty spots of Bonn no tourist
should miss: the old Godesburg and the nearby Godesberg Spa.

The Godesburg is an ancient thirteenth century castle overlooking the river Rhine. Its ground floor has been remodelled into
a magnificent restaurant. The ancient tower remains unchanged.
The architects handling the remodelling job showed good taste.
A casual visitor feels he has returned to the 13th century. The
breathtaking view of the Rhine is one of Germany's most picturesque sights. — Bad Godesberg is situated on the other side of the
mountain; actually a Bonn suburb, it has become part of the city
itself. Its main hotel, the Rhein-hotel Dreesen, is the place where
Hitler met Chamberlain before the Munich pact was signed. The
Dreesen played a major part in Hitler's rise to power. The infamous
meeting between the Führer and steel magnate Thyssen took place
here. The agreement by which the Ruhr barons financed Hitler's
election campaigns were signed at the Dreesen. The hotel's atmosphere is unusual. Impressive but cold. The halls and the huge
dining terrace next to the Rhine are taken right out of a Wagnerian

operatic scenario. Hitler's preference for this hotel is understandable.

Very late at night I strolled across the almost deserted market place and chatted with an old Bonn burgher, whose views represented those of many old-timers. "What do I think of the government? Hang them all! This used to be a small, quiet town. Look at it now! Nothing but big-shots visiting us. Who pays for all that? I'll give you one good guess! The Kaiser, Weimar, Hitler, Adenauer, Erhard? Whom do I like best? I tell you whom I like best, Beethoven. We haven't had a decent government for the past 85 years. Ever since I can remember things were bad. Back to the good old times? They weren't that good! I wish the government had stayed in Berlin. I sure don't want them here. Is there anything I can do about it? No. So why talk about it?"

The average Bonn citizen resents the sudden importance gained by his home town.

CHAPTER III

WEST GERMANY'S RELATIONS WITH ISRAEL

Very few people outside Germany have ever heard the name of Dr. Hans Schirmer. He is a senior civil servant working in West Germany's Ministry for Foreign Affairs. His position is that of *Vortragender Legationsrat*, Counsellor to the Foreign Minister. Legation counsellors are in charge of specific geographic areas of the foreign service. Dr. Schirmer handles the Federal Republic's relations with all Near-Eastern countries. This includes Israel and the Arab nations. West German recognition of Israel and the subsequent worsening of relations between Bonn and Cairo, officially the work of Chancellor Erhard and Foreign Minister Schroeder was actually engineered by Dr. Schirmer, whose friendship for Israel and the Jewish people is admitted by most members of the Bonn diplomatic corps. — I was therefore much surprised when I learned that Dr. Schirmer had once been a prominent member of the Nazi hierarchy.

During 1964 the East German Government published a *Brown Book*, listing the past sins of all former Nazis working in prominent West German Government jobs. It contained the following remarks about Dr. Schirmer:

The key position of the Foreign Office's Near-East Department is held by a diplomat given his post at the specific orders of Heinrich Himmler's Reich's security office. Hans Schirmer, former SS-*Obersturmführer*, was detailed to the Foreign Office in 1939 as a so-called liaison officer. Later he was transferred to Croatia, a Nazi satellite state during the Second World War, where he acted in his capacity as *Obersturmbannführer* and member of the SS. Hitler decorated Schirmer with the "Knight's Cross", Nazi Germany's highest decoration. — Later Schirmer joined the Ribbentrop office and was detailed to handle propaganda broadcasts to the Arab area, with the intent of preparing the Arabs for eventual conquest.

Since I considered Schirmer the most influential of all Foreign Service employees, I had requested a special interview with him. At first the request had been denied. "Why don't you see Foreign Minister Schroeder instead?" I was asked. "After all, Schroeder is the Minister in charge. Schirmer is only one of his assistants." But I repeated my request. Schroeder's views are known to most journalists. Realizing that Schirmer, though in a subordinate position, was the Near-East Department's key man, I preferred a Schirmer interview to one with the Foreign Minister.

Eventually permission was granted. Time limit: fifteen minutes. When I left the office of West Germany's most enigmatic diplomat, I had stayed more than two hours.

Dr. Hans Schirmer appears to be a friendly elderly gentleman. Having jumped the hurdles surrounding his office, I found the interview easy. During the first few minutes I tried to find out whether Schirmer still harboured traces of Nazi sentiments. The answer to this question is NO. Schirmer considers Israel to be the Near East's most stable nation and feels Hitler's anti-Semitism was by far the worst of his many crimes. During my West German trip I interviewed many former Nazis. None showed as much abhorrence at what had happened as did Dr. Schirmer. Could his strong anti-Nazi sentiments be a cloak hiding his true feelings? To test this possibility I constantly returned with minor questions to the underlying problem: "What do you think of convicted war criminals working for Nasser? Would you like to see Dr. Joseph Mengele extradited from Paraguay? Would you like to have Nasser extradite Dr. Eisele from Egypt? How do you feel about Israel's Jordan river water project? Do you prefer relations with Israel to ties with Egypt?" Some of my questions were deliberately crude, since I employed tactics used by prosecutors cross-examining potentially hostile witnesses. At the end of the interview I concluded: "Either Schirmer is the most unmitigated liar I ever met or else he was speaking the truth". I believe he meant what he said.

After one hour the picture of West Germany's Near-East policy began to take shape. I had never been able to understand why Germany had on the one hand delivered military supplies to Israel, yet had steadfastly refused to recognize her; and why she suddenly changed tactics, broke with Egypt and exchanged ambassadors with Tel-Aviv. The official reason for Bonn's near-break with Egypt had been Walter Ulbricht's Cairo visit.

The Hallstein doctrine, which guides West German diplomacy,

would have made a Bonn-Cairo break mandatory if Nasser had formally recognized East Germany; but this never happened. Bonn could therefore have continued its former cordial relations with Cairo.

West German diplomatic appraisal of Near-East conditions is based on three assumption: First, no matter what they may say, the Arab States will not attack Israel unless they feel they have the military backing of a major power. Second, the only major power which might conceivably endorse an Arab attack against Israel is the Soviet Union. Third, the Soviet Union will not endorse an Arab attack against Israel as long as she is assured of the use of warm-water ports in the area.

Bonn believes Soviet policy to be the continuation of Czarist policy — to ensure access to ports connecting with the Mediterranean. Of all wars fought by Russia most were fought to ensure this right. The hostility between Britain and Czarist Russia during the 19th century was caused by Britain's unwillingness to grant Russia this access. Russia's involvement in the First World War on the allied side was caused by Russia's desire to conquer and hold Constantinople.

"The following developments would ensure Near-Eastern peace", Schirmer explained:

A basic agreement between the USA and the USSR allowing Soviet access to a warm-water port. This concession would have to be the price for peace in the area. Our policy is based on the assumption that no war in the Near East is possible without the active cooperation of the USSR and that no Russian help will be given the Arabs as long as the possibility of a USA-USSR settlement exists. The United States is strongly committed in the Far East. She will not seek additional areas of friction. United States-Soviet relations in this part of the world have been comparatively peaceful during the past few years. This is why we finally established diplomatic relations with Israel. We wanted to do it for many years as a simple act of moral restitution. Our government wishes to make up for the Nazi regime's guilt. For many years the Near-East situation had been too precarious to risk this step. In 1965 we finally took the chance.

Dr. Schirmer added: "Please do not quote me. Please do not print what I said. It is confidential information."

For the first time in my life as a journalist I decided to break a confidence and print what I had learned as privileged information. It was a difficult decision to make. But I felt that I had discovered a vital diplomatic secret which, if shared by the public at large, might help to create more stable conditions in that part of the world. I hope Dr. Schirmer will eventually forgive my indiscretion.

Many people have complained about the great number of former Nazis who kept their positions in the Federal Republic. The Foreign Office is said to contain a particularly large percentage of former Hitlerites. Factually some of the complaints are true. But most of the conclusions are subject to qualification.

The German diplomatic service has always been the most "civil service" minded branch of the government. Before 1918 German diplomats served the Kaiser to the point of aping their ruler's tactlessness and ill manners. In 1918 the same men worked for the Weimar Republic, serving their new rulers grudgingly but faithfully. In 1933 the Foreign Service abruptly switched its allegiance to Hitler. And in 1945 they once again became democrats. Many former Nazi diplomats circumvented denazification proceedings by exchanging affidavits of alleged past pro-democratic sentiments. These affidavits — nicknamed *Persilscheine,* after one of Germany's better known detergents, helped most "old party comrades" to remain in the Federal Republic's newly established diplomatic service. But these ex-Nazis did less actual damage than most anti-Nazi authors and journalists would ascribe to them. As true civil servants they experienced a complete and automatic change of heart with the change-over from Nazism to democracy. Opportunists? Of course! They were craftsmen of the diplomatic trade anxious to serve whatever government happened to be in charge. I do not doubt that should West Germany suddenly go communist (a one to ten million shot), the men of the Foreign Service would immediately become dogmatic communists and work for the new regime. *

---

* Some writers have taken a darker view of the German civil service. Franz L. Neumann, for example, referred to the bureaucracy of the Weimar period in the following acerbic terms:

"The German Civil Service Union with about 1,000,000 members called itself 'politically neutral'. Political neutrality in Germany invariably meant opposition to democracy and support of nationalist forces who claimed to be the sole defenders of national interests."

And: "It is to the German civil service that Nazism owed most." See *German Democracy 1950*, International Conciliation Pamphlet No. 461, Carnegie Endowment for International Peace, New York, 1950, pp. 263 and 264.

Dr. Hans Schirmer is primarily a German diplomat. The outside world will consider it a paradox that a former SS-officer is in charge of West German relations with Israel. Bonn accepts it as a completely logical development. Who am I to sit in judgment?

CHAPTER IV

THE SOCIAL DEMOCRATS

I had used my first two days in Bonn to visit government offices. My third day was set aside for the opposition party, the Social Democrats, headed by West Berlin's Mayor Willy Brandt. Third deputy leader Stephan Thomas, one of the party's political wheelhorses, received me at SPD headquarters. Little known outside Germany, Thomas is one of the men responsible for Social Democratic political strategy. His official title is Chief of the party's "Eastern section".

Thomas is a tall, athletic sexagenarian who speaks excellent English; he is one of the few German parliamentarians who speaks it without the trace of a foreign accent. "Understandable", he explained. "In a sense I am an American college professor; during my sabbatical leave, or whenever I have the time, I fly to the USA and lecture at Hunter College and other American universities."

My first question dealt with Social Democratic chances of ever winning a parliamentary majority.

"Eventually we will win", was Thomas' comment. "If we do, I propose to form a grand alliance with the present government party, the Christian Democrats. Our country is engaged in a cold war with the East. The Berlin situation is intolerable. We live in dangerous times for our country and for the entire West; to protect ourselves we require emergency legislation. A grand coalition with the Christian Democrats is essential."

My second question was: "You are heading the Social Democrats' Section East. Does this mean that you will negotiate with the Warsaw Pact nations or the GDR?" "Not at all", he answered, the Communists of East Germany are our mortal enemies. They have to be fought. I am not popular in East Berlin. In fact, should I venture into that city I would certainly be arrested. The German

Democratic Republic? There is no such thing. Let us call it the
Soviet occupation zone!"

Thomas' opinions are typical of the Social Democratic right
wing. This century-old Marxist party has completely changed
its original aims and convictions. Today's SPD (the German
abbreviation for Social Democratic Party) shows stronger opposition
to compromise in the cold war than do most centre parties. Thomas
is known to be strongly anti-Soviet and anti-GDR. But other SPD
leaders like Erler and Brandt share his basic feelings. The SPD as
a party has changed every single plank of its original platform.
During a party meeting held three years ago at Bad Godesberg the
SPD dropped all revolutionary aims and became strongly nationalist. Today's SPD is a nationalistic middle-of-the-road group. A
North American analogy which doesn't exactly fit but which helps
to make its transformations intelligible is the record of the
Republican party of the USA founded during the 1850's on
Jeffersonian and anti-slavery tenets. When in July 1964 the GOP's
southern delegates helped to nominate Barry Goldwater at San
Francisco's Cow Palace with rebel yells, the Republicans had
become perhaps the world's only other political group emulating
the complete turnabout exhibited by West Germany's Social Democrats.   This change of heart of Germany's socialists has had far-
reaching effects in Europe as a whole. Socialism as such began in
Germany with Karl Marx and Friedrich Engels; after a turbulent
early history August Bebel and Wilhelm Liebknecht founded the
precursor of the present-day Social Democratic Party in 1869. Its
original aims were the expropriation of the larger landowners and
industrialists and the introduction of practical socialism. During
the 1870's and 1880's the SPD's aims became more radical. When
two SPD sympathizers (Hoedel and Nobiling) attempted to assassi-
nate Emperor Wilhelm I (May 11 and June 2, 1878), special laws
were promulgated against the Party: these laws remained on the
statute books until 1900 — but they proved ineffective. During
the election of 1877, 493,288 people had voted the SPD ticket. In
1890 the Party received 1,427,300 votes; in 1907 it had grown to
3,259,000 — they received 29 per cent of all votes.

Germany's SPD battled against an entrenched military feudal-
ism. This explains why the German Social Democrats became more
radical than the socialists of Western Europe. The British Labour
Party developed in a constitutional monarchy with a post-feudal
tradition of two centuries. Hence British Labour never borrowed

many of the more revolutionary Marxist concepts. In Germany, the social conditions of the late 19th century led toward the radicalization of the SPD.

The Social Democrats remained revolutionary and uncompromising until the outbreak of the First World War. In August 1914 they experienced their first change of heart. Less than three months before the outbreak of war they had been a pacifist group. After war was declared most SPD deputies voted for war credits. One notable exception was Karl Liebknecht, a young member and leader of the Party's left wing. After the revolution of 1918 the SPD became Germany's governing party. Almost immediately they split into two opposing groups. The leftist group, led by Karl Liebknecht and Rosa Luxemburg, wanted to follow the original party program. The SPD's conservative wing, led by Friedrich Ebert, suggested a more pragmatic approach. The conservatives' views prevailed. Karl Liebknecht and Rosa Luxemburg were murdered January 15, 1919. The Weimar Constitution was primarily the work of the Party's conservative wing. Its aims were noble; but its proportional voting system and its politicking to which the German electorate was completely unaccustomed bore the seeds of its own destruction. The SPD moved more to the right. Finally it started to lose ground to the newly emerging Nazi Party. The Nazis had borrowed a number of the SPD's original theories and combined them with illogical hatred for minority groups and fanatic nationalism; the program became attractive to a nation which had never accepted the fact that it had lost the war. But nationalism and anti-Semitism alone would not have sky-rocketed the Nazi Party. The deciding factor of Nazi success lay in the use of socialist slogans originally propagated by August Bebel and slightly altered to 20th century conditions — "Freedom and bread" — "Break the chain of the bankers' rule", etc. The SPD's dissident leftist group had formed the Spartacus Federation which later changed into the Communist Party. During the early 1930's the battle for German power was primarily fought between the Nazis (a nationalist party with socialist slogans) and the Communists (a socialist party with international aims). The SPD stood helplessly between the two opposing groups. Its decision of 1918 had emasculated its voters' appeal. The Communists almost won the battle. Two facts finally defeated them: the Nazis had more money (heavy industry financed them); and the Communists lost a small but decisive percentage of their votes to the Social Democrats. In many vital disputes the

SPD preferred the Nazis to the Communists. The left was split and
the right was united. The degeneration of the SPD, which had
begun in 1914 and culminated in 1918 opened the way to Hitler's
rule.

The experiences of these turbulent years are the cause of
today's SPD's chameleon-like behaviour. The SPD leadership feels
that the German electorate needs a healthy dose of nationalism.
The hard line taken by the SPD in the Berlin crisis toward East-
West relations and future German reunification is the direct result
of the Party's belief: "We lost to the Nazis because our platform
was not nationalistic; the Hitler movement succeeded in charging
the loss of World War I to our account. The German people wish
a reunification of the two German States; the expellee groups are
fighting for a chance to return to their native soil; unless our
party platform takes these facts into consideration we may be
wiped out at election time." These are the considerations which
have changed the revolutionary SPD into a conservative party.
From the point of view of their own political future and fortunes
some of these considerations appear valid. The SPD has never
been able to form a national government in the Federal Republic.
But as a group they actually grew. In the Bundestag the SPD
steadily increased its number of deputies. In 1949 it elected 131;
in 1953, 151; in 1957, 169 members of the SPD entered parliament.
In 1961, 190 made the grade.,

The ruling Adenauer-Erhard party cannot match this record.
In 1953 it elected 243 deputies. In 1957 it counted 270. In 1961 it
dropped to 242. The end result was that the SPD was on its way
up; the CDU (Adenauer-Erhard party) went downhill. But the
Social Democrats never quite made it. Adenauer and his successor
Erhard were able to hold onto the reigns of government by forming a coalition with the Federal Republic's smallest party, the
Free Democrats. Proportionately, the SPD has actually grown into
West Germany's largest party. In 1961, 36.2 per cent of the electorate
voted for them, compared to 35.8 per cent for the Christian Democratic Union (CDU). But the CDU made up for this deficiency
with the help of its Bavarian offshoot, the CSU, which cornered
9.6 per cent of all votes.

West Germany operates under one of the world's most complicated election systems. Each voter votes twice. Once he votes for the
deputy of his constituency; this vote is counted in the same
manner as American or British votes. Whoever receives the most

votes is elected; all others are out. The second vote is given to a specific political party and is added up under the proportional voting system. West Germany has learned from the Weimar fiasco when a host of splinter groups rendered the Reichstag impotent. To get representatives into the Bundestag under the proportional system, a party must corner at least 5 per cent of all votes cast. Any group receiving less than 5 per cent of the total vote is wiped out. Through this complicated system of electoral checks and balances, the Federal Republic of today has but four parties: the CDU which governs with the Christian Social Union (CSU), its Bavarian offshoot, the FDP (Free Democrats), and the SPD — actually the largest of the four. But the manoeuvres of the other three have sent it into a permanent political wilderness. Its appeal to nationalism helped to make it the numerically largest group, but not large enough to obtain a workable parliamentary majority.

Its nationalism has led it into unusual political situations. It has gained support among the expellee organizations, groups in which neo-Nazis hold vital positions of leadership. One of the presiding officers of the Sudeten-German organization is Wenzel Jaksch, an old SPD member. During the early 1930's Jaksch had been an active Sudeten-German socialist. When the Nazis took over his homeland in the fall of 1938, Jaksch fled to London where he shared exile with Ex-President Benes and other SPD leaders. After the war he returned to Germany and started organizing Sudeten-German expellee groups. I read most of his speeches. It is almost inconceivable that they were made by an alleged social democrat. Jacksch demands the return of the Sudetenland to West Germany. He lauds folkloristic festivals of the youth movement. (While folk dances and folk songs are popular almost everywhere nowadays they always have a distinct meaning for Sudeten Germans and are usually equated with Nazism.) Not all Sudeten organizations are nationalistic. The North American group under the leadership of Henry Weisbach of Toronto, one of Jaksch's former SPD colleagues and close collaborators during the late 1930's, has followed the line of the original SPD. They are at odds with the nationalistic aims of the Bonn group. But the West German branch heads the entire network of expellee organizations and Jaksch and his followers toe the post-Godesberg SPD line; they control the home organization. West Germany's controversial Minister of Transport, Hans-Christian Seebohm, has echoed the

sentiments of the Jaksch group. It is difficult to see any difference between SPD policy and those of the centre parties. Perhaps the SPD veers slightly to the right of the CDU.

Whenever I met SPD politicians I asked the same question: "What are your policies? How do they differ from those of the CDU and Free Democrats?" It is interesting to note that more than half of the questioned men could not come up with a simple answer. Mayor Willy Brandt gave me the most concise reply. He said: "The CDU has a Christian-democratic basis and Federalistic leanings; the SPD has a socialist basis and a centralized conception. The foreign policies of the two parties are almost identical."

After two days of travel in the Federal Republic I concluded that the SPD and the CDU were as similar as Southern Democrats and conservative Republicans. When I ended my entire trip I knew I had been wrong. The similarity was even greater than that of the two competing American groups — tweedle-dum and tweedle-dee.

CHAPTER V

BONN'S PRESS OFFICE

Nazi Germany had been the world's first country to elevate its chief propagandist to ministerial status. All governments maintain press offices and information centres; all try to create favourable public images of themselves and often use crude or dishonest methods to further their aims. No country used propaganda more crudely than the Hitler regime.

The German people remembered this lesson. When the Federal Republic was first established no provisions were made for an information centre; this state of affairs changed within a year. The West German Press Office was established. During the next five years it shared Bonn's most hectic rate of expansion. But it never reached ministerial status. Today's Press Office commands one of the town's main thoroughfares. Its size, appearance and staff exceed that of the Ministry for Foreign Affairs. It is harder to enter the Federal Press building than almost any other government offices. The head of the Press Office is a senior civil servant who might for all practical purposes just as well bear the title of "Minister of Information". The most prominent of all Press chiefs has been Felix von Eckhardt who since 1952 has been in charge of the department most of the time. In his book *The New Germany and the Old Nazis* (Random House, New York, 1961) German-born author T.H. Tetens accuses Eckhardt of having been one of Nazidom's most popular writers of film scripts. Eckhardt's deputy, Dr. Werner Krueger, is described as a graduate of Dr. Goebbels' Propaganda Ministry.

The charges are factually correct but the author's conclusions are open to interpretation. Von Eckhardt had been a young script writer and — following the trend of the times — did write for Nazi-sponsored film companies. Dr. Krueger had been an employee of

the Propaganda Ministry's press section. But neither man had
ever been an active Nazi Party member or shown any open Nazi
sympathies. The Press Office, like the Ministry for Foreign Affairs,
is run by a group of coldly efficient civil servants who serve
whatever government rules Germany at a particular time. Presently
Bonn's Press Office is trying to influence world opinion along the
lines of the policies advocated by Professor Hallstein: only West
Germany has the right to speak for the entire German people; the
Ulbricht government is an illegal government kept in office
against the will of its people by Soviet bayonets; the ultimate goal
of Federal foreign policy is the eventual reunification of both
German states and the correction of the Oder-Neisse line (the
GDR's present eastern border) in favour of a future united Germany.

Officially the Press Office is subordinate to the Federal Chancellery and for many years had been supervised by Secretary of
State Dr. Hans Globke, West Germany's most controversial senior
official. Globke had been a faithful servant of Nazi dogma and had
authored the commentary to Hitler's infamous anti-Semitic
Nuremberg laws. The presence of this man in West Germany's top
civil service position caused considerable controversy. The resentment was fully justified. One cannot explain Globke's actions as
those of a political opportunist; they were the actions of a convinced
hard-core Nazi. His inclusion in the Adenauer government as
Secretary of State was scandalous.

Globke was sentenced to life imprisonment in absentia by the
East German Government. Shortly after this trial he left the
political scene. Since his welcome departure the policies guiding
the Press Office have relaxed considerably. The revamped Information Ministry still aims at a unified Germany of the future. But
no outright Nazi influence remains.

Following the example set by the Foreign Ministry the Press
Office is divided into geographic sections. Each department is
headed by a *Referent*. All press relations with the United States
and Canada were handled by E.C. Privat at the time of my visit —
a man crowding retirement age. He received me in a jovial mood
and took me to lunch in Bonn's world-famous restaurant Mater-
nus. My reception was one of his last official acts. He has since
been honourably retired and lives on his ample Government pension.

Privat had been the head of the German Government network

which sought to create West Germany's "image" in North America's German-language press. He seemed satisfied with his success: "Only two newspapers on the entire continent do not print our press releases verbatim", he complained. "One is New York's *Aufbau*. The other is your confounded *Montrealer Nachrichten*. We really don't mind the *Aufbau*'s line. They are liberal and reasonable. They are staunch friends of the Federal Republic. They represent the very best in German-Jewish thinking. They call East Germany by its proper name: the "Soviet occupation zone". But you *Nachrichten* people? You spoil our perfect record. Why do you mention that there are two German states? There is but one lawful German state. I hope your trip through this part of the world will finally convince you!"

My assurance that I had come to form an unbiased opinion did not register with Privat. "I am an interested reader of the *Montrealer Nachrichten*", he continued. "I will pay you this compliment: once I have picked up your paper I can never put it down until I have read every word from beginning to end. What you write is brilliant — brilliantly wrong! Tell me, when did the Soviet zone ever hold free elections? Why doesn't Ulbricht call a plebiscite so that his people can decide whether they are in favour of his regime? They wouldn't dare! Ninety per cent of their citizens would defect if they had the chance!"

Privat confided that he had personally trained young Wolfgang Scheur, Montreal's liberal West German Press Attaché. "We have learned much since the days of the Nazis. We reject all crude attempts to influence foreign thinking. Our task is simple: to present ourselves and our country as we really are. We do not try to brainwash anyone. Hitler's propagandists were political warriors. We are merely press agents."

As a final gesture, E.C. Privat arranged an appointment with Miss Adelheid von Veltheim, head of a Government-sponsored organization called "Society for an Indivisible Germany". It turned out to be one of the most interesting interviews during my stay in Bonn. The *Kuratorium,* as the society is called in German, maintains a small suite of offices on one of Bonn's seamier streets. The von Veltheims are members of an old Prussian aristocratic family who played an important part in Imperial Germany. They also played a key role in the abortive anti-Hitler coup of July 20, 1944. By some miracle Adelheid von Veltheim, a young girl at the time, escaped with her life. Today she is a middle-aged woman trying to recapture the past. The *Kuratorium* was meant to become an effective medium of propaganda. Somewhere along the line it missed its goal. It attempts to reach the East German public by radio, TV and leaflets. It organizes West German memorial services each June 17, the anniversary of an anti-Ulbricht demonstration in East Berlin. It maintains liaison with most of the nationalistic expellee organizations. Somehow Adelheid von Veltheim managed to retain a sincere belief in the justice and necessity of her work. "We wish to rebuild a united Germany. We do not want to achieve this by war. I hate war. We will win by remoulding the hearts and minds of our kinfolk across the line. If we can reach them across the barbed wire, if we can stay in touch with them long enough, everything will eventually be alright. We work for Germany, not for a nationalistic dictatorship. Eventually we will succeed!"

I told her that in my opinion the *Kuratorium* had failed to understand the trend of European history. My explanations fell on deaf ears. "You do not understand — we will eventually win because everything we represent is good and noble — our country is entitled to unify if our people will it — the sins of Hitler must not forever be held against the German people!"

The sun was setting across the Rhine when I left Adelheid von Veltheim's office. For the first time during my trip I was sad. The woman had been sincere — but she belonged to another age. Her world had collapsed when the German Reich evaporated. It is not likely to be rebuilt either by brute force or lofty idealism.

CHAPTER VI

SOFT SPOT IN
GERMAN-CANADIAN RELATIONS

On the fourth day of my Bonn visit a situation I had put in motion myself caught up with me. When I returned to my hotel a member of the local SPCA and a live young seal were waiting for me. I had to pose for pictures and grant a series of TV interviews.

More than a year earlier I had published a short story dealing with the mass killing of Canadian seals on the Magdalen Islands in the Gulf of St. Lawrence. Our news photographer Uwe Koenemann had flown over the islands during the sealing season of March 1964; he had shot a sequence of pictures which showed baby seals being skinned while alive. The hunters would hit them on the head or snout, hoping the blow would kill. Then, without first assuring themselves of the death of their unfortunate quarry, they would begin to open the animal and tear off the pelt. Very often the baby seals were still alive; they would wriggle under the hands of their torturers; they would let out agonizing screams and move their skinned bodies minutes after the hunters had left them. All these facts were clearly discernible in the film which was turned over to the CBC's French Network and shown by the Government-owned body. The public was able to view the film on Montreal's Channel Two.

After I had examined Koenemann's film and interviewed eye witnesses I described the events in a short news story entitled *Die Mordinsel* (Murder Island) in the *Montrealer Nachrichten*. It was quickly reprinted by three of West Germany's largest publications: the *Hamburger Morgenpost, Heim und Welt* and *Wochenend*. From these sources the story circulated in twenty-six countries and was eventually published in 168 newspapers. The director of the Frankfurt Zoo, famous zoologist Professor Grzimek, ordered the film and caused it to be shown over West Germany's television network, to the consternation of an embarrassed Department of Fisheries in Ottawa. To my great surprise the article thus became the most widely published story I had ever written. For I had never intended it to be more than a brief comment on man's inhumanity to dumb animals.

I had first published the story under my pen-name, Freddy Weiss. But my true identity soon became known. I was invited to speak before eight national SPCA organizations and had to turn them down due to lack of time. In no country did the story receive wider publicity than in West Germany. I was told that close to forty million people had read it in one form or another.

The extended publicity my story received caused chain reactions I had never intended. The Canadian Department of Fisheries in Ottawa, under the Hon. Mr. Robichaud, was inundated by a flood of protest letters. More than 100,000 letters and telegrams were received from West Germany alone. The Canadian Government passed legislation after my story appeared, banning the skinning-alive of baby seals. The annual catch was limited to 50,000 for the St. Lawrence Gulf area (no limitation was set for the more important Newfoundland coast area). Weight and size of clubs used by hunters were regulated by new Government decrees. The Minister of Fisheries had a serious problem on his hands: how to cope with an aroused world opinion abroad, and the Leader of the Opposition at home; Mr. Diefenbaker brought the matter up in Parliament. Mr. Robichaud had to promise that the Government would speedily look into the matter.

Mr. Robichaud's office issued much literature. Ottawa had to admit that the number of seals had greatly diminished during the past few years. A Department of Fisheries spokesman flatly denied that any baby seals had ever been skinned alive (a statement belied by Koenemann's film). These constant denials caused the query: if seals had never been skinned alive, why did the newly promulgated regulations specifically forbid this practice?

The great seal controversy between the German publishing industry and the Ottawa Government took on overtones to which I, as the author of the controversy, could not possibly subscribe. West-German neo-Nazis, twisting the rules of logic, would argue: "The cruelties committed by Canadians against their seals far exceed our own cruelties committed against the Jews. Canadians are no better than we are." Actually, both types of cruelty are inexcusable, if not quite comparable. Several West-German organizations started to help our campaign to save the Canadian harp seal, including the German SPCA, spearheaded by its Hamburg chapter. Its presiding officer Kertscher issued press releases and organized publicity across the entire European continent. Another group, the Federation against the Abuse of Animals took up the fight in southern Germany, Austria and Switzerland. Of all assistance none was more valuable than that of Professor Grzimek who familiarized West Germany's television audience with the seal massacres. Very soon the Canadian Embassy in Bonn became one of the battle centres of the great seal fight. Canada's interests were well protected by the Embassy's Press Attaché, W.M. Jarvis. Mr. Jarvis wrote excellent German. At first he tried to dictate personal answers to the protest mail reaching his desk. Unfortunately — from his point of view — most of his letters somehow managed to end up on my desk, since the addressees, very often *Nachrichten* readers, would mail them to me. His choice of explanations often missed the intended mark — in one of his early letters Mr. Jarvis wrote: "While the clubbing of baby seals could hardly be called a refined hunting method, the effects of the clubbing are nevertheless humane...". Such letters usually called for printed editorial comment; incidents of this type kept the "great seal controversy" alive for more than a year.

Eventually Mr. Jarvis learned his lesson. Later inquiries were answered by mailing a short preprinted explanation of the Canadian Government's official position. When I reached Bonn, I immediately tried to visit Mr. Jarvis. I felt the urge to meet the man with whom I had "crossed swords" so often. "For Heaven's sake, don't!" was E.C. Privat's friendly advice. "He is far too angry with you. You are the West German Government's guest; we don't want you to get into trouble!"

I never met Mr. Jarvis. I never learned whether he was old or young, tall or short. I know that he tried to defend the indefensible position of the Ottawa Department of Fisheries. This was the way it should have been, for it was the job for which Mr. Jarvis had been hired; just as it had been my job as a journalist to publish the report about the seal massacres.

The seal controversy has greatly worsened German-Canadian relations and has influenced the average German's image of Canada more than any other non-political event since the end of the Second World War. Canada's corrective legislation came too late to change the impression caused by the original cruelties.

CHAPTER VII

DUSSELDORF — EUROPE'S MINIATURE NEW YORK

Bonn is a medium-sized university town in its own right; but it is also part of a huge urban area of almost five million people; Bonn and Cologne have grown into each other. The suburbs of Cologne, Duisburg and Essen are interlocked. The urban district of the Rhineland and Ruhr has become a modern megalopolis plagued by chronic shortages of housing, water and utility services. Düsseldorf, the administrative centre of many of West Germany's largest business concerns, is situated at the periphery of the giant metropolis. It was my next port of call. I used the local electric railway to reach it.

It takes less than an hour to reach Düsseldorf from Bonn. I have rarely seen a greater difference between two cities. Düsseldorf is the most Americanized of all German towns; its degree of westernization exceeds that of Frankfurt. Düsseldorf can look back on a centuries-old existence as a village (its very name means village on the river Düssel). As a large city it is comparatively young. Since 1945 its population has more than doubled. It became the capital of the Federal Republic's largest state (Rheinland-Westphalen), the administrative seat of her largest business firms and the centre of West Germany's reestablished small Jewish community. All this explains Düsseldorf's fantastic rate of growth.

No one entering this teeming community for the first time would believe that it numbers only 750,000 people. It gives the impression of being a town of two million. Huge skyscrapers have gone up everywhere — the tallest copies the style of New York's United Nations building. Elevated highways spring up in the middle of town and end some miles further with equal abruptness. Automobile traffic has reached a crescendo parallelled only by

Paris and Munich. The Königsalle, Düsseldorf's Broadway, resembles the Champs Elysées of Paris. Its people are smartly dressed and seem to be in a perpetual hurry. The average person tends to copy the New Yorker's behaviour during rush-hour. People dress and act like Americans; all this makes Düsseldorf look like a miniature New York.

Almost every German town experienced a postwar real estate boom. But nowhere did it reach the fantastic proportions of Düsseldorf. The last land sale before the Second World War brought a price of 80,000 marks for an average sized building lot on the Königsallee. A similar sale in 1965 topped fourteen million marks, almost 150 times the market value of 1939. The purchasing power of the mark has decreased to approximately one-third of its value during the same period.

Less than a generation ago Cologne was the undisputed queen of the Rhineland. Düsseldorf was considered a small, uncouth country town. Today Düsseldorf has outdistanced Cologne. The growth of the town created an atmosphere of rivalry between Düsseldorf and Cologne which has been compared to that of Dallas and Fort Worth. But it goes further than the Texas feud, for there is nothing good-natured or humorous about it. The rivalry is fought with bitterness and rancour. To generalize broadly, the people of Cologne are Catholic, placid and stubborn (Konrad Adenauer is one of Cologne's best known sons); the citizens of Düsseldorf are ambitious, money-minded and uninterested in most cultural activities (even though their town has become a centre of art exhibitions).

Their different approach to the problem of neo-Nazism can be summed up in two statements I heard. An elderly Cologne burgher deeply regretted the crimes committed against the Jewish people. He said: "It was terrible to betray all principles of humanity. The crimes brought shame and punishment on the German people." A highly placed Düsseldorf government employee said: "It was criminal of the Nazis to destroy the Jewish people, one of the most successful business groups. Their persecution actually was worse than criminal, it was bad business!"

Düsseldorf's citizens react similarly toward their greatest son, the German-Jewish poet Heinrich Heine. Heine, born to a poor Jewish family in 1797, left Düsseldorf at a relatively early age. He was a pitiless critic of the political conditions of his day; no monument stands in his honour in West Germany, and no street had been named after him before 1945. When Hitler came to power Heine's books were burned and his name erased from German school books. After 1945 the Düsseldorf city fathers finally named a major traffic artery after him. They discussed whether a monument should be erected to him and turned the idea down. The only Heine monument on German soil is in East Berlin. The house where Heine was born is situated less than five minutes from the street named after him — the Heinrich Heine Allee, in the heart of the old town. I asked no less than five people to tell me the exact location of the house. No one knew it. I finally found it myself by sheer accident. A small decrepit sign said: "Heinrich Heine was born here in 1797". The house was in a bad state of disrepair. After seeing Goethe's birthplace in Frankfurt and Beethoven's home in Bonn, the discovery of Heine's shabby original home proved anticlimactic. Had Düsseldorf really overcome its Nazi past? Actually it has. After visiting Europe's miniature New York for two days I came to the conclusion that Düsseldorf would extend similar treatment to any non-Jewish composer or poet born there. Düsseldorfers just do not care. They lack the time to reflect. Poetry and music take last place in Rheinland-Westphalen's capital city.

CHAPTER VIII

WEST GERMANY'S CONTROVERSIAL INDUSTRIALISTS

It took me less than an hour's car drive to reach the Krupp works from Düsseldorf. They are located at Essen, the heart of the Ruhr district. Krupp accounts for a major part of Essen's industrial production. Since the war of 1870 which Alfred Krupp's improved steel production won for Prussia and which helped create the Second German Reich, Krupp has been Germany's largest and most influential munitions maker.

After 1945 the Krupp plants were dismantled and forbidden ever again to produce war machinery. But today the complex once more produces guns, mortars, airplanes and some of the more complicated machinery of the nuclear war age.

During the Hitler years Krupp had been instrumental in arming the Nazi war machine. After 1938 the firm had acquired shipyards formerly owned by Jews. During the war years Krupp employed 97,952 war prisoners, concentration camp inmates and foreign workers pressed into labour gangs. After the war's end the head of the Krupp works, Gustav von Bohlen und Halbach, lay paralyzed in a small Austrian town. Alfried Krupp, the family's youngest managing member (born in 1907) was arrested by the Allies and tried in Nuremberg as a war criminal. He was convicted and sentenced to twelve years imprisonment; United States authorities prepared the case for the prosecution.

In 1951 he was released from prison, having served only three years. During the same years his holdings, which had been seized by the government, were returned to him. Between 1951 and 1965 the Krupp firms multiplied their sales, rebuilt their armament plants and reestablished themselves as the Federal Republic's most important war materials producer. Today Alfried Krupp von

Bohlen und Halbach heads West Germany's largest concern. It consists of 104 business firms. Their sales total six billion marks a year.

Personally Alfried Krupp is a pleasant man. He appears polite, business-like and clean cut. He rejects Nazism — at least today — the record of his Nuremberg war crimes trial showed strong Nazi sympathies during the Hitler years. "Nazism was a colossal failure", he commented during our short interview. "Yes, we did make mistakes." He tried to minimize Krupp's role in employing and exploiting concentration camp inmates. "The government sent them to us. We had no choice — during war time we had to employ them. Their working for us saved their lives; otherwise the Nazis would undoubtedly have killed them immediately."

Ever since the Big Bertha guns, named after Alfried's mother, had sent artillery shells into Paris during the First World War, the name of Krupp has become one of the most hated of German family names. Many Europeans worry about Krupp's reappearance and this concern is shared by all "East block" countries, whose citizens served the firm as forced labourers during the Second World War. This makes Krupp not only the largest but also the most controversial of all German industrialists.

The feud between the Krupp family and the progressive political forces of Germany runs deep. The last of the Krupps (the present owner is descended from the Krupp family through his mother — the male line died out) was Friedrich Alfred Krupp, a jovial man, who preferred Italy to his native Essen. During July of 1902 the social democratic newspaper *Vorwärts* accused Friedrich Krupp of homosexuality. The charge was never formally proven and Krupp instituted a libel action. In the course of the following months Krupp suffered a nervous breakdown and died under mysterious circumstances at his palatial home, the Villa Hügel in Essen, on November 22, 1902. His death was attributed to a heart attack and may actually have been suicide. His daughter Bertha, then sixteen years old, became the heiress of one of Europe's great fortunes. In 1906 she married Gustav von Bohlen und Halbach, who by special Imperial permission took on the family name of Krupp. The death of Friedrich Krupp, only forty-nine years old at the time, was blamed on the Social Democratic Party. The hatred against progressive movements which haunts all political and economic actions of the surviving members of the family, dates back to the death of the last of the male Krupps.

Germany's second controversial industrialist is not as well known as the Krupp family; Friedrich Flick organized several of Germany's large steel mills. Flick had been one of the earliest financers of the Nazi Party. During November of 1932 he transferred to Heinrich Himmler an "advance payment" of 100,000 marks. At the time, the Nazis were not yet in power. During 1933 and 1934 the Steelworks Riesa, an affiliate of the Flick concern, paid 30,000 marks to the Nazi Party. Flick took over a number of Jewish-owned firms and once stated that he considered himself to be "Goering's commissioner". During the war he acquired a number of trusteeships in occupied Europe. In November 1940 he sent a letter to Goering in which he requested a share of Lorraine's iron-ore industry. Goering obliged. His firm employed approximately 40,000 concentration camp inmates, war prisoners and forced labourers. After the war Flick was convicted of war crimes and sentenced to seven years imprisonment. On February 5, 1951, less than four years later, Flick was released. Today he controls a huge industrial empire and is said to finance Germany's nuclear research. He owns or controls some eighty different firms in the mining industry, including several which are active in the uranium-producing Black Forest region.

The predominance of the Krupp and Flick concerns in West Germany's industrial set-up is one of the major causes for the grave suspicion with which "East block" countries look toward Bonn.

CHAPTER IX

THE HAMBURG PRESS BARONS

No German city suffered more war damage than Hamburg, the first town to be hit by a major bombing attack. Between 1942 and 1945 Hamburg lived through more air alerts than any other large community, including London. The RAF launched its most devastating series of attacks during the ten days between July 24 and August 3, 1943. On the morning of August 4 more than 6,000 city blocks of Hamburg were completely gutted; close to 800,000 people were homeless and almost 70,000 civilians lay buried under the rubble of the dying city.

Hamburg has been completely rebuilt. Few signs of war damage remain. Its houses have been recreated in their original style. Casual visitors find it hard to believe that less than twenty-three years ago the city had practically ceased to exist.

I reached Hamburg by air from Essen. The first impression belies the fact that it is West Germany's largest city and the hub of its import and export trade. For Hamburg's suburbs give it a "small town" appearance.

Hamburg has become the nerve centre of the Federal Republic's large newspaper chains. Before the war, Leipzig had been headquarters for the Reich's book publishers. The large periodicals had their head offices in Berlin. The Ullstein concern, leading publishers of the Weimar Republic, changed hands when Hitler came to power. Most of the large Berlin newspapers vegetated during the Nazi era. But even while distributing Nazi propaganda, they never completely lost their original identity. After 1945 most West German book publishers moved to Stuttgart while Leipzig continued as East Germany's book capital. The huge newspaper concerns of Berlin moved to Hamburg.

The Federal Republic has a number of world-famous periodicals. The most influential group is controlled by publishing tycoon Axel Springer. The most controversial is *Der Spiegel* (The Mirror) founded and managed by Rudolf Augstein. Axel Springer and Rudolf Augstein have one thing in common. Both started from scratch after 1945. Both wield tremendous influence in West Germany. Both are gifted newspaper men. At this point the apparent similarities end. Augstein is a liberal. (Many Germans call him leftist, but on close scrutiny the label evaporates.) He crticizes militarism, bureaucratic excess and neo-Nazis in sensitive government jobs. Once in a while he launches a series of articles calculated to inflame and irritate West German nationalists. "I regret that once again I feel obliged to foul my own nest." With these words Augstein introduced an article which explained Imperial Germany's guilt for the outbreak of World War I. While Germans at large have accepted the fact that Hitler caused World War II, few agree with the Allies' contention of the Fatherland's responsibility for World War I.

Axel Springer, on the other hand, leans heavily toward German nationalism. He rejects neo-Nazism but underscores the Federal Republic's right to speak for the entire German people. He is fanatically anti-GDR. He has kept the Berlin tension at boiling point.

The huge skyscraper housing the Axel Springer offices in Berlin is built almost directly on the East-West boundary. The upper floors of the building can be used to shower East Berlin streets with anti-communist leaflets. In at least one instance a tunnel was dug from the building's basement underneath the wall to help some East Berliners escape. During this incident an East German border guard was killed — causing a further deterioration of an already dangerous situation.

Augstein and Springer became West Germany's chief literary antagonists. Their feud is not caused by mere political dissension. It reaches a personal level. Springer is a tall, distinguished-looking man. His luck with ladies is proverbial. He is married for the fourth time and succeeds in remaining on friendly terms with his three ex-wives. Augstein is different. Devoted to his liberal principles, he is less spectacular than Springer. His success with women is not as great as that of his competitor and insiders hint that this fact may be one of the underlying causes of the newspaper feud. But the cleavage between the Springer and Augstein firms goes much deeper. Springer has been called the William Randolph Hearst of the Federal Republic. Springer's *Bildzeitung,* the largest unit of his far flung newspaper empire, compares to the old *Journal-American.* Like Hearst, Springer will use nationalism and hammer away at it. His news stories and reporting resemble the heady journalism of Hearst's early days. If Hearst had helped to prepare the emotional atmosphere that exploded into the Spanish-American War, Springer is one of the architects of the smouldering Berlin crisis. "Wall of Shame", "Barrier of Infamy", "Concentration Camp Fence" are slogans coined by the Springer press and hammered into the collective mind of the Federal Republic's readers. The East Germans accuse the *Bildzeitung* of luring potential East German defectors to prearranged meetings near the wall where tunnels were dug from the West into East Berlin territory — then alerting the East German *Vopos* to create martyrs. The truth of this charge has never been proven, but the rumour itself has become a symptom of the Berlin crisis.

Springer's empire bears a striking resemblance to the Ullstein concern which went under after Hitler's rise to power. Springer not only copied Ullstein's original set-up, but hired every former Ullstein employee available. Springer's personal assistant Vollhardt started with Ullstein, and quite a few other former Ullstein men who emigrated during Hitler's early years are working for Springer today. Thus Springer is the only large German publishing house with German Jews among its top policy makers. The Springer newspapers include weekly illustrated papers as well as dailies. Not all of them cater to sensationalism. This domain is left to its largest paper, the *Bildzeitung.*

Augstein on the other hand owns but one publication, *Der Spiegel.* In its format the *Spiegel* resembles America's *Time* magazine. The style is similar — at this point though all similarity ends. Augstein's newsmagazine is liberal in the Rooseveltian New Deal sense. *Der Spiegel* is loved by West German intellectuals, disliked by conservatives and despised by neo-Nazis. This undercurrent of hatred and frustration suddenly exploded some years ago into the "Affaire *Spiegel*". Augstein and several of his closest collaborators were arrested for treason. This scandal (also known as the "Strauss Affaire" after its other central figure) made the *Spiegel* world-famous and became a test case of Germany's newly emergent democratic spirit. Democracy won. For the first time in its turbulent history public opinion questioned actions by governmental authority.

The case started with the publication of an article dealing with German defence strategy against potential attack from the East. The article, entitled *Bedingt Abwehrbereit* (conditionally able to resist) appeared in issue No. 41 of October 10, 1962. In it, *Spiegel* editor Conrad Ahlers criticized German defence policies and described at great length certain occurrences at the NATO forces' German fall manoeuvres ("Fallex '62'). The article dealing with "Fallex '62" did not contain classified information. Similar stories were published in most NATO countries and were carried by a number of American and British newspapers. The German army objected. Dr. Friedrich August Freiherr von der Heydte, a military spokesman, published an article in a Würzburg daily newspaper in which he stated: "*Der Spiegel* has gone beyond the limits of normal reporting. By publishing these facts it committed high treason!"

Franz Joseph Strauss, West Germany's controversial Minister of Defence, now entered the scene. Years ago Augstein had published details of a corruption scandal (the FIBAG case) in which Strauss had allegedly been involved. Strauss had sued for libel. Eventually the case had been settled out of court. Ever since then Strauss had tried to get even with the *Spiegel*. Now he saw his chance. He caused the treason case to be prosecuted without advising Minister of Justice Stammberger. For many centuries the German army had prosecuted such cases without civilian interference. Strauss simply followed in the footsteps of generations of Prussian and German defence ministers before him. But for the first time in German history civilian authority was to question the military's semi-judicial actions. The "Affaire *Spiegel*" is filled with illegal arrests and extraditions. (The worst breach of judicial etiquette: Strauss ordered Spanish authorities by long-distance telephone to hold vacationing Conrad Ahlers and spirit him back to Germany in the middle of the night without the formality of an extradition demand.) Augstein and his co-workers had been arrested, but they were cleared. Defence Minister Strauss lost his portfolio, but not his political influence. Augstein had won a complete moral victory.

The *Spiegel* case is closed. Its political consequences still reverberate in the Federal Republic, and will not be forgotten for many years to come. Its ultimate effects can be summed up as follows. Highhanded action by military and other government offices against newspapers have slowed down considerably, but have not stopped completely. Both adversaries withdrew to their corners.

Most German journalists ape some of the traits of their American colleagues. Sometimes they go a few steps further. I was invited to an editorial board meeting of the *Bildzeitung*. It was a fascinating experience. Fifteen men sat around a huge table in a smoke-filled room. A never-ending stream of copy boys rushed through swinging doors. News tickers clicked, intercoms hummed and eight telephones rang without interruption. The scene was utter confusion; yet, two pages of the *Bildzeitung* slowly took form. The atmosphere reminded me of an old-type Hollywood film spoofing the life of a large metropolitan newspaper office.

Der Spiegel shares a building with several other large West German publications. The Springer concern owns its own skyscraper. The lower floors are left to the hard-working employees of the Fifth Estate. The three top floors are reserved for the brass. The oak-pannelled walls and heavy rugs are those of all large corporation offices. The three chief executives take their lunch on a huge glass-encased terrace overlooking Hamburg. I was invited to lunch by Vollhardt, Springer's right-hand man. He gave me a quick run-down of some of Springer's aims. After I had interviewed him for two hours, the actions of enigmatic Axel Springer became clearer to me. The East German Government sees him as a sinister force bent on a course of cheap and dangerous nationalism. The West Germans consider him their most Americanized newspaper publisher — one who put the Federal Republic back into the field of international journalism. Actually he is a brilliant businessman anxious to expand his holdings and increase his profits. I gained the impression that Springer might easily change his entire political line if he felt public opinion demanded it. Augstein wants to influence public opinion; Springer wishes to profit by it. This appears to be their main difference. Augstein and Springer are not their country's only newspaper magnates. But they are the most important men in their field, the two top figures who between them have influenced the trend of West Germany's post-war journalism.

CHAPTER X

WEST GERMANY'S TOP NAZI HUNTER

Chief prosecuting attorney Erwin Schuele heads the West German War Crimes Investigating Office at Ludwigsburg near Stuttgart. Former Chancellor Adenauer had created the Ludwigsburg centre by Government directive, when it had become woefully clear that many Nazi criminals were escaping punishment through legal loopholes. Under German law a criminal may either be prosecuted in the locality where the crime was committed, or at his present domicile. But most war crimes were committed outside Germany proper, and very few Nazi criminals maintained domicile in West Germany.

The prosecuting attorneys of the *Länder* (states) making up the West German Federation frequently failed to make their prosecution stick. After the war's end the occupying powers had handled war crimes cases. In the territory which later became the Federal German Republic the American prosecutors quickly lost their zest to bring Nazis to trial. A few particularly dangerous criminals had been condemned to death but US Appeal Courts had commuted the death sentences into prison terms. After a few years the killers, originally slated to hang, were freed. The most notorious of these cases is that of former Dachau concentration camp doctor Hans Eisele, who fled to Egypt after the American authorities had freed him. The German prosecutor who wanted to rearrest him was thwarted.

The Bonn government has been accused of laxity in the prosecution of known Nazi criminals. This charge is not to be taken at face value. Official German policy aims to bring all war criminals to trial. The Chancellor himself has gone on record that no major Nazi should go unpunished. When accused Nazi bigwigs successfully cheated justice by jumping from one jurisdiction to another, Adenauer created the "Ludwigsburg Centre for the Investigation of War Crimes".

The office is an investigating agency — like Scotland Yard — specializing in tracing and capturing known Nazi criminals. After the fugitives had been apprehended and the incriminating material assembled, the Ludwigsburg office would turn over defendant and evidence to the *Land* claiming proper jurisdiction — usually the area in which the accused had his last known domicile. The complicated mass of evidence used at the great Auschwitz trial, which occupied the German criminal courts for more than two years, had been collected by a Ludwigsburg team. The centre has been instrumental in gathering evidence for all similar trials.

Adenauer picked an energetic prosecutor named Erwin Schuele to head the Ludwigsburg bureau. His official title was *Oberstaatsanwalt* (Chief Prosecutor). He set up a very efficient office staff; brought in a team of trained criminologists and investigators and started to assemble a complicated filing system listing all known Nazis and their crimes. Under Schuele's orders the Ludwigsburg office started on a world-wide hunt for known war criminals. Many were extradited and brought to trial. Schuele did not always succeed. But no one doubted that he tried his very best to capture, prosecute and convict the elite of the Third Reich.

Schuele was held in almost universal esteem as a staunch antiNazi fighter when in October 1964 a stunned public learned the following facts: Erwin Schuele had once been a member of the SA (Nazi stormtrooper organization) which he had joined in 1933. In 1935 he had become a full-fledged Nazi Party member. He served as a staff member of the German 215th Infantry Division during the war and in this connection was accused of participating in atrocities committed near the Leningrad front. After the war a Soviet court had convicted him of war crimes and sentenced him to twenty-five years at hard labour. He received a pardon several years later and was repatriated to West Germany.

Originally the East German Government had placed these grave charges against Schuele. Similar charges against other West German officials had frequently failed to stand up under close examination. In Schuele's case the charges were substantiated. During a press conference in January 1965 he stated: "It is true that I was a member of the Nazi Party. I had to join, because I wanted to finish my university studies. When I finally recognized Hitler's

madness and sadism, I worked actively against Nazism. Today I am
doing my best to bring all war criminals to justice."

The case of Erwin Schuele, virtually unknown outside Germany
proper, became one of the Federal Republic's causes célèbres. A
chief Nazi prosecutor who had himself been a Nazi! "Why not
appoint a reformed gangster as chief warden of our top security
jail, or a former embezzler as president of our National Bank?
quipped the *Spandauer Volksblatt*, West Berlin's most lively newspaper. "It is unheard of to appoint an ex-Nazi to the sensitive job
of hunting down other Nazis... it is an insult to those who suffered
during the Hitler dictatorship. Is there no one left in Bonn who
knows the difference between good taste and outrageous tactlessness?" (*Spandauer Volksblatt*, West Berlin — February 16, 1965).
The German public hotly debated the Schuele case during late 1964
and 1965. When the East German Government published its *Brown
Book*, Erwin Schuele rated a long paragraph. Several West German
newspapers came to the assistance of the embattled prosecutor. *Der
Spiegel* spearheaded his defence. It carefully examined Schuele's
record as an anti-Nazi prosecutor and summed up its findings:
"Schuele is doing a good job hunting down his former comrades.
He once was a Nazi himself; he has reformed. There is some
element of doubt, and when in doubt we must find for the accused.
Based on his recent record, Schuele seems to be the country's most
useful former Nazi Party member..."

Before his past suddenly caught up with him, Schuele had
granted many interviews. But in late 1964 he retired to the Ludwigsburg centre and refused to admit journalists. He became one
of the most difficult of all highly placed West German public
servants to meet. When Bonn promised me an opportunity to interview Schuele, I gladly accepted. The meeting was set for Monday,
July 12, 1965. I had left Hamburg two days before for a short
break; the Government had flown me to my home town of Nuremberg for a weekend of rest. (It turned out to be the most hectic
time of my entire trip.) From Nuremberg I travelled to Stuttgart by
train — the trip was my first experience with German trains
since 1933. As a Government guest I had been placed in a first class
compartment. German travel habits have not changed much during
the past generation. Every one still travelled "second class" — all
second class compartments were overcrowded, while I was the sole
passenger of an entire railway car of first class compartments.
The German economic miracle has not been able to convince

travellers to go first class! Stuttgart is one of Germany's loveliest cities. Like Rome and San Francisco it is built on several steep hills. None of the war's big air raids hit Stuttgart; yet, at the war's end, the town had been 80 per cent destroyed.

Today Württemberg-Baden's capital is completely rebuilt. It has become South-West Germany's industrial capital. During the Third Reich Württemberg never took strongly to Nazism — it was the state which gave the Nazis the smallest percentage of votes in the last free German election (March 5, 1933). The Swabians, who inhabit Württemberg, have the reputation of being level-headed and hard-working. Famous men born in or near Stuttgart are the poet Friedrich Schiller and the philosopher Friedrich Hegel — the writer who more than any other influenced the thinking of Karl Marx.

Stuttgart has one of Germany's loveliest hotels, the Schlossgartenhotel. The town's traffic problems are something to behold. Stuttgart is also the home of Germany's highest and most unusual television tower, a needle-like structure whose architect must have been an avid reader of science fiction magazines. Just below the tower's top is a glass-encased area of three stories. The upper floor serves as a lookout; the others contain a luxurious restaurant, unlike any other eating place I have ever seen.

Ludwigsburg, the home of the war crimes bureau, is a small eighteenth century town ten miles outside Stuttgart. It once served as the residence of a runaway Grand Duke of Württemberg who did not get along with his parliament and took up residence at Ludwigsburg where he built a luxurious baroque castle. A local jail was constructed nearby to house the Grand Duke's enemies. Later on it was enlarged and today it serves as the Stuttgart district jail. It does not house Nazi prisoners, but common criminals. The offices of the war crimes centre are located in the administrative buildings inside the prison walls. Erwin Schuele's visitors must pass through the huge prison gates where they are processed by the jail's personnel. If there should ever be a serious riot at Ludwigsburg jail, the carefully assembled evidence of the Nazi hunters would be in jeopardy.

Erwin Schuele, the Federal Republic's most controversial public servant, awaited me with a handshake and a friendly "Guten Morgen, how are you?" He is a medium-built elderly gentleman, who bears a striking resemblance to the American actor playing the role of Lieutenant Tragg in TV's Perry Mason series. His manner is friendly — but when I looked into his steel-blue eyes, I felt that this man would be without pity where criminals are concerned.

After a secretary had served us the inevitable hot coffee and cookies, I asked the first and most obvious question: "Was there any special reason why you — a former Nazi Party member — have chosen to hunt down your former colleagues?" "It's not really too surprising", he answered. "Only a man who once was a Nazi himself can visualize the horror Nazism brought to the world. I studied Nazi dogma. I learned that hatred and contempt for human rights was the very essence of Nazism. When I joined I had not known these things. For a few years I — like most other Germans — was hypnotized by Hitler. During the war I served on the Eastern front. When I saw the crimes committed in the name of the German people I became a convinced anti-Nazi. I decided right then and there that those crimes must be stopped and punished and the criminals who perpetrated them must be brought to justice. In my own mind I joined the war crimes centre long before it was established."

During the following hour, Schuele explained the workings of his bureau. More than one hundred trained investigators have searched the archives of most European countries for records of Nazi crimes. There is excellent cooperation between his office and Polish government agencies (approximately 70 per cent of all murders were committed in Poland). There is good liaison between Ludwigsburg and most Western and Eastern countries, with one notable exception: relations between East Berlin and Ludwigsburg are strained — East German officials have never forgiven or forgotten Schuele's former political association. They do not give him much cooperation. The results of the investigators' efforts are stored in three medium-sized rooms adjoining Schuele's private office. The secret of this amazing concentration is microfilm. More than 100,000 files dealing with the record of Nazi crimes have been photographed on microfilm and are kept in three huge fireproof cabinets. The organization of the centre is so efficient that any wanted document can be found within eight seconds. I timed it.

The names of all known Nazi criminals are listed on small white cards in a complex card-filing system. Each card contains a brief biographical sketch of the criminal, his assumed whereabouts (in case he has not yet been caught) and a list of the charges against him. A second card-index system contains a list of all known Nazi crimes and a third the names of all known Nazi victims. The third set is incomplete. "Almost impossible to find out the exact number of people murdered in the camps", Schuele explained. "It is even more difficult to find their names; in most instances the 'production records' of the extermination camps were handled on carload scale!" One of the ghastliest documents I saw at the war crimes centre was the typewritten report of Christian Wirth, former commander of the Belzec extermination camp. "It gives me great pleasure to advise you", Wirth's letter to the Reich Security Office in Berlin read, "that the Belzec production has risen from forty-seven carloads to sixty-five carloads this week. The use of gas crystals has proven to be far more efficient than the carbon monoxide we used before." It is almost inconceivable that "production" meant mass murder, and that "carloads" meant lots of eighty to ninety human beings. The murder record of Belzec has been tabulated at a sum total of 650,000 people — and there was not a single survivor! One heavy file contains car-loading schedules of the *Reichsbahn*. The Nazis took great care not to list their victims by name; but they were equally scrupulous in keeping careful tab on all railway cars which carried them to their death. Each car is listed by initials, numbers and dates of arrival. In one instance I found a shipping manifest unlike any other I have ever seen. It used the German word *Ware* (merchandise) to indicate the number of murder victims. Railway car "Zwickau 34785" delivered 89 pieces of merchandise ("89 *Stück Ware*") to the extermination camp at Sobibor on July 18, 1943. In this particular case the Ludwigsburg office has been able to trace the shipment further. The "merchandise" were young children from the Lodz ghetto being carried to their death.

The walls of the largest office contain rows of neatly bound correspondence files. It looks like any other business office, except for the horrible inscriptions of the *Leitzordner*. Five thick files are filled with Eichmann's personal correspondence, — Eichman 1 — Eichmann 2 — (he must have been a prolific letter writer), "Auschwitz 1" — "Auschwitz 2", "Majdanek", "Stutthof", "Sobibor" — a horrible sequence of names made infamous by the Hitler dictatorship.

I was able to trace the last group of Nuremberg Jews carried to their death March 15, 1942. They were brought to Izbicka near Krasnystaw — from there to their final destination at Belzec. One of them was my late uncle, Dr. Otto Bloch.

Schuele invited me to check on any particular criminal or series of crimes — "We list many thousands of criminals; since your time is limited, check on one or two of your own choice, so that you may learn how our system works." I decided to check on two particularly brutal mass killers: Christian Wirth, nicknamed *Der wilde Christian* (wild Christian), camp commander of Belzec; and Oscar Dirlewanger, head of one of the most dreaded *Einsatztruppen* in the Soviet Union who had killed more than 100,000 people.

Within five seconds Schuele handed me two white cards. I learned that Wirth had been killed by Jugoslav Partisans in Istria during the war and that his widow, whose Stuttgart address and telephone number are listed, receives a German Government pension. ("No matter how we look at it, the wife is not guilty of her husband's crimes", explained Schuele.) The list of crimes ascribed to Wirth looked almost harmless on paper — until I read the cross-reference cards in the crime-card index. "Action #4 — 44,229 people killed, for details see cards 11894 and 11895. Action #5 (Belzec), approximately 650,000 people killed, see card #11975". — Dirlewanger's card answered one important question. He had been reported alive in both South America and Egypt. But Dirlewanger is definitely dead. Shortly after his capture he was questioned by a French military investigation team who did not treat him too gently. He died shortly after the inquiry. "We wanted to be certain of his death", Schuele explained. "We exhumed his body. We compared the dental chart kept by his dentist with the teeth of the corpse. It checked out. We knew Dirlewanger had suffered a head injury during World War I. An X-ray of his skull was on file. It corresponded to the skull of the corpse we exhumed. Dirlewanger had once lost a toe in a hunting accident. The body we exhumed had only four toes on the left foot. There is no doubt, Dirlewanger is definitely dead."

The war crimes bureau never takes the death of a wanted criminal for granted until there is irrefutable proof. "Most people believe Martin Bormann dead", Schuele explained. "Perhaps he is. But for us he remains alive until we have complete proof of his death." The prosecutor gave me a few little known facts about Bormann's family. "Bormann's two sons joined a monastery to atone for their father's crimes. Both believe him to be dead. But meanwhile we are checking all clues for Bormann's possible whereabouts. He has been reported in Chile, Bolivia, Argentina, Brazil and Paraguay. So far all these leads have proven false."

Sometimes Schuele traces his quarry without being able to bring them to trial. The best known case of a mass murderer gone scotfree is that of Walter Rauff, inventor of the moveable death van. Rauff would commandeer ordinary furniture vans, then extend the exhaust pipe into the truck's interior. The van would be loaded with murder victims and slowly driven to the burial plots prepared in advance. On arrival, the entire "cargo" was dead.

Schuele found Rauff a prosperous businessman in Chile. He asked the Chilean authorities to arrest and extradite the mass killer. He was arrested — and promptly freed by a Chilean judge. Under Chilean law no mass murderer can be prosecuted more than ten years after the date of the murder. Today Rauff still runs his expanding Chilean interests and has organized a local neo-Nazi group. Another criminal not brought to trial by Schuele is Dr. Hans Eisele. The notorious Dachau concentration camp doctor lives in Egypt. Nasser refused to extradite him. Under Egyptian law murderers can only be prosecuted fifteen years after the date of the crime.

The Ludwigsburg centre cooperates with the police departments of many nations and exchanges valuable information with most of them. Relations between Ludwigsburg and Israel are usually cordial. I asked Schuele whether his office could have extradited Eichmann, if they had found him before the Israeli secret service spirited him out of Argentina.

"Argentina would have been obliged to extradite him, because murder enjoys no statute of limitations under Argentine law. But our chances of getting Eichmann would have been slim. He would have jumped the border and crossed into Paraguay; this is what Auschwitz doctor Joseph Mengele did when he knew we were on his track." "Do you think that Israel did the right thing by spiriting him out of the country?" I asked. "Officially I cannot approve the Israeli action. Unofficially — well, at least they got him, didn't they?" I felt that Ludwigsburg approved the Israeli coup against Eichmann. "One of our main problems is the refusal of the International Police Organization to classify Nazi crimes as murders. They consider them to be 'political crimes'. Consequently, Interpol does not help us to track down Nazis."

Schuele shed some light on another situation I had not realized existed. "Cooperation between US and German authorities in the apprehension of war criminals has not always been satisfactory. Since 1952 our prosecutors had been looking for certain documents dealing with Nazi crimes. We knew that the US authorities had the files in their possession. We did not know what branch of the US services guarded them. All enquiries to Washington drew denials. Finally I learned that a former US Army officer of German descent named Schumacher had photographed some of the documents for his own private library. Schumacher resided in Berlin. I visited him and he loaned me the documents. They were vitally important and helped our prosecution of the Auschwitz concentration camp guards. Schumacher also told us the location of the missing documents: Alexandria, Virginia. When we confronted Washington with the facts they finally granted us access to the documents. They have served us well ever since. Individual Americans are not always helpful. Some years ago I wrote to American author Gerald Reitlinger who had written a book about Nazi crimes. I asked him to loan us certain documents. Reitlinger answered briefly stating that he was no longer interested in Nazi crimes. He now concerned himself with the art of glass painting."

Schuele explained the case of the concentration camp commander of Treblinka. Nobody knew his name or whereabouts. To his victims he had been known by the nickname *Lallka,* a Polish word meaning doll. None could properly describe him. Finally one of the few surviving inmates remembered the address of Lallka's wife. The prisoner had been instructed to mail parcels to the commander's family containing valuables stolen from his victims. Lallka's identity suddenly became known. His name was Kurt Franz, and he ran a prosperous beer garden in Düsseldorf. Presently he is being tried before the Düsseldorf courts for mass murder. When police searched his home, they found a photo album with many pictures of Franz's activities in Treblinka. The album was inscribed: "The most wonderful days of my life!" — Sometimes defendants are convicted but their sentences are too short. Schuele takes those cases to the appellate court. The second in command of the Belzec concentration camp, *Oberscharführer* Oberhauser, received a sentence of four and one half years. Schuele appealed the sentence. Another convicted mass killer named Fellencz received a similarly light sentence. After Schuele's appeal the sentence was increased.

Schuele gave me some details of the great Auschwitz trial in which several defendants received the maximum sentence of life imprisonment (West Germany has abolished the death penalty). At the time of my visit the court had begun its final deliberations. "We have brought many criminals to trial and have avenged many crimes. Unfortunately there remain a great number of crimes which will never be punished. The Nazis worked thoroughly and butchered every single eye witness. This saved the camp personnel of Sobibor and Majdanek and was the cause of the inadequate sentence meted out to Oberhauser for the Belzec crimes.

"Not a single survivor remains of the death camp at Sobibor. The Jews were brought there in huge trucks. They were gassed on arrival. In some camps there were crude attempts to hide the ultimate purpose of the death-dealing machinery. Gas chambers would be marked as "Baths and delousing centre". In Sobibor the gas ovens and crematoria were in full view. When the cars arrived at the siding the people knew at once what was in store for them. They refused to disembark. A team of auxiliary SS-men used long bullwhips to get them out. The result of these whippings which left a number of the weaker prisoners dead on the railway siding, resulted in a phenomenon which the camp commander jokingly called "the rose carpet of Sobibor". The entire platform was covered with bloodstains. Eventually most of the victims would be driven into the chambers and gassed. Only the camp commander and one SS-man survived. The commander gave us his statement, then committed suicide. No one was ever tried for the Sobibor murders. More than 500,000 people perished there.

"There are only two survivors of Belzec. One of them of course is *Oberscharführer* Oberhauser. We tried him. But there were no witnesses to fall back on. There remained one single document, the so-called Gerstein report. Gerstein was the other survivor. He was an unusual man. A religious anti-Nazi who had somehow been able to conceal his views from the Nazi leadership. He became one of the Reich concentration camp inspectors and he visited the camp at Belzec during August 1942. He gave us his sworn statement on May 4, 1945 at Rottweil. (Actually it was given to the occupation authorities who some years later turned it over to us.) Shortly after making the statement Gerstein escaped custody. He has never been found. We assume that he was killed by his fellow-criminals for the damaging evidence he gave us. The Gerstein report became the most powerful evidence for our trial of Oberhauser. But it lacked judicial value — the witness making the deposition had vanished and could not be cross-examined. His statement was introduced by our prosecutor as a "deathbed statement". The defence immediately objected. Where was our proof that Gerstein had really died? Finally the judge disallowed the admission of the report. Very

few people have read this document. One of those who did was
author Rolf Hochhuth. His famous play *The Deputy* is based on
the Gerstein report. One other person knew of the events related
by Gerstein, the prelate representing the Vatican in Berlin. Was
Pius XII really informed of the report? I am not certain. Hochhuth
seems to think so — his *Deputy* is based o nthe assumption that
he was. Did the Pope act and speak up against these crimes?
Please, Mr. Lust, don't ask me this question. I do not know! I
only run the war crimes centre. My personal beliefs and opinions
matter little!"

Schuele went to the vault and returned with a long typewritten
document, signed Kurt Gerstein. Gerstein must have been under
great emotional stress at the time. His signature is hardly legible.
Obviously, his hand had trembled. "Very few people ever studied
this document", Schuele explained. "I cannot allow you to photostat
it. But you may make notes or even copy it word for word. Take
your time!" During the next thirty minutes I copied one of
recorded history's most ghastly documents. The fact that my uncle
had been among the victims did not make my task any easier. Here
are the results of my labour:

The next morning we proceeded to Belzec. They had built a
small railway yard near a hill north of the highway Lublin-Lem-
berg, left of the demarcation line. South of the highway stood a
few houses with a sign: Special command post of the *Waffen*-SS,
Belzec. Since the commander of the entire extermination machinery,
Police Captain Wirth, had not yet arrived, Globocneck (the officer
who accompanied me) introduced me to SS-*Hauptsturmführer*
Obermeyer. He only showed me the things he was obliged to show.
I did not see any corpses that afternoon; but a terrible stench
covered the entire region. Millions of flies were everywhere — it
was the smell I had encountered in the great cattle abattoirs
of Oranienburg. Close to the small railway station stood a huge
shed, the so-called 'dressing room', with a counter for valuables.
Behind it, a room with approximately one hundred chairs, the
'hairdressing room'; a small road lined with birch trees and fenced
off by barbed wire on both sides. At the end of the road a bath-
house surrounded by flowerbeds; a small staircase leading to three
rooms, 15 by 15 feet, 6 feet high, closed off by wooden doors. At
the opposite end, barely visible from where we stood, bigger gates.
As a ghastly joke, the Star of David was nailed to the roof. At the
building's main entrance a sign: Heckenholt Foundation. This
is all I could see that afternoon.

The next morning they woke me up shortly before seven. I
was told that the first transport would arrive in ten minutes. A few
minutes later a train pulled in from Lemberg, containing forty-
five cars and 6,700 people. 1,452 were dead on arrival. Behind the
small barred windows I could see children, pale and frightened,
the fear of death clearly written in their faces. Also men and
women. The train came to a halt. Two hundred Ukrainian auxilia-
ries tear open the doors and start using their whips. A loudspeaker blares out instructions: Undress completely; this includes
artificial limbs and false teeth; leave your valuables at the counter
— no receipts will be given; leave all eye glasses there too. After you
are completely undressed, tie your shoes together carefully (this
was imperative; otherwise it would have been impossible to salvage
the shoes for further use by German civilians). All girls and women
into the hairdressers' — they will cut your hair short ('they put the
women's hair into huge potato bags — for later use in some special
U-Boat equipment', explained the *Unterscharführer* in charge of
the operation). All the people start to march. They walk naked
along the alley. A pretty girl leads the procession — men, women
and children — some of them hobbling with the help of others, all
nude. I stand with Captain Wirth upstairs between the "bathrooms"
on the roof of the building. The people walk up, women
with small babies in their arms — all enter the death chambers. A
tall SS-man tells them in a pastoral voice: Don't worry, nothing
will happen to you; just take a deep breath when you are inside
to kill your germs, we have epidemics here — yes, the men will have
to work; but the women don't have to work unless they themselves
wish it. These words are enough to dispel the doubts of some of
the victims. They walk into the death chambers; but most people
know what's in store for them. Many people are praying. They
hesitate, but they enter the death chambers, driven by the crowd
behind them who in turn are driven by the leather whips of the
Ukrainian auxiliary SS. Most people enter without protest. But a
middle-aged woman curses the murderers. 'Our blood will be upon
you', she screams at Wirth. 'We will be avenged!' Wirth uses his
bullwhip on her, she receives five blows in her face. Then she too
disappears into the death chamber. How I wish I could have died
with them! But I know I must find out what happens here, I must
warn the world of the crimes perpetrated here. The death chambers
are crowded. This is what Wirth had ordered — crowd them
in! 700-800 people on 225 square feet! The prisoners stand on each
others' feet. Now I finally understand why the building is called
Heckenholt Foundation. Heckenholt is the technician servicing
the Diesel motor whose fumes are used to kill the victims. Heckenholt also built the murder plant and death chambers. But the

motor won't start. Captain Wirth is furious that this failure
occurs during my visit. He uses his whip on the Ukrainian auxiliary
SS-man who tries to help Heckenholt. Ten minutes — twenty
minutes — thirty minutes — the motor won't start! Meanwhile the
victims stay in the small chambers awaiting death. I can hear them
scream and sob inside. The hour mark passes. The motor still won't
start. It takes another hour to get the motor in working order;
finally, at long last, after two hours and forty nine minutes — my
stop watch has registered the exact time — the motor starts. Another
twenty-five minutes go by. Many people are dead now. I can see
it clearly through the chambers' small windows. Thirty minutes —
thirty-five minutes. Now everyone is dead!

At the opposite side Jews of the work command open the
gates. The dead stand silent — upright — like pillars of marble.
There is no space for them to fall in. One can still recognize
families — fathers grasping the hands of their children — husbands
holding the hands of their wives. It is hard for the labour gang to
separate the dead. They tear them apart and drag them to a
huge mass grave which had been prepared some 100 yards behind
the buildings — the death chambers have to be readied for the next
load. Corpses of children are hurled through the air for quicker
burial — a ghastly ball game with human beings. Finally they are
buried and earth is thrown over 3,200 dead. Only a few arms and
heads can still be seen — sticking from the earth.

The criminals of Belzec have never been properly punished.
Camp commander Wirth was killed by Jugoslav Partisans in Istria.
Obermeyer escaped and lives somewhere in South America. And
Oberhauser received only four and a half years in the penitentiary.
Why? No eye witnesses survived — the Gerstein report is a sworn
statement but the man who made the deposition cannot be found
anywhere.

It took me ten minutes to reason and talk coherently after I had
copied the Gerstein report. Schuele had expected this reaction. A
glass of whiskey and a cup of black coffee were served. I needed
both. "Perhaps you understand now what we are fighting for"
Schuele said. "Today's Germany tries her best to atone for the
crimes that were committed. This is why our bureau was established. It is impossible to bring the dead back. At least we will
try to find those criminals who survived. We cannot really undo
the wrong that was committed. We all know that!"

I had spent most of the day at Ludwigsburg. I was glad to
escape the depressing atmosphere of the war crimes centre. The

limousine which the West German Government had thoughtfully provided for me returned me to Stuttgart and its beautiful lights. I wanted to be alone. I asked the chauffeur to drive me to Stuttgart's huge Television tower and dismissed him. I spent the rest of the evening on the tower's lookout platform. Below me lay Stuttgart, bathed in thousands of lights, home of close to a million Germans. Many of Stuttgart's people have never learned of the crimes committed in their name and recorded in Ludwigsburg. The young people of today were not even born during the Nazi era. Do all of them share the guilt as some Americans and Canadians believe? Actually they do not. For very few Germans could have known in 1933 what Hitler was capable of. When they clearly recognized the character of the Nazi regime they had helped into power it was too late to act. The unlimited resources of an unprincipled police state smothered every attempt to overthrow the regime. When the Nazis were driven from power, when the people learned what had really happened, they were aghast and horrified at the crimes committed in their name. With few exceptions today's Germany attempts to bring the Nazi criminals to trial and liquidate the heritage of horror.

A Catholic priest approached me: "I read your article in this morning's paper and recognized you from your picture", he introduced himself. "I understand you were to interview Chief prosecutor Erwin Schuele. Did you, actually?" When I confirmed this he asked me for my impressions.

The evening was still young. I wanted to talk to someone. I gave the Father a brief outline of what I had learned and seen. Tears came to his eyes. "There is nothing I can really say", he stated. "Our nation simply lost its mind. This sometimes happens to individuals. We will have to accept the fact it could happen to entire nations. It makes me think of the beginning of Dante's *Inferno*:

> Midway the journey of this life I was aware
> That I had strayed into a dark forest
> And the right path appeared not anywhere. . .

This happened to our nation. Now we are trying to extricate ourselves. It is a question of conscience, individual and collective conscience. We have started to punish a few of the guilty. But are the Nazi crimes not the crimes of mankind? Why did the outside world encourage Hitler during his early years? Why did they

permit the reoccupation of the Rhineland? Why did other nations
refuse to accept an unlimited number of Jewish refugees? All
the murder victims of Belzec and the other death factories could
have been saved. Was there no room for them in the wide-open
spaces of the United States or the Soviet Union? Or Canada?
Australia? South Africa? Could these nations not have absorbed
the six million? It would have been so easy for them! No, their
failure does not diminish our guilt. Members of our nation committed the murders. As a nation, the Germany of 1933 was guilty
of mass murders. And let that foreign nation which is entirely
innocent cast the first stone!"

The priest bade me goodnight and left. Below me the lights
of Stuttgart were slowly going out. Twenty years after victory
the scars of war have all but disappeared. The cities have been
rebuilt. German industry is running full blast. The German
people experience the biggest economic boom of their violent history. Only the murder victims remain very dead.

CHAPTER XI

WEST GERMANY'S POLITICAL VACUUM

Stuttgart was to be the last town of my itinerary in West Germany proper. I had travelled through the Federal Republic for almost three weeks. It was time to record my impressions of the country's political condition.

My editor-in-chief had asked three simple questions: "Who do you think will win the next Federal elections? What will be the consequences of these elections? Would there be any appreciable difference in German foreign policy if the Social Democrats ever formed a government?"

I had set aside ten minutes to cable brief, concise answers. When the allotted time was up, I had not yet reached any conclusions. I paced across a hotel room whose floor was covered with torn-up cable drafts. I continued to compare notes and tried to draw up an intelligent analysis. I could reach none that made any sense. — After two hours I finally sent my home paper a cable which might go down in the annals of journalism as the most nondescript analysis ever sent home by a pundit: "Don't know who will win STOP won't make any difference anyway STOP nothing will change here STOP German voters don't care either way STOP please don't fire me STOP regards."

The abdication of West German Social Democrats as a fighting organization and the emasculation of their original social philosophy has left West Germany without an actual opposition party. The Weimar Republic's proportional election law had created a large number of splinter groups: eventually democratic process collapsed and the Nazis took over. When the three Western occupation powers turned over their zones to local German leaders laws were promulgated to govern the slowly emerging West German

State. These laws called for the establishment of electoral districts fashioned after the Anglo-Saxon electoral system. Thus the allied military authorities had set the pattern for West Germany's *Grundgesetz*, the Fundamental Law which became the new state's constitution. Half of the members of parliament are elected under this Anglo-Saxon system, the other half by the old proportional voting procedure. The authors of West Germany's constitution wanted to avoid the pitfalls of Weimar-type splinter parties; in order to be represented at all, a party must receive at least five per cent of all votes cast; political groups falling below the five per cent mark are struck off the electoral list. Their votes are lost.

This was an innovation for Germany. Historically the new rules were as new and strange to the people of West Germany, as communism was to East Germany. The most important consequence was the elimination of small political parties. After twelve years only three parties are left. During the first few elections the CDU, the party of Adenauer and Erhard, reached an absolute parliamentary majority and could rule alone. In later elections they fell short of a majority but continued to rule in coalition with the small "Free Democrats", the party of Erich Mende. The Social Democrats, although numerically the largest party since 1961, never had a chance to form a government. Since the "economic miracle" worked in favour of the ruling CDU, the socialists dropped all pretences of socialism. Prosperity proved a better social equalizer than any socialist platform.

There are no parties of the extreme right or left in parliament. The Communists were outlawed. This law was highly controversial and was hotly debated at all levels. It was received with mixed feelings by liberals who believed in the individual's right of free political choice. The Government issued a two-pronged explanation for their anti-Communist edict: The Communists had not received five per cent of the total vote and therefore had lost their right to sit in parliament; and the banning of the KPD (German Communist Party) made it legally possible also to ban neo-Nazi groups.

Most of the country's young intellectuals rejected this type of reasoning. They argued that since the KPD had not reached the minimum of five per cent of the votes, banning them was unnecessary; it was a symbolic act without practical justification. Besides, Communism and Nazism were not out of the same mould and should not be compared. — The Socialist Reich Party had been banned several months after the Communist obliteration. Smaller pro-Nazi groups which served the members of the dispossessed Reich party as political abode were not banned. West Germany's openly pro-Nazi newspaper *German National and Soldiers' Journal* of Munich also continued to publish. But all Communist papers were shut down.

In Germany's stormy past economic factors had always been reflected in the composition of her parliament. Recessions had caused a radicalization of the voters which went far beyond the comparable developments in other Western countries. Hitler had been given his first chance by the German inflation of the early 1920's; he almost made it — he lost the Beer Hall Putsch of 1923 by sheer accident. The great depression of the early thirties pushed the Nazis back into the limelight, after the business boom of the twenties had almost wiped them out. In the last free German elections of March 5, 1933 they polled forty-three per cent of all votes. The very same depression which had brought Roosevelt and his moderate New Dealers into power in the United States, made a fanatic party of extremists masters of Germany.

In today's West Germany small parties cannot exist; they are wiped out. Since the country is experiencing an unprecedented boom, the parties of the centre (today's Social Democrats are one of them) corner all the votes. People who are dissatisfied with present conditions are unable to express their disenchantment politically. There is no party for them to vote for. No serious political arguments go on in Bonn's parliament. The dialogue between Franz Joseph Strauss, controversial boss of Bavaria's CSU, and men like Willy Brandt or Fritz Erler, are rooted in personality differences, not opinions. West Germany is experiencing a situation properly described as a political vacuum.

One generation ago the shrill discussions between the Weimar Republic's political parties threatened the peace of the world. In an editorial of March 1932, the London *Times* stated: "The German factions are the world's most ill-tempered political groups. They do not wish to cooperate in the management of their country's affairs. They want to tear each other to pieces. Their internecine fighting makes onlookers forget that they are all citizens of the same land."

When we examine the two German states of today, we find that there is little serious political controversy among the parties of West Germany; there is equally little argument between the parties of East Germany. But the cleavage that existed between Germans of the right and of the left before 1933 still lives on today. The disputes which once took place in the old Reichstag now fill the air waves between Bonn and East Berlin. They are carried on by the two contesting German governments. During the late 1940's, a great German population exchange took place. Active socialists and communists living in the three Western occupation zones found their activities hampered by local authorities. They simply moved to the Soviet zone, where they felt politically at home. Former Nazi Party members and other rightists who had reason to fear the avenging anger of the Soviet authorities, moved to the West. When the Federal Republic was proclaimed in 1948 and started to function in 1949, most hard-core socialists of West German birth had already established themselves in the Soviet zone. Most rightists and conservatives had moved to the Federal Republic. This exchange of politically active citizens continued until the great Berlin wall was built in 1961. The exodus of rightist East Germans into West Germany weakened the influence of East Germany's remaining anti-socialist opposition; and the transfer of pro-communist West Germans to the GDR had a similar effect on West Germany's parliament. The emasculation of the opposition spirit in West Germany's political life today is a direct consequence of the large-scale population exchange between the two states. As internal opposition in both states decreased, the dispute between the two opposing German regimes became more vociferous. The cleavage between the Ulbricht and Erhard governments is serious — but no more serious than the battle between the parties of the right and of the left had been in the Reichstag of the Weimar Republic. In this shrill dialogue between the German factions the Federal Republic represents the voters of the right and centre, and the German Democratic Republic those of the left. The principle of non-compromise between the two German states is simply the political continuation of the principle of non-compromise which existed between the opposing groups of the Weimar Republic. They find their expression in the Federal Republic's Hallstein doctrine, a set of rules first formulated by Professor Hallstein, one of the planners of the European Economic Community (EEC). According to Hallstein, the East German Government has no legal status and exercises its powers against the will of its citizens. It cannot be recognized and is unworthy of diplomatic relations. Bonn refuses to deal with any state recognizing East Germany. If a country accredited to Bonn should suddenly recognize the Ulbricht regime, all diplomatic relations between West Germany and the offending state would cease. There is one notable exception. West Germany maintains diplomatic relations with the Soviet Union, even though Moscow recognizes East Germany. This policy of non-recognition goes further. Bonn refuses to honour East German passports. It will not enter into discussions with the Ulbricht government. No official cultural ties exist. Federal authorities refuse to sign any documents on which the signature of an East German official also appears. No negotiations are ever carried out between the two German governments. If an urgent matter has to be settled, Bonn ostensibly contacts Moscow. The Federal Republic considers East Germany to be a country occupied by Soviet troops. East Germany's name is boycotted by the West German press; the country is simply called "The Soviet-occupied zone of Germany" — abbreviated to "the zone". This complete political, economic and cultural boycott (the Hallstein doctrine aims at dogmatic totality and does not allow the slightest pragmatic compromise) has created a serious, warlike atmosphere in the heart of Europe. The consequences of the boycott — it can be likened to a political and spiritual blockade — reach into every East German household. GDR citizens may not travel unhindered in West Germany and other NATO countries. Their football and ice hockey teams cannot take part in international meets. Their scientists can't participate in international conferences. This isolation is deliberately planned by the Hallstein doctrine. It aims at creating dissatisfaction and dissension in the East German population. In this respect the doctrine has not been successful — like all measures of applied force it has created a reaction of truculence and anger in East Germany.

The opposing aims of the two German states are easy to define. Bonn wants to unite the two states; after reunification it aims at a change of the eastern borders imposed after the end of the Second World War — by peaceful means if possible. East Germany on the other hand tries to defend and maintain her statehood and in order to gain allies for the maintenance of her western border, she has accepted the facts of her eastern border. The GDR therefore defends the status quo, the conditions of post-war Europe. West Germany aims at the status quo ante — a single German state with the borders of 1937, the last year before Hitler tried to change them by force of arms. These political aims are openly proclaimed to the world at large. Bonn publishes huge quantities of maps of Germany which hang in every single government office of the Federal Republic and in every consular or ambassadorial bureau abroad. The maps show the borders of the German State, as it looked in 1937. The westernmost part is coloured in deep red and is marked "Federal Republic"; the middle section appears one shade lighter marked "Central Germany — Soviet-occupied Zone". The east sectors are one additional shade lighter and are marked "East Germany, under temporary Polish and Soviet administration". The East German State actually occupies the central part of the maps; the areas which the maps mark as "East Germany" are the districts beyond the Oder and Neisse rivers which were given to Poland and the USSR after Hitler's defeat and which have become integral parts of the two victorious states. The implications of these maps are clear. They represent the political and potentially military aims of West Germany. In West German schools, where this feeling of a "single, united Germany" is instilled into the Federal Republic's youth, these three parts of Germany are commonly called West Germany (meaning the Federal Republic), Central Germany (meaning the GDR) and East Germany (meaning the lost lands beyond the Oder and Neisse rivers).

Bonn's ultimate goal is therefore a single, undivided German state under the economic and political principles of the present Bonn Constitution. All major West German political parties agree to these principles — smaller parties who might disagree have not been able to elect members to the Federal parliament. On major issues of foreign policy a complete vacuum exists in the Bonn parliament. Debates are limited to minor disagreements. Occasionally an individualistic deputy might rise and make a short, controversial speech. But there are no major political debates. There is little leeway for opposing opinion.

During the summer of 1964 a more serious debate threatened to change the political calm. The Government had attempted to pass emergency legislation. These so-called *Notstandsgesetze* were meant to become effective in case of war or threatened war. The proposed laws granted sweeping powers to the Government in case of a sudden emergency. This debate aroused West German voters. For Hitler's rise to power had been heralded by similar developments. During the last year of the Weimar Republic Presidential decrees under section 48 of the Weimar Constitution had set aside constitutional government. Eventually Hitler became Chancellor and stifled all remaining opposition by similar emergency laws.

If the issue of the *Notstandsgesetze* could have been brought to a plebiscite in 1964, the voters might have defeated them. Some liberal newspapers and magazines questioned their wisdom. *Der Spiegel* devoted considerable space to the event. The new laws created fear and anger in East Germany (actually, this had been one of the reasons for their promulgation). A West German magazine, the *Blätter für deutsche und internationale Politik* of Cologne, had openly stated: "These emergency laws are the first step in the establishment of a West German dictatorship". The article, entitled *"Griff nach der Diktatur"* was reprinted in many foreign newspapers. But most West Germans soon forgot about the controversial statutes. Parliament enacted them and they became law.

Does the lack of parliamentary factions of the extreme right and left mean that no radical groups exist in West Germany? Most communists have moved to the GDR, but a few remained behind. They go along with the organization of peace marches, influence the policies of a splinter party which never quite made parliament (the German Peace Union — DFU), and edit a few magazines and small newspapers. Under the Bonn Constitution an office resembling the FBI or RCMP has been created, the *Amt für Verfassungsschutz* (Office for the Protection of the Constitution). Since the Communist Party is illegal, all Communist organizers are subject to fines and imprisonment. The same applies to Nazi and neo-Nazi groups. It is one of East Berlin's perennial complaints that these laws are weighted heavily against leftist extremists and that Nazis are rarely prosecuted. Actually, the *Amt für Verfassungsschutz* does act against Nazis whenever the opportunity arises. But Nazis often operate in areas where they are protected by the local population. Communists are rarely helped by the public. This is the underlying reason why the *Amt* catches more Communists than Nazis.

According to East Berlin, the Federal Republic is a neo-Nazi state. Most civil servants and public figures are accused of a Nazi past. The population is believed to be Nazi-infested. East German newspapers often publish cartoons in which members of the Erhard cabinet are dressed in Nazi uniforms. This helps to convince the East German public that a Nazi state exists which aims at the destruction of the German Democratic Republic, thus dramatizing the dangers of the Hallstein doctrine. Actually these allegations are untrue. West Germany is a basically conservative state using the Anglo-Saxon principles of self-government, slightly altered to fit specific German needs. A few Nazis and Nazi-infested areas remain; they are not strong enough to exercise any appreciable influence on the conduct of the government. Bonn is not ruled by the principles of Adolf Hitler. It is ruled by the principles of the old Weimar parties of the centre and the conservative right — by ideas which could have stemmed from the brains of Bruening or Hugenberg, the leaders of the pre-Hitler Centre and Conservative parties. The amazing lack of political imagination of present-day West Germany is the consequence of the unspoken cooperation between the three political parties for the purpose of conducting a firm, uncompromising policy against the GDR.

A few highly-placed officials do have a Nazi past. Most of these men are opportunists; they had served the Weimar Republic; when Hitler came to power, they became Nazis. When the Allies set up their military government, they put themselves at their conquerors' disposal. Today they work for the Federal Republic. A few of the older officials had served the Kaiser in their younger days. Should there ever be another change of government, they would undoubtedly change their position again. Since Nazism has fallen into disrepute, most of these men are desperately anxious to hide their Nazi past. The danger that these men could work openly for a reestablishment of Nazi aims or principles is remote. East Berlin's hysterical reaction against their very existence appears unjustified. The employment or non-employment of these "old Nazis" therefore becomes an issue of political ethics, but its bearing on everyday political events can be exaggerated.

The same might be said for those actual Nazis who have not repented their past sins. Most of them can be found in small towns and villages; they tend to equate German patriotism with Nazi creed. Anyone criticizing the Third Reich becomes a *Schweinehund* in their eyes, an unpatriotic scoundrel fouling his own nest. None of these groups is represented in the present Federal Parliament. Nazi influence remains strong in the different expellee organizations, and only in connection with these groups does Nazism remain potentially dangerous. The *Witikobund* openly demands the return of the Sudeten territories. Several other organizations reject the Oder-Neisse border agreed to by the Potsdam Conference. Some expellee groups would openly risk war to regain their lost homeland. Expellee organizations often wear private uniforms reminiscent of the Nazi style. Meetings and marches outside the Berlin wall have been organized by these groups, causing a series of potentially dangerous incidents. They repeat many of the former Nazi slogans. They attract the disenchanted members of the population. A substantial part of the former expellees have found new jobs and have completely rebuilt their lives in West Germany. Not every former Sudeten German is a member of the extremist *Witikobund*. The percentage of actual or potential Nazis among expellees is slightly larger than the national average. But it rarely exceeds ten per cent of any one group.

The shrill dialogue between the two German states reaches crescendo force every time the Nazi issue is mentioned. One of East Germany's major complaints is that Bonn has never denazified its civil service. The complaint is basically correct. I mentioned that the former Nazi association of these civil servants is rarely dangerous to the cause of democracy. But the constant reminders from the East fill the hearts of these ex-Nazis with fear and apprehension. They are afraid of East Berlin's revelations of their past. They had done their very best to hide their political skeletons in their closets. The GDR's very existence constitutes a mortal danger to these people. Their collective fear gives further strength to Bonn's wish to eradicate the GDR.

The West German Government wavers between two basic foreign policy approaches. One group, identified by Chancellor Erhard and Foreign Minister Schroeder wishes to strengthen US commitment in Europe. This group objects to the independent course taken by France's DeGaulle and wants to put all of West Germany's military and political eggs into the Washington basket. The second group, identified by former Chancellor Adenauer and Bavaria's controversial Franz Joseph Strauss opposes the American alliance in its present form and tries to build a "third force of Western Europe". They applaud an independent French policy; their mood is anti-American. They aim at a completely independent Western Europe. To assure their immediate political success, they would grant temporary leadership of this European alliance to DeGaulle. But West Germany would emerge as the alliance's strongest member.* This group wants to solve the "problem of

---

* "It is a fallacy to argue that Germany would cease to be dangerous if she were integrated economically, politically, and militarily, into a Western European political and military federation. Such a federation would in many

the Soviet-occupied zone" from a position of strength and "European solidarity". Their very existence has helped to moderate the cold war between Washington and Moscow more than any other single event. Moscow has never forgotten the lessons of the Second World War, and a large segment of American public opinion still remembers the dangerous years between 1941 and 1945. Its influence is often minimized, but never denied. West German foreign policy is aimed at the neutralization of this seat of potential anti-German hostility. Bonn can rightfully claim that for the first time in three generations German foreign policy has been partially successful. Twenty years after the end of history's most murderous war, the nation which started it all has been fully accepted by the Western powers as a peace-loving entity. As far as the younger German generation is concerned, this change of character is at least partially credible.

---

ways resemble a cartel — and the Germans are masters in the manipulation of cartels." See Franz L. Neumann, *German Democracy 1950*, p. 286.

WEST GERMANY'S JEWISH COMMUNITY

When Hitler came to power 550,000 Jews lived in Germany. During the first few years of the Nazi regime, 150,000 emigrated. The first serious anti-Semitic pogrom occurred November 10, 1938 during the so-called *Kristallnacht*. Between 1938 and 1940, when the "phony" war turned into a "Blitz", another 130,000 had left. The remaining 270,000 stayed behind and were caught in the holocaust. When the war ended, 2,000 German Jews had survived, living underground in Germany. Approximately 8,000 German-Jewish survivors returned from the death camps. This derelict group of 10,000 people was all that remained of Germany's once prosperous Jewish community of 550,000.

Most survivors had but one thought — to leave Germany and move to another country. The memories of past suffering proved too much for the few German Jews who had escaped. All survivors shared a deep-seated distrust of everything German. Their attitude could be summed up in the words of one of the leaders of the reestablished community: "How can we trust a German now? Anyone of them might have been among the concentration camp murderers!" Two years after the war's end the German-Jewish population of what had by then become the three Western occupation zones had shrunk to less than 7,000.

Today, more than twenty years after the end of Nazism, West Germany's Jewish population has grown to 25,000. Eight thousand of this group live in West Berlin — the rest in the Federal Republic. This increase which all reasonable observers would have considered impossible fifteen years ago, is mainly the work of two leading members of the Jewish community: Karl Marx, publisher of the *Allgemeine*, the country's largest and best known Jewish

newspaper, and Hendrik van Dam, Secretary-General of West
Germany's Jewish communities. Their success was helped by a
relatively enlightened policy at high government level.

Düsseldorf is the nerve centre of the Federal Republic's Jewish community. There the *Allgemeine* is published, and the community headquarters are located nearby. Düsseldorf's largest synagogue used to stand in the Ziethenstrasse. During the *Kristallnacht* it was burned to the ground. The West German Government rebuilt it at government expense and turned it over to the
Jewish community. Karl Marx's newspaper takes up the building's top floor; van Dam's offices are several blocks away.

Karl Marx (no relative of the founder of communism) is a
very old man. His working hours are limited. Much of his time
is spent at Baden-Baden and other resorts. But his occasional presence is essential for the return of German Jews. Marx is the only
man completely trusted by both the West German Government
and the bulk of the German-Jewish population. Van Dam, a man
in his late fifties, is the more energetic of the two. He did most
of the spade work needed to revive the community. His methods
are less diplomatic than those of Marx — but most of the negotiations for financial restitution are the work of van Dam. "Without
him, there might not have been any worthwhile restitution payments", is the comment of most community leaders. For better
or for worse, the present state of relations between the Federal
Government and its Jewish citizens is the work of these two men.
This relationship is expressed in a complicated mass of restitution
laws. The principle of restitution is attacked by both sides. Most
Jews consider it completely insufficient for the suffering and
losses they had to endure. Those Germans who retain any anti-
Jewish prejudice believe them to be excessive. And the small
group of surviving Nazis use the restitution payments as propaganda material. "All our money is given to undeserving Jews who
survived. Germany will go bankrupt because of these payments",
is their steady complaint. The increase in the cost of living is
cleverly blamed on Jewish restitution payments by neo-Nazis. In
reality these payments amount to less than one per cent of the
Federal Republic's annual budget.

What is the truth of restitution payments? If we take the
word's meaning literally, the payments miss the mark by some
90 per cent. People whose bank accounts were confiscated receive
approximately eight cents on the dollar. Since the mark was de-

valued at the rate of 10 to 1 in 1948, a varying devaluation loss is charged against all bank accounts. A similar percentage is paid for lost income. No one may collect more than the salary of a senior civil servant. A business tycoon may have lost an annual income of ten million marks. A salaried director of an insurance company may have been deprived of an annual salary of 20,000 marks. Both claimants will receive the same settlement: 12,000 marks for each year lost. The 12,000 marks are then devalued at the rate of 5 to 1,* thus, 2,400 German marks is the maximum amount collectible for each year of lost income. If a claimant lived through the entire Hitler years, he will receive 24,000 marks, or $6,000. The smallness of these amounts creates considerable anger among the recipients.

There are two types of restitution payments: repayment by individuals and restitution by the Government. Individuals can be sued to return assets they illegally seized. The Government pays for assets seized by the Nazi Party or the Hitler government. It also pays for physical damages suffered by concentration camp survivors. Young people who had to interrupt their schooling receive a total of 10,000 marks for their loss. Actual out-of-pocket expenses for the costs of emigration are also reimbursed — again devalued at the rate of 10 to 1. The only loss for which full restitution is made is loss of furniture or jewelry. For furnishings and valuables had not lost their value at the rate of 10 to 1 at the time of the mark's devaluation. Exact proof of loss must be given — and the German Government is stricter than any North American insurance company would be. Affidavits mean little. There must be corroborating evidence. Since the Hitler years were lawless years, precious little evidence is available. Most North American claimants would scoff at the organization of German restitution payments. But to the Nazi persecutees the payments give sufficient money for a fresh start.

What kind of life awaits returning Jews in West Germany? The Federal Republic has enacted laws making anti-Semitic statements a criminal offence. There are no openly anti-Jewish newspapers (the few remaining pro-Nazi papers — Munich's *National and Soldier's Journal* is foremost — do not publish anti-Semitic articles). Anyone making anti-Semitic remarks is quickly arrested.

---

* The mark was usually devalued at ten to one, but in some cases of persecutees it was devalued at five to one.

Jews are permitted to enter all professions. Nevertheless, they are
not happy.

Latent anti-Semitism still exists. It can be felt in small towns.
The villages of Franconia and Schleswig-Holstein still are hot-
beds of anti-Semitism. The names of Bamberg and Würzburg
have become infamous throughout the world. In Bamberg, Nazis
splashed paint over Jewish cemetery monuments and painted
anti-Semitic slogans on walls and homes. In Würzburg an anti-
Nazi doctor had discovered the Nazi past of one of the town's
presiding judges and published his findings. The doctor and his
entire family had to leave Würzburg to save their lives. "The
threats and physical violence I had to undergo had become in-
sufferable", he explained during a press interview after his flight.
Neo-Nazis control the public life of Schleswig-Holstein. When the
Protestant Minister of Wesselburen attacked Nazism in a sermon,
his church remained empty. Nobody attended his services any
longer. The pastor also had to leave.

There is another side to the coin. In large urban areas (like
Berlin, Frankfurt and Stuttgart) not much anti-Semitism remains.
The young West German generation tends to be less anti-Semitic
than their elders — friendship for West Germany's small Jewish
community often serves them to express hostility against their
pro-Nazi elders. This dialogue between the two German generations has been described in many novels and plays. The parents
were often Nazi Party members; the youngsters question their
motive and common sense. But in practice this dialogue does not
always take place. To some extent the older generation influences
the thinking processes of young Germans. The most pernicious
influence is exercised by the remaining pro-Nazi teachers — particularly high-school teachers. The case of *Studienrat* (high-school
professor) Zind became a cause célèbre throughout the world.
Zind, a fanatic Nazi, had taught his classes the inherent justice
and wisdom of Hitler's anti-Jewish laws; he had also insulted
several Jewish citizens in public — a criminal offence under present
West-German law. When the police came to arrest him, he fled
to Egypt where he now heads a department of President Nasser's
Information Service.

A large segment of German officialdom tries to make amends
too obviously. Officials sometimes extend preferential treatment
to Jews; in most instances the recipients are embarrassed and even
harassed by these actions. "We want to be treated like anyone

else — neither better or worse", was the explanation of a Jewish
businessman who complained to me about this particular aspect
of present-day Jewish life in Germany. Most returning Jews are
elderly people who want to live out their remaining years in the
surroundings of their earlier life. The West German Government
grants 6,000 marks ($1,500) to all former persecutees who return.
This gift helps many older people make their soul-searching
decision. To return, or not to return. Young Jews rarely resettle
in Germany. Those few younger Jews who make West Germany
their home are not former residents. They are Jewish citizens of
South American countries where the arrival of German Nazis
after the war created an unpleasant political climate. This population exchange between countries like Argentina and Paraguay
on the one hand and West Germany on the other has its unusual
aspects. The flight of former German Nazis to Argentina and
Paraguay is well known. But it is virtually unknown that for each
German Nazi reaching these countries at least one South American
Jew has immigrated to West Germany. Former German Jews who
left the country when Hitler came to power rarely return. If the
emigrant was in his teens or twenties at the time, he never goes
back. Many families broke up over this issue. A rich German-Jewish brewer returned from Israel to his native Bavaria to claim his
holdings (he had left Germany in his forties and his sons had
been in their teens). Both sons refused to return. One worked as
a longshoreman in New York, the other lived in an Israeli Kibbutz. Both were poor. The father wanted his sons to take over his
business and threatened them with complete disinheritance. The
sons remained adamant. The father lives in Bavaria, a lonely
multi-millionaire. There are thousands of similar cases. The cruelties of the Nazi regime are too well remembered. The young generation, more impressionable and more idealistic than their elders,
have never forgotten. This inability to forget is one of the main
characteristics of German-Jewish life today. German Jewry suffers
from a doubly inverted age pyramid. Many old people and a few
very young. But the age group thirty to fifty is virtually extinct.

Has the small group of German Jews made an impact on West
Germany's cultural, economic or political life? There are cases
where individual Jews have made a success of their careers. One
of the larger Munich banks, F. Feuchtwanger & Co., is a Jewish
firm. There are others. But generally speaking, no Jewish influence can be felt in the West German economy, or its cultural or

political life. Before 1933 Jews contributed considerably to the
Germany of their day. Today their influence is minimal. It is
difficult to define it by percentages. Today's Jewish population
approximates six per cent of its pre-Hitler numbers. But their
economic or cultural efforts do not reach six per cent of the pre-
Hitler community's achievements. In a sense they try to hide
their talents. The wounds are still too fresh. "Look what happened
to us the last time we tried to develop Jewish talent in the arts
and sciences. The horrible consequences of our attempt to become
well-established in German political life are hard to forget. Let
us live simply, away from the limelight. And, please, don't quote
me!" These were the parting words of one of West Germany's
most prominent Jewish figures.

THE AFFLUENT SOCIETY, WESTERN STYLE

When the victorious Allies toppled to Nazi empire, they occupied a bankrupt country; its cities were burnt to rubble, its industry was virtually destroyed, its financial resources spent. Without food shipments and massive help from the conquerors a large part of the population might have perished. This is the view that we accept almost unquestioningly and it is the one which is most prevalent and which is projected officially or semi-officially in West Germany.

From other sources, especially an official American investigation that occurred at the war's close, it is far less certain that Germany's industrial plant was decisively destroyed in the Allied bombing raids and their aftermath. Teams of American economic and industrial experts were flown in and were checking the industrial installations on the ground in Germany within the shortest possible time after the shooting stopped. There can be hardly any doubt about their accuracy or objectivity. They were investigating the efficacy of their own military strategy, personnel, planes and bombs. They had no motive to understate the damage — on the contrary. Their widely respected over-all report, known as *The United States Strategic Bombing Survey (European War)*, published on September 30, 1945, goes so far as to state that "The majority of industrial plants, those that served strategically unimportant industries and were in locations that escaped area attacks were undamaged". The members of the Survey were also able to confirm that the index of total German armament production had actually risen until the third quarter of 1944; that raw material supplies, parts and accessories were deemed adequate by the Germans themselves for an increase in output of 20 per cent in the last quarter of 1944.

The misconception — if misconception it was — concerning the degree of damage to German industry was based on two faulty analogies. Observers and commentators drew too close parallels between the destruction of flats and dwellings, on the one hand, and the more durable factories and machine tools on the other. Secondly, they assumed that because the factory buildings themselves were destroyed, to a greater or lesser extent, that the machine tools within them were equally damaged. Both these assumptions proved to be largely incorrect, as we shall see. However high the piles of rubble rose in some cities and industrial areas — and they were high — the consequent loss of industrial capacity did not follow. Concretely, the comparison between the degree of destruction of all types of German industrial buildings and the machine tools within those buildings — based on a broad sample — showed a ratio of 42 to 46 per cent average destruction for buildings accompanied by an average machine tool damage of no more than 23 to 25 per cent. The Report makes absolutely clear that while serious damage was done to specific segments of the German economy — especially oil, steel, and transportation, "the Allies did not attempt to destroy the German economy as a whole". It went on to state that "There is no evidence that shortages of civilian goods reached a point where the German authorities were forced to transfer resources from war production in order to prevent disintegration on the home front". Food rationing was kept up until the spring of 1945 (the war in Germany ended with the formal ratification of German surrender signed in Berlin, May 9, 1945) and it was mainly the transportation failure, late in 1944, and the consequent coal shortage which thereafter caused civilian production to decline precipitously.

To cite such contradictory evidence is not to deny that things were in a very disorganized state in Germany at the end of the war, or that the average German lived under appalling conditions in 1945 to 1946. It is rather to throw light on the ensuing economic developments in Germany. For however much disagreement there may be about the state of the German economy in the middle of 1945, there is no doubt at all about what followed.

Five short years later the Federal Republic was on her way to becoming the richest country in Western Europe. The national product outranked all but two Western nations, Britain and the

United States. What caused this amazing metamorphosis? West
Germans will say: "Our economic miracle; the currency reform
of 1948 triggered the biggest boom Germany has ever known.
New fortunes were made and old ones were multiplied. Basically
we did it ourselves, with the United States helping us occasionally."

Many non-Germans will answer, "The United States poured
untold millions into the West German economy because she wanted to build up her former enemy as a reliable ally in the cold
war". Which of the two answers is valid? After examining the
details of the "economic miracle" I came to the conclusion that
neither answer was wholly valid. The destruction of Germany's
housing and industrial machinery — so far as it went — set the
scene for her post-war boom. Entire cities had to be rebuilt. Industries needed to be established or refurbished, although not
to the extent that we have been led to believe. The reconstruction
could not have been achieved so quickly without the help of American capital, but the need for it was not quite as drastic as has
been painted.

There is another factor which tends to be easily overlooked—
or swept under the rug — these days. The "rape of Europe" had
added immeasurably to the wealth of Germany. For more than
five years, the resources, labour, and industry of the occupied
countries underpinned the economy of the Reich and untold
treasures were carried back home. This extended one-way drain
cannot be ignored in explaining West Germany's miraculous recovery after the War.

The war years had changed the life pattern of most Germans.
At the turn of the century the country's main characteristics were
its ability to work hard and to accumulate wealth. The growth of
savings accounts, the constant buildup of assets and decrease of
liabilities, was a national trend. After two world wars and two
inflations, the people's zest to save had all but evaporated. They
began to follow the American example: earn big money and spend
most of it; improve the level of income, not the bank account.
This change of the national spending pattern inflated credit,
pushed up production and sales figures, and made West German
living levels the highest in Europe — second only to those of the
United States and Canada.

Inflation has always been Germany's great phobia. After the
First World War the great inflation of the early 1920's destroyed

all of the nation's savings. The mark had been devalued at the fantastic rate of one to one trillion. (In 1923 the United States dollar sold at four trillion, 200 billion marks.) This monster inflation had wiped out Germany's middle class and created a small social stratum of war profiteers. The pauperized middle class became the Nazi Party's main source of strength.

In 1923, to stabilize the mark, Reichsbank President Helfferich had devised a plan to use German public land as a new currency basis. His stabilization was no less sensational than the "miracle" of 1948, and the basic results were somewhat similar — an industrial boom which created the prosperity of the late 1920's. Germans once again started to save and hoard their earnings. The *Rentenmark* devised by Helfferich eventually became the *Reichsmark*.* During the great depression of the early 1930's unemployment started to eat up the people's savings. The Second World War wiped them out completely. This economic history was another important condition for the Federal Republic's continuing boom of the 1950's and 1960's.

Ludwig Erhard, Konrad Adenauer's Minister of Economics, is credited with planning the "miracle". Actually, Erhard's approach resembles that of his predecessor Helfferich, the miracle man of 1923. The influx of American capital, absent in 1923 in this form, but available in 1948 in huge quantities, accounted for the "miracle's" quicker tempo. The events of 1920-23 turned the once prosperous middle class into paupers bent on revenge. The currency reform of 1948 elevated the entire working population to middle-class status. It created something completely new in German history: a society without strong class distinctions. These developments were overlooked by the socialist theoreticians. Unemployment all but disappeared from the German scene. A scarcity of workers made itself felt. It was overcome to some extent by the importation of large groups of foreign workers. These worked at menial jobs no longer acceptable to the "German children of the economic miracle". In past decades Germans had disliked foreigners in their midst. The foreign workers

---

* It has been pointed out to me with justice that the Dawes Plan and the foreign loan of 800,000,000 gold marks were vital in Germany's emergence from bankruptcy at this time. (See George P. Auld, *The Dawes Plan and the New Economics*, New York, 1927, and the brilliant book on the post-Versailles period by Etienne Mantoux, *The Carthaginian Peace, or the Economic Consequences of Mr. Keynes*, Lond., Oxford U. Press, 1946.)

of the 1960's are not hated. They simply occupy the lowest rung
of West Germany's social ladder — they have taken positions formerly held by a German proletariat suddenly grown affluent. The
number of foreigners working in Germany is often overestimated.
In 1962, the last year in which a complete set of figures was published, they numbered 710,000. 580,000 were men, 130,000 women.
Heading the list were Italians (266,000), Spaniards (87,000), Greeks
(69,000), followed by the Dutch (53,000) and Austrians (47,000).
Of the rest 9,000 came from the "East block". About 30 per cent
of the foreign workers were employed in the iron and metal
industries, and 25 per cent in the building trade. Most foreign
workers sent their earnings abroad — for 1962 the total figure for
transferred funds was 1,600 million marks.

American workers like to show their prosperity by acquiring
large consumer durable items. This applies only partly to the
German worker. Inflation fears still haunt the country's economy.
Many Germans have gone on a gold-buying spree. (Gold may be
sold freely by all German banks.) Gold bars and gold coins have
become West Germany's most amazing status symbol. When I
visited the home of an old foreman working for Krupp, he proudly
took me into his living room, removed a picture and opened a
small wall-safe of the type shown in older Hollywood society
movies. He lovingly (no other expression fits) removed four small
gold bars and a collection of gold coins, placing them on the table.
Other family members crowded around the hoard with gleaming
eyes, as he told me the history of his gold. The treasure represented
his life's savings between 1950 and 1965. He owned no car ("I
can't afford one — it costs too much money") and uses his bike
to travel to and from his job. "Next winter we will travel to
Spain", he explained. "We all like to travel a bit." Travel, particularly winter travel, has become another status symbol of Germany's affluent society. For the average citizen the points of travel
include Southern Europe, the Near East and North Africa. Few
middle-class Germans travel as far as the United States or Canada.
These longer trips are reserved for the economic elite — who
have invented rather unusual junkets. Guided tours to hitherto
restricted places like Timbuktu and Saudi Arabia (Mecca is ex-
cluded — non-believers are not admitted there), and the com-
mercialized harems of semi-professional entrepreneurs of the Near
East.

By North American standards the average citizen's income is

rather modest. In 1962 the average German household's monthly income was DM 718.02 ($179.50). People today have 71 per cent more money at their disposal than in 1953 — indicating an increase in real purchasing power of approximately 40 per cent in nine years. Twenty-five per cent of all incomes is used for "on the spot" purchases — items other than food, shelter, clothing and insurance. The corresponding figure for 1953 had been 9 per cent. This increase in purchasing power has further stimulated the economic boom, even though total income figures are much smaller than those of American or Canadian workers. What are the average German worker's everyday luxury needs? These figures also changed greatly since the war. According to a tabulation reaching into 18,000 households, the average German consumes each year 1,390 cigarettes, 73 cigars, five ounces of fine-cut and 1.1 ounce of coarse-cut tobacco. He drinks 214 pints of beer, 16.7 pints of wine and 3.6 pints of hard liquor. He consumes 2.2 pints of champagne and 3.9 pints of fruit juice (West Germans are the world's only people who drink almost as much champagne as apple or grapefruit juice); the mineral water consumption stands at eleven pints per year.

The country's gross national product amounted to 77 billion 600 million marks in 1962 and has grown some 10 per cent since. Comparing the figures of 1962 with those of 1950, the building trades account for the most important increase (403 per cent); agriculture and forestry for the smallest (175 per cent); other items which multiplied during the first fifteen years of the Federal Republic's existence are manufacturing (358 per cent); transport and communications (282 per cent); banking and insurance (an amazing 439 per cent), and rents (314 per cent).

West Germans feel that one of the reasons for their prosperity is the existence of the European Common Market, an organization whose course is a matter of contention between France's DeGaulle and West Germany's Erhard. The Benelux countries and Italy round out this rather unusual partnership which had aided Germany's economic recovery during the first few years after the war. Since the summer of 1965 it has hindered rather than assisted the German economic potential. France's role in the Common Market has become an issue of heated controversy among the Market's senior members. France's main interest lies in the unhindered distribution of her agricultural surplus. Germany aims at controlling the sale of consumer durable goods while trying to keep out France's agricultural surplus. German landowners have one of Bonn's strongest parliamentary lobbies. They have declared war on France's attempt to "dump" farm products into the Common Market. At the time of writing the organization's future does not look very bright.

Against this background of economic solvency, West Germans have developed a climate of cultural consciousness. They have produced a number of talented young writers, whose political views veer toward the left. Günter Grass is probably the most brilliant, Rolf Hochhuth the most controversial, Peter Weiss the most sincere. Hochhuth's drama, *The Deputy*, in which he accuses Pius XII and the Holy See of criminal silence on Hitler's mass murders, has created a furore not only in West Germany but in the world at large. Hochhuth's position in Catholic West Germany became untenable after his work was published. He retired to Switzerland. Grass has written some of West Germany's most widely read novels. (*Dog Years* and *The Tin Drum* are the best known.) The latter novel has been read by many and understood by very few.

Grass has become a pamphleteer for the Social Democrats. Together with Rolf Hochhuth and Peter Weiss he launched a frontal attack against the "atmosphere of fat complacency prevalent in the Federal Republic". This caused the most amusing literary outburst of postwar German history. Grass and his friends annoyed the usually stolid Erhard. The Chancellor issued a brief statement in which he said: "The literary men attacking us can be compared to a horde of Pinscher (a breed of small dogs popular in Germany) whose bark is worse than their bite". — This statement almost lost Erhard the last Federal election. "Anti-intellectualism" had been one of the trademarks of the Nazi years. The Chancellor's ill-tempered outburst against young Germany's intellectual elite caused an embarrassing chain reaction.

The Federal Republic has experienced a renaissance of her theatres and operas (most small German towns have their own opera houses; opera has become one of Germany's prevalent art forms). Richard Wagner lost much of his prewar popularity. ("The genius of the German people is better expressed by Beethoven than by Wagner", one of Adenauer's statements is basically true.) East Germany's Bert Brecht Ensemble has played to standing-room audiences in Hamburg and West Berlin. The country has developed one form of entertainment less well-known in other parts of the world, the "political cabaret", a small theatre which is a cross between the legitimate stage and a night club. In these cabarets political satirists poke fun at events and figures in public life. (Later I learned that these cabarets exist in East Germany as well — they have become one of the few public places where outright criticism of the government is tolerated.)

West German movies concentrate on melodrama. German comedies are rarely funny to North American audiences. ("As a people Germans do not like comedy or comedians"; this statement made more than a century ago by the philosopher Arthur Schopenhauer still holds true.) The country's most unusual writer of adventure stories, Karl May, has experienced a renaissance. His best known stories, describing the nineteenth century conflict between the white settlers and Indians in North America, and the conditions of the Near East under Turkish rule, have been made into films — a British actor, Stewart Granger, plays the leading role. Every Karl May film is assured of box office records.

May was one of Germany's most puzzling writers. He never set foot in the United States or the Near East, yet he told amazing tales of his imaginary travels to these countries. He always takes the centre of the stage, describing himself as a fearless hero defending the good and punishing evil. During his lifetime May was widely attacked. He died a broken man in 1913. His stories are not "true" in the usual sense. But there is little doubt that he believed them to have been true — daydreams of a poor, weak person glorifying himself. May was exceptional in the sense that he set down his daydreams and became one of his country's most prolific writers. I cannot quite share the contempt heaped on the man during his lifetime and after his death. He was a literary genius whose sick mind achieved marvellous things. He had the misfortune to be Hitler's favourite writer. (Actually May had been a deeply religious man trying to teach the brotherhood of man in his novels — a trait completely lost on his reader Adolf Hitler.) Because of the admiration heaped on him by the Nazi government May has become persona non grata in East Germany, where he lived and worked during most of his lifetime. He was a native of Radebeul, a small town near Dresden.

Grand opera and Karl May — the zenith and nadir of German intellectual life today, the *Wohlstandsgesellschaft* — West Germany's affluent society which has not yet become accustomed to its new finery.

THE WORLD BETWEEN

CHAPTER I

WEST BERLIN — THE COLD WAR'S FRONTIER TOWN

The average North American thinks of West Berlin as a be-leaguered bastion of Western freedom situated at the very heart of political turbulence. Actually it is quite easy to reach West Berlin. Its outward appearance is peaceful and prosperous. The town is connected with West Germany by two super-highways, several rail lines and three air corridors. Train passengers and travellers using the highway have to clear East German check-points. Air travellers avoid this procedure. In less than two hours from most major German centres they reach West Berlin's Tempelhof airfield, the only major air terminal situated so close to a modern metropolis. It is an unusual experience to leave one's plane and then walk a mere three blocks to the centre of a large city.

I boarded a Pan American plane at Stuttgart. (One of the anomalies of the Berlin situation is that every major airline may serve Berlin, except the German airline *Lufthansa*.) Less than two hours later I stood on West Berlin's main thoroughfare, the Kurfürstendamm. My Berlin trip which had taken so much planning, had turned out less eventful than a Toronto-Montreal flight.

For those who knew Berlin before the Second World War a return visit will be disappointing. The former capital has ceased to be a world centre. Bonn has become the country's capital. The administrative headquarters of German banking and industry have moved to Frankfurt and Düsseldorf; the publishing trade went to Stuttgart and Hamburg; the stock exchange still maintains a branch office in Berlin, but it has lost much of its former importance. In 1933 sixty-two per cent of all people listed in *Who's Who* lived in Berlin. Today this figure has dropped to less than fifteen per cent. To people who knew Berlin at the height of its glory, the town has become second rate. Berliners always used to be smart and arrogant. (*Kess* is the Berlin slang word describing this state of mind.) This quality has not changed; but the city's beat has become more hectic. Berlin's collective mind is formed by the belief that it is "surrounded by the enemy". Politically and psychologically Berlin is a frontier town in which Communists have taken the role of raiding Indians, and the West Berliners that of white settlers holding their ground in the midst of potential — and sometimes actual — attack. This hectic atmosphere quickly infects the visitor. Guided tours of the Western side of the great Berlin wall whip up the tourist's hitherto dormant feeling of political responsibility. The wish to free this noble, embattled city is common to almost all Western visitors. It is a feeling shared equally by leading Western political leaders and the anonymous visitor from Tuscaloosa and Waukegan. President Kennedy's famous statement *"Ich bin ein Berliner"* certainly came from his heart. The thought represents the feeling of most Western tourists, and dispensing the ingredients which cause this elating "spirit of the fighting West" is West Berlin's most important industry.

I did not prove immune to infection. I had come from prosperous, reasonable, down-to-earth West Germany, where thoughts like "German reunification", "embattled Berlin", and "the West's bastion against the Godless East" belong to a few well-advertised expellee organizations and to all political office seekers at election time. The rest of West German public opinion is surprisingly realistic. In West Berlin all this changes. The overwhelming majority of West Germans pay occasional lip service to nationalistic schemes. The more progressive groups, such as college students and young writers, openly scoff at them. In West Berlin the tables are turned. Most students of the "Free University of Berlin" believe in the ultimate necessity of using arms and securing Berlin's freedom. It is easy to whip up a crowd for quickie demonstrations against East Berlin's Communists. People who would be openly opposed to warlike actions if they lived in West Germany proper, usually are in the forefront at West Berlin demonstrations. The city has become an operational centre for groups wishing to change the results of the Second World War. It is an irritant next door to East Germany's nerve centre. The deep concern felt for the Berlin problem by most responsible Western and Eastern statesmen anxious to keep the world peace becomes apparent to every traveller visiting both parts of Berlin; all he has to do is to check the facts in both parts of town. It takes some time before the impressions fall into place and begin to form a pattern of reason. It took me one full week of visiting all parts of both West and East Berlin before I could even begin to rationalize the problem.

When I left Stuttgart I bid goodbye to *Inter Nationes,* the West German organization which had guided me through the country. In West Berlin a young lady representing the West Berlin Press Office awaited me. She was a young, married college student who worked to help with her studies. Unlike her West German colleagues she hoped to emigrate as soon as possible. "West Berlin is a dying city", she confided, "No, I do not believe there will be war. But everybody who is anybody either has already left or is planning to. Berlin is the past. Frankfurt, Düsseldorf and Munich are the future. I dislike the past. I live for the future. I want to get out!"

The Kurfürstendamm is West Berlin's Broadway. This is more than a figure of speech. The similarity of the two thoroughfares is amazing. Except for the German signs, the "Ku-Damm", as it is popularly known, resembles the area between New York's 40th and 57th Streets. The district around the gutted Kaiser Wilhelm Memorial Church is a carbon copy of Times Square, complete with automats, hot-dog stands, cheap little movie theatres and teenage crowds which cannot be distinguished from their Times Square opposite numbers except by the German language.

The Memorial Church merits a few lines; it is no doubt the most outrageous piece of postwar construction on view. The original church had been gutted in one of the major air raids. The town planners left the ruins of the old building intact — a memorial to the futility of war. This was a noble thought. Unfortunately the town planners followed up the original idea by rebuilding the church next door as a modern skyscraper with glass panels and stainless steel ornaments. It looks like an ill-conceived miniature Empire State Building. In Berlin slang the new church is called *Gasamt Gott* — God's office block.

The "Ku-Damm" also is the heart of Berlin night life. It boasts several night clubs for homosexuals, a practice officially frowned upon in other world capitals. In Berlin it exists openly. Some other buildings merit attention. The Berlin Hilton — next to the one in Athens — is the most luxurious of all Hilton hotels. The huge Europahaus attempts to copy New York's Rockfeller Center.

A few large West German business firms have branched out into West Berlin — often for political reasons. Axel Springer built his skyscraper directly on the East-West border. Flight tunnels underneath the wall were dug to or from the Springer basement. When an East German policeman was killed by a Springer employee the West Berlin Government clamped down on their "digging activities".

West Berlin is not entirely urban, as most North Americans believe. There are wide stretches of land which are completely rural. The Grunewald, a forested and landscaped area, stretches for many miles around the outskirts of town. The Wannsee is a pretty lake near the border. Actually, West Berlin's legal status in the Federal Republic is that of a *Land* (state), with a state parliament and an executive government. The parliament, or *Abgeordnetenhaus,* is elected by West Berlin's entire population. The *Abgeordnetenhaus* in turn elects the Lord Mayor — at the moment this office is held by Willy Brandt. The Lord Mayor, whose office compares to that of a state governor, then names the actual mayor who attends to the daily tasks of city administration. This important office is presently held by Heinrich Albertz. The cabinet of the Lord Mayor is referred to as "The Senate".

Berlin's unsettled status stems from the time when the town was split into four occupation zones and administered by a four-power council. When later the three Western-occupied parts of Germany formed the Federal Republic, and the Soviet-occupied zone became the German Democratic Republic (GDR), each state wanted to annex Berlin. As a temporary compromise, the four-power status was officially continued but the rights of the council were rigidly cut to the point of non-existence. Today its rights are primarily symbolic and one of the few remaining functions of the Four-Power Council is the guarding of the major Nazi war criminals in Spandau prison. West Germany considers West Berlin to be one of her *Länder* and East Germany maintains that West Berlin is a "Free City" and not part of the Federal Republic. Most East German actions hampering free access to West Berlin are caused by her policy of not recognizing the political union between West Berlin and West Germany. The Federal Republic pays lip service to this state of affairs by one solitary compromise: West Berlin elects members to West Germany's *Bundestag* (parliament), but these members do not have the right to vote. They sit in the *Bundestag* as observers. But they are allowed to make speeches. And these speeches serve to remind the world of West Berlin's precarious position.

To most Western newspaper readers West Berlin is an exposed outpost of Western civilization — a beleaguered garrison of freedom. To most Eastern newspaper readers West Berlin is a beehive of spy activities, an advance post of American and West German imperialism. Both points of view are overdrawn, but any writer trying to analyze the recurring difficulties between West and East Germany must bear them in mind. To Western observers, the access routes to Berlin constitute basic rights which must not be touched by the East German Government. To Eastern observers, these routes cutting across the territory of East Germany are used to ferry vicious spies into the nerve centre of the German Socialist State and to supply a hostile army in their midst. Whenever the East German Government feels that "too many spies or too many arms" are carried across, they tighten the border controls and slow down traffic. This Eastern action never fails to evoke great indignation in the West, since the supply routes to "heroic Berlin are once again threatened".

The worst crisis of the past few years occurred when the West German *Bundestag* suddenly decided to hold a meeting in West Berlin. The East Germans do not recognize West Berlin as part of the Federal Republic. They felt that West Germany's parliament had decided to sit in a neutral area where it held no right of sovereignty. The controversial session was held in a building less than 300 yards away from the wall, which by East German standards constitutes the "border of the GDR". The West German action spelled one word to East Berlin: Provocation! The East German authorities clamped down on autoroute traffic and halted all trains. But the *Bundestag* deputies used the air routes and all arrived safely in West Berlin. The session was held in the Congress Hall, not far from the old Reichstag, within shouting distance of the wall. The East Germans now started a provocation of their own. Just as the parliament's session began, a formation of Russian MIG-fighters started manoeuvres directly overhead at 1,000 miles an hour. Whenever the sound barrier is broken, sounds resembling artillery fire develop. During the following two hours it became impossible for the *Bundestag* members to continue their session. The noise drowned out their loudspeakers and amplifiers.

The third world war could have started at this point. Each side had provoked the other. Fortunately there were no further incidents and the Western governments politely suggested to Bonn that the Bundestag should not attempt to sit in Berlin for some time to come.

The Four-Power Council maintains another atrophied function: solitary rounds of military vehicles representing the four occupying powers. In East Berlin I was suddenly confronted by an American jeep with three GI's and one officer, driving along Karl Marx Allee. I learned that American military vehicles enter East Berlin from time to time to symbolize Western rights conferred by the Four-Power Statute. This sort of thing is a constant irritant. The East German Government never tried to end the practice, but turned its propaganda guns against these "visiting GI's". "Child run over by American army jeep"; "old woman brushed aside by sneering GI's"; "traffic constable who tried to stop jeep from crossing a red light run down and killed", are some of the headlines appearing in East Berlin's press. Are American soldiers actually running amok in East Berlin, as some of these stories would indicate? I tried to learn the answer. But each story disintegrated as I tried to run it down. "Someone saw a woman being run over", was the answer I received from an East German city editor. But he could not tell me the date it had happened, nor the woman's name. The roster of East Berlin traffic constables does not contain the name of any member run down by a military vehicle and the stories do not seem to stand up to close analysis.

Spandau, the prison where the three remaining major war criminals (Hess, Schirach, Speer) are kept, actually stands on West Berlin soil. The four Powers alternate in the jail's management. The three prisoners are probably the world's most difficult persons to interview. I had applied for permission to see Rudolf Hess — but was turned down. The closest I got to Europe's most enigmatic personality was one Soviet guard who had done duty outside Hess's cell several months ago. "Hess is not crazy", the guard, a staff sergeant, told me in excellent German. "You understand that we are not permitted to talk to the prisoners; but they often try to talk to us. Hess however is very talkative. I was detailed one day to walk the prisoners in the prison yard. Hess, now an old man, his hair completely gray, heard the noise of some air activity. "Lots of airplanes", he said. "Isn't it terrible how bad the weather is? I used to be able to pilot planes myself. Have they changed much during the past twenty years?" Then he tried to ask me about world conditions. Finally he asked me for books and newspapers. I referred his request to the prison authorities. I have no way of knowing whether he ever got them. One set of books he had requested were the works of the German philosopher Hegel. He also wanted to know whether President Kennedy would come to Berlin again. Apparently he had not heard of the assassination. No, I did not tell him. Hess insane? Dont make me laugh! Crazy people do not read Hegel!"

Willy Brandt, West Berlin's fighting Lord Mayor, heads the Social Democratic Party. West Berlin's parliament, the *Abgeordnetenhaus*, presently contains eighty-nine SPD men (Social Democrats), forty-one Christian Democrats and ten Free Democrats. The Social Democrats, who represent the opposition in the Federal Parliament in Bonn, rule West Berlin. The CDU, which governs in Bonn, head's West Berlin's opposition. But the West German pattern is repeated in Berlin. There is little difference between the SPD and the CDU. I doubt whether an "upheaval" in the Berlin *Abgeordnetenhaus* would result in a different domestic and foreign policy, or a change in cold-war policies.

West Berlin has a number of beauty spots. One of them is the Zoo. Next to the Frankfurt Zoo, it is undoubtedly the best known West German animal park. East Berlin's *Tierpark* actually far surpasses the West Berlin Zoo, but since few West Berlin visitors ever venture into East Berlin, West Berlin's Zoo remains one of the visitors' lasting impressions.

August 13, 1961 is a day not easily forgotten by West and East Berliners alike. On that date the East German Government built the great Berlin wall and ended all outgoing and incoming traffic. I had always wondered how such a huge structure could suddenly have been built on a given day. When I visited East Berlin I learned of the mechanics which had been applied to reach this sudden isolation. A solid wall of East German soldiers had served as a temporary barrier across Berlin, while a host of workmen feverishly built one of history's ugliest structures. Forgetting all the political pros and cons, the Berlin wall is one of the most unsightly enclosures I have ever seen. Unlike most prison or fortification walls the Berlin wall was built so quickly that on its Western side it looks forbidding, unfinished and raw. Only part of its entire length consists of concrete blocks and cement. The remainder is constituted of barbed wire fortifications or by retaining walls and buildings which have been torn down except for the parts now forming an integral part of the wall. For several miles the river Spree forms the border between the two halves of Berlin. No wall exists there — only wire entanglements on the river's eastern bank. Few visitors can approach the wall without a preconceived set of values. To the Western observer it is a monument to infamy, the confining wall of a monster concentration camp, the Eastern rulers' frank admission that they cannot hold on to their population without resorting to brute force. To the Eastern observer it is a barrier wisely drawn to protect the GDR against subversive foreign infiltration, to keep out vicious currency speculators trying to enrich themselves at the expense of the East German economy, and the "border of the state" which no East German may cross without a proper passport and exit visa. One fact stands out above all others. The wall is ugly. It tends to isolate West Berlin. From the standpoint of psychological warfare it militates against East Germany. What caused the GDR to erect this unsightly structure? There must have been overriding reasons, for by its very existence the wall harms the East German Government's image.

Most Westerners believe the wall was built to hold back the flow of refugees from East Germany. The GDR lost approximately two million citizens — most of them young and middle-aged people whom she could ill afford to lose. The old and the very young remained behind creating an economic problem. Since their wage earners had left them behind, the East German State had to support them. During my stay in East Berlin I learned that while the refugee problem had been pressing, it was secondary to another vital problem, economic drain. Both East and West German marks are pegged at the same exchange rate. But in West Berlin East marks could be bought for a fraction of their official price. East German workers employed in West Berlin received their salary in West German currency. They would exchange their West marks into East marks at the favourable West Berlin exchange rate, bring their inflated salaries back to East Berlin, buy East German goods at Government-controlled low prices. They would then bring these cheaply bought goods into West Berlin where they sold them against West marks, again, exchanging the proceeds of their sales into East marks at the depressed West Berlin exchange rate. A simple worker could become a millionaire within a few months and many of them did — at the expense of the East German economy. This situation caused most skilled East Berlin workers to look for jobs in West Berlin and resulted in a

GDR labour shortage. In turn, the labour shortage further increased the economic problems of the East and accentuated the difference in value of the two currencies.

Some people had indeed fled the GDR for political reasons. But it is plausible to assume that most had followed the lure of better pay in the same manner in which many young Canadians migrate to the United States. During the summer of 1961 the situation had suddenly become critical. The Ulbricht government decided to build the wall primarily to stop the drain on its economy and to keep the increasing flow of migrants at home. The wall achieved this purpose. East German emigration to the West decreased to a trickle — some refugees still reached West Berlin through tunnels, ladders and other courageous escape routes. They made world headlines, but their number no longer mattered sufficiently to have a depressing effect on East Germany's labour situation. More important was the fact that the illegal import of East marks had come to an abrupt halt. I had last seen East Berlin during the summer of 1962 when the wall was only one year old. I was astonished at the great changes and improvements made by the city in three years.

The wall helps East Berlin's economy. It does not harm West Berlin's affluence. But it dealt it a serious psychological blow. The wall brought home to most West Berliners the complete geographic isolation of their city. East Berlin admits foreigners through "Checkpoint Charlie", and West Germans through several other checkpoints. But West Berliners are forbidden to cross. During the past few years temporary permits, the so called *Passierscheine,* have been issued during holiday seasons to West Berliners visiting relatives in the Eastern sector. During the rest of the year West Berliners are not admitted.

Their reaction against the wall was one of fury. This is understandable. The wall's western side became an excellent propaganda vehicle for the West Berlin Government. Not all official actions were wise. Every few yards huge white and red signs appear on the west side of the wall: "KZ" (the German abbreviation for "concentration camp"); "We will never recognize the Oder-Neisse line". At important intersections huge parade stands have been erected enabling tourists to look across to East Berlin. These stands are covered with signs: "Ascend at your own risk". When I had reached one of the highest of these unique structures, the one near the Bernauer Strasse (twenty feet high) I was almost disappointed that nobody tried to shoot at me from the other side. The most photographed spot of the Berlin wall is the section separating the Linden from West Berlin, in front of the Brandenburg Gate which actually stands on East Berlin soil. Here two huge stands have been erected on the west side and one small one on the east side; the eastern stand is out of bounds to the general public. The western stands are used by all Berlin tourists. Photographers often offer their services to visitors wishing to mail home a snapshot of themselves with the threatening wall and the pretty Brandenburg Gate in the background. The wall also cuts across one of old Berlin's most famous landmarks; the Potsdamer Platz. This square had once been the hub of Berlin vehicular traffic. Today it has become a no-man's land, framed by a high section of the wall and barbed-wire entanglements. Several clever West Berlin businessmen have erected a photo stand on the western side, selling pictures of the Square as it once looked. It was the only spot on the wall's western side where I was stopped by two armed. West Berlin policemen. I was allowed to proceed after flashing my press card.

At the Potsdamer Platz I was able to take a good look across the wall. I noted a carefully raked sandbank on the wall's eastern side. "Easy to recognize footsteps — that is why they do it! Any potential escapee would be spotted within seconds", was the explanation of one of the policemen.

Escapees spotted by East German border guards are shot at — sometimes killed. This practice has created a number of martyrs whose names are inscribed with appropriate brief biographical notes on the wall's west side near the place where they met their death. I checked all the names I could identify — thirty-two of them — and found that twenty-four actually represented killed escapees. The remaining eight I could not identify. They may have been conceived in the imagination of one of the many hundreds of West Berlin press agents.

Most Westerners assume that all flight tunnels are dug from East to West. Actually I was unable to identify a single East-West tunnel. Most tunnels are dug from West Berlin into East Berlin in the hope of spiriting out certain individuals. Some of these "tunnel diggers" are semi-professional entrepreneurs working for high fees. In at least three instances prospective "tunnel engineers" are now before West German courts, charged with "obtaining money under false pretences". "Illegal contract, unenforceable in a court of law", is the line of all three defence attorneys. "To enter forcibly a hostile jurisdiction is an act of war, and the results of warlike acts can never be predetermined!" The three accused had collected large fees in advance, then had failed to dig the tunnel. One of the men has meanwhile been sentenced to four years in prison.

The hectic border town atmosphere shows in a quick and angry exchange of accusations. East and West Berlin both have TV stations. Obviously, both channels can be viewed by each side. To listen to West Berlin telecasts is not a punishable offence under East German law. East Berliners often tune in on West Berlin. "We never make laws which cannot be enforced", a highly placed East-German official explained to me later. "Since we cannot stop our people from viewing West Berlin stations, we don't call it a crime. We don't particularly like the practice but there is little we can do to stop it." The exchange of East and West Berlin epithets is worth hearing. "Another poor escapee was killed this morning" roared West Berlin's channel on the evening of my visit. "Nonsense", answered its East Berlin opposite number. "A West Berlin common criminal had fled jail and one of the guards shot him while he was trying to flee East." I have never been able to find out which side was right.

The West and East flaunt each other's martyrs across the dividing line. Huge pictures of East Berlin's "murdered heroes" can be clearly seen from the West. "Murdered people's heroes" are members of the *Vopo*, the armed peoples' police, who were killed by escapees or by rifle fire from the West. The West in turn exhibits huge posters across the wall, showing larger than life-sized pictures of killed escapees. This battle royal of the West Berlin Press Office and the East Berlin Information Ministry some-times reaches amusing proportions near the wall. Some of the huge caricatures and drawings shown across the wall are really witty. Near the Bernauerstrasse the West shows a huge picture of a concentration camp victim trying to break his chains. The caption: "One day he will be free!" On the opposing side the caricature is of a monocle-wearing Prussian officer of the old school in a swastika-adorned West German army uniform. The caption: "Says you!" Another rather amusing Eastern poster near the Potsdamer Platz: the eagle (West Germany's heraldic animal) with its claws pulled and its injured head bandaged. Inscription: a hard-to-translate Berlin slang expression: *"Siehste, das haste davon!"* (Well, that's all you get out of it!) The sardonic humour of this typical Berlin exchange is often lost on the North American tourist.

The wall's impact on West Berliners is entirely negative. On the Eastern side the wall's existence is not felt so keenly, for East Berlin is the geographic centre of a state. Its people have the possibility of extended tours into suburbs and the open country. They can make trips to the Baltic or to the mountains of Saxony and Thuringia. West Berliners feel hopelessly hemmed in and thwarted. This state of mind creates an emotional illness which I chose to call "Berlinitis", to the consternation of my West Berlin contacts who after much thinking and soul-searching finally admitted its existence: Narrow provincialism and nationalism seeking to expand and break the surrounding chains at all cost. In a sense this feeling of utter frustration which haunts the West Berliner can be understood and appreciated. But it is the underlying cause of the many recurring Berlin crises and of the strain in that sensitive part of the world. It left me with the impression that today's Berlin situation is potentially more dangerous to world peace than many other better advertised global trouble spots. "Berlinitis" shows up in the most unlikely places. One of them is the legitimate stage. Berlin has one of Germany's best "political cabarets", the *Stachelschweine* (hedgehogs). In Munich and Hamburg the cabaret jokes are amusing and relaxing. They are directed at perennials like Adenauer's untiring old age, Erhard's corpulence, and Strauss's lack of tact and political finesse. But the *Stachelschweine* deals in angry and bitter comedy. (Until I attended a performance I would have considered this word combination a paradox; but it is the only way to properly convey the impressions created by the cabaret.) Between sketches dealing with standbys like legalized prostitution and bureaucracy of the Town Planning Commission (the Kaiser Wilhelm Memorial Church Commission must be the world's most kidded planning commission), the stage shows a vicious Walter Ulbricht ordering the murder of innocent women and children and a bleeding escapee running into West Berlin's City Hall crying for help. Instead of giving immediate medical attention the administrators have him fill out a four-page questionnaire. In another sketch, two escapees try to get away from East German border guards. When the *Vopos* finally catch up with their quarry it develops that all they wanted was to join in the escape. I left the *Stachelschweine* with a sad heart and a bitter taste in my mouth. I had the intense feeling that the two opposing sides are utterly irreconcilable! This mentality may prepare the coming of the next (and last) world war.

West Berlin's Press Office is some distance from the heart of town. The building is much smaller than that of the Bonn office. But the atmosphere there is more hectic. It is organized as "Department III of the Senate Chancellery". Its head is a member of the ruling Social Democratic Party and a close associate of Lord Mayor Willy Brandt.

My interview with the head of the Press Office lasted more than three hours. Less than twenty minutes of the time was devoted to discussion. The remaining two hours and forty minutes (I timed it exactly) were wasted on innumerable telephone calls. The press officer had no less than four telephones on his desk. Very often they rang simultaneously. The official's ability to concentrate was admirable. During my visit a well-dressed young man rushed in and exchanged pleasantries and other small talk in flawless German without the trace of a foreign accent. I was amazed when the young caller introduced himself as the representative of the official Soviet News Agency TASS. I marvelled at the seemingly amicable relationship between the Soviet newsman and the head of the West Berlin Press Office at this focal point of the cold war. "Why not?" was the Russian's answer to my query. "Why take such things personally?"

I had been promised an interview with Willy Brandt, but he was out of town. The federal election campaign had started to gather steam. I had interviewed and spoken to Brandt during my short stay in Nuremberg some five days earlier, where he had held an election rally. Brandt who in Western eyes represents "West Berlin's indomitable will to survive" is a strange man. During the Hitler years he lived abroad, working against the Nazi Government. This fact damaged him politically both with rightists and leftists. The nationalists dislike all former emigrés, and some leftists prefer those who lived out the Hitler years in German concentration camps or underground. Actually Brandt's exile saved his life. Most observers are certain that he would not have survived in a camp. Brandt is an easy-going Social Democrat with a severe case of "Berlinitis". He is convinced that the East Germans wish to engulf, starve out, and eventually annex West Berlin. Consequently he has advocated a tough policy against the East. He heartily endorses the construction of escape tunnels and had at one time suggested armed forays into East Berlin territory "whenever or wherever humanity demands it". These views are shared by the *Bildzeitung*, the largest of the Springer papers. In his own way Brandt is as nationalistic as West Germany's Franz Joseph Strauss. The pre-Hitler SPD leaders would have great difficulty identifying with the theories and policies of today's leader Willy Brandt.

I was able to interview Heinrich Albertz, governing Mayor of West Berlin. Albertz is second in command. In practice he makes most of the decisions and shoulders the heaviest administrative burden. Albertz is less outspoken than Brandt. He favours cooperation with East German authorities in all instances where basic problems of "survival" and "recognition of the Ulbricht regime" are not involved. Albertz was the West German official credited with the successful conclusion of the *Passierschein* agreement, which enabled West Berliners to visit their East Berlin relatives during the Christmas season. But Albertz shares the basic Berlin concept, "We are surrounded by the Soviet zone, a territory whose government rules without the consent of the governed and which therefore lacks legal authority". The GDR — to Albertz as well as to his colleagues — is a political vacuum, a non-existent entity. "We prefer to negotiate with the Soviet authorities about all matters pertaining to the Soviet sector", Albertz explained. "Legally no East German Government exists. At best, we consider it to be the agent of the occupying power. It was in this capacity that we dealt with them in connection with the *Passierschein* agreement."

West Berlin's City Hall Square has been renamed "President Kennedy Square". Many West Berlin streets are named after Americans. The John Foster Dulles Allee and General Clay Avenue are two of West Berlin's best known thoroughfares. Citizens of West Germany proper either accept or reject the NATO Alliance, depending on their political views. Most people simply take it for granted. But to West Berliners the NATO Alliance and the protection it alleges are vital. Barring the extreme left it is hardly ever criticized in West Berlin. Of all American visitors of the last decade none has left a stronger impact than President Kennedy. Lyndon Johnson does not reach his predecessor's popularity in West Berlin. Johnson and Eisenhower are generally respected (although Johnson's Vietnam policy is strongly criticized by the average West Berliner), but Kennedy captured the heart of the city. During the days following his assassination most West Berlin night clubs were closed, theatres shut their doors and people cried openly in the streets. The Kennedy monument is never left without freshly cut flowers — very often children bring small bunches of wild flowers. This attraction between Berlin and the late President had been mutual. I had met Mr. Kennedy during the winter of 1958 at Montego Bay's (Jamaica) Round Hill Hotel. I had tried to interview the Senator from Massachusetts for my paper. My German accent must have been discernible, for Mr. Kennedy said to me at once "You seem to be German — do you come from Berlin?" When I answered that while I was a "Southerner" from Bavaria, I knew Berlin and had been there recently, Kennedy began questioning me about Berlin streets and landmarks. Had they changed much? I never finished interviewing the Senator. Instead Mr. Kennedy interviewed me about Berlin — he showed an amazing familiarity with the town's scenery. I never saw Mr. Kennedy again, but I was reminded of his interest when I saw the Kennedy Monument in Berlin. I believe the late President would have liked to see his monument in this particular spot.

I spent the afternoon inspecting the *Hansaviertel,* a well-designed giant real-estate development sporting modern multi-family dwellings. The *Hansaviertel* is built in an area which had been completely gutted by air raids. The houses are modern and resemble American and Canadian residential projects.

The last two hours of my stay in West Berlin were spent in Ploetzensee. The name of this quiet Berlin suburb once spelled terror to Hitler's enemies. Berlin's top security prison stood there. When Hitler came to power his most dangerous enemies were assigned cells in Ploetzensee. It was a regular prison not a concentration camp. During the war years Ploetzensee was reserved for those to be tried before the dreaded "People's Court". Most of the army generals and resistance leaders who organized the ill-fated coup of July 24, 1944 were executed in Ploetzensee.

Today the former prison has become a shrine, dedicated to the memory of the German resistance. Unlike many other shrines Ploetzensee is dignified and does not try to appeal to sensation seekers. The room where Erich von Witzleben, Karl Goerdeler and their fellow-conspirators were hanged has remained unchanged. The victims were hanged from butcher hooks. Piano strings were used in place of ordinary rope. Since no trap doors were provided death came through slow asphyxiation. Two SS men made colour movies of the executions for Hitler's personal edification. There is a simple inscription above the death chamber: "To the victims of the Hitler dictatorship — 1933-1945". Many people visit the shrine. Some 200 schoolboys paid their respects during my visit, accompanied by their teachers. A brass plate outside the prison gives the names of those killed in Ploetzensee. It contains some illustrious names which belie the widely held belief that no German underground ever existed: Julius Leber, newspaper editor; Wilhelm Leuschner, trade union leader; Helmuth Huebener, oddly enough a member of the Mormon Church (I had never realized that there were Mormons in Germany), who was executed on his seventeenth birthday. Ulrich von Hassel, ambassador; Ernst von Harnack, Chief Administrator of Merseburg; Alfred Delp, Jesuit Priest; Eva-Marie Buch, book dealer; Johannes Popitz, former Prussian Minister of Finance; Joseph Wirmer, trade union leader — and many others. Over five thousand men and women, mostly members of the German underground, were executed in Ploetzensee. Near the shrine's exit the dying words of Father Delp are chiselled into the former prison wall: "Bread is vital — but freedom is more vital than bread!"

Father Delp's execution took place February 2, 1945. His dying words became the slogan of the German resistance fighters during the closing days of the war.

CHAPTER II

CHECKPOINT CHARLIE

To the average West Berliner, the Berlin wall represents the symbol of a hated dictatorship. To the East Berliner, it is merely the border of the State. Like any other border, it is closed to those who would cross it illegally. Lawful travellers are processed at a number of officially designated borderpoints. Considering the fact that the two political entities separated by the wall do not recognize each other, and that an almost warlike atmosphere exists between them, a large number of people cross each day. In an attempt to organize this movement, the East German Government designated certain points to every category of travellers. West Germans are served by two checkpoints. West Berliners (when admitted during the holiday season) at still another. The point serving allied personnel and nationals is situated near the former Anhalt Railway station. Its official name is "border crossing point Friedrichstrasse". But it is far better known by its nickname "Checkpoint Charlie".

Nobody could tell me with any degree of certainty how this nickname originated. The most likely explanation lies in the original designation of border points by letters of the alphabet. The Friedrichstrasse crossing was "Point C" and following the tradition which calls the season's Caribbean hurricanes by girls' names in alphabetical order, "Point C" soon became known as "Checkpoint Charlie".

Berlin is the most famous of all divided cities; but there are others whose plight is infinitely worse. Last March I had occasion to visit Jerusalem. This biblical town is also cut in two by a dividing line consisting of walls, barbed wire entanglements and other impediments. Only one legal checkpoint exists, the Mandelbaum

Gate. Compared to that forbidding gate (which is not a gate at all
but an open stretch of highway), "Checkpoint Charlie" is doing a
land-office business. The Mandelbaum Gate is tightly closed all
year except during the Christmas holidays.

The checkpoint's border arrangements are entirely one-sided.
Behind the wall's eastern side are the office barracks of the GDR.
On the west side — nothing, barring a small cottage in which
American soldiers check out military vehicles crossing the line.
Private persons and non-military vehicles are neither stopped nor
checked on the West Berlin side. "The explanation is simple; we
do not recognize the existence of the wall or of a border", explained the American officer of the day doing checkpoint duty. A
great number of tourists cross into East Berlin on one-day permits.
Any allied citizen may report to "Charlie", stand in line (because
of the large crowds waiting to visit the "forbidden city" of East
Berlin, it takes approximately half an hour to cross during the
summer months) and get his visa. The tourist shows his passport
— he must be in possession of a non-German passport — and gets
his one-day permit in form of a rubber stamp. He is then asked to
declare the amount of foreign money carried by him. He is obliged
to buy his Eastmarks from the Government-chartered bank at the
checkpoint (five marks is the obligatory minimum). He should
also declare valuable cameras, typewriters and other high-priced
consumer goods. ("This allows him to take out his property when
he leaves; for the export of consumer goods bought in East Germany is subject to a Government permit", was the explanation of
the chief customs officer at the point.) The East German officials
try their best to make everyone feel at ease. Sometimes their smiles
seem forced. But they keep on smiling. On the wall a happy
Walter Ulbricht beams at the arriving tourists. Beneath the huge
portrait a sign in eight languages: "The German Democratic Republic, the only true Germany, welcomes you!" The back of the
customs and immigration shack is crowded with three tables; they
are covered with a variety of pamphlets dealing with the Berlin
problem. I noticed French, English, German, Italian, Spanish,
Dutch, Flemish, Swedish, Danish and even Finnish pamphlets.
Their titles vary: *The Truth about the Wall; Globke's Criminal
Career; West Germany is a Neo-Nazi State; The Conspiracy of
the Expellee Organizations.* I did not find any anti-American pamphlets at the checkpoint. The official anger is directed against
Bonn and the "revanchist clique of ex-Nazis", who, as East Ger-

mans see it, hold all West German positions of influence. The absence of anti-American pamphlets is understandable. The GDR's Information Ministry, the publisher of the pamphlets, is anxious to win the friendship and confidence of the American tourists. The checkpoint serves not only as the point of entry, but also as point of exit. Many tourists take home some of the pamphlets. I read most of them. Some of their facts appear correct, others are exaggerated, a few are completely unfounded. But their tenor is no worse than that of similar West Berlin pamphlets sold or given away on the wall's western side.

Every allied visitor wishing to enter East Berlin must clear through "Charlie". No exception is made even for the most prominent visitors. A few well known Americans who crossed here are former Vice-President Nixon and Senator Ted Kennedy, the slain President's youngest brother. Like their lesser known fellow citizens, the VIP's are asked to show their passports and apply for their permit East German cameramen usually snap pictures of their entry. An unsmiling Nixon and a smiling Ted Kennedy look down from a huge signboard hanging near the bench where the passports are stamped. West German officialdom refuses to recognize the very existence of the GDR. This applies not only to diplomatic channels but to the most insignificant activities as well. One of the basic rules of West Berlin Press Club members has been their blank refusal to cross into East Berlin (at least officially). I had been bluntly advised by the officer in charge that I would be dropped one block from "Charlie" and would have to cross by myself as a pedestrian. To this day I have no idea what caused them to change their minds. But half an hour before my intended border crossing I received a telephone call from the Press Chief at my hotel. "We have decided to drive you over and deliver you to our East Berlin opposite number, the Society *Neue Heimat*. Please be ready. The limousine will pick you up in ten minutes!"

Five minutes later — the Germans are a very punctual people — the car had arrived. The chauffeur was a young West Berlin college student with a British passport. The young man looked typically German and — as I soon found out — hardly spoke any English which he had just started to study in school. He was born in Berlin and had never in his life been outside the city. "My British passport? Simple. It's on the level!" he told me in Berlin slang which is hard to understand for anyone who has never lived there. "My mother was born in Britain. I retained her British citizenship. It pays, you know!"

The arrival of an official West German Press Office limousine caused a minor sensation at the checkpoint. The official handling passport examinations ordered me out of the queue which I had joined and asked me to enter his private office. "Oh yes, we were expecting you", the captain in charge told me. "How come they bring you over in an official car? This has never happened before. They don't recognize us — we do not exist. So their car is actually driving into a perfect vacuum!" The captain laughed. "No, we don't really mind. They wouldn't allow one of our press cars in West Berlin — I am sure of that! But we'll clear their press car. The boy can drive you to the *Neue Heimat!*"

After I had bought the mandatory five Eastmarks we proceeded quickly to the *Neue Heimat*. Amusingly enough, these offices are located in the former Propaganda Ministry of infamous Dr. Goebbels — the only major Nazi government building not destroyed during the siege of Berlin. Upon arrival the sensation of a West Berlin Press car parking in front of the East German office was repeated. The doorman refused to let me enter. "This is too unusual — has never happened before — I must consult my superiors. Don't you move, just stay where you are..." "Do as you like", my young chauffeur told him, "but until you get organized I will show my passenger the former government buildings. I am a licensed tourist guide." But just as he was about to start on his completely unscheduled guided tour, he was called back. "Will you please enter — I am sorry I refused you before." Apparently the doorman had received his instructions from upstairs. Five minutes later I had made my first contact in the German Democratic Republic.

THE EAST

CHAPTER I

BERLIN, GERMAN DEMOCRATIC REPUBLIC

East Germany is a country which likes to be known by its initials GDR. The name "East Germany" is rarely used by its citizens and causes raised eyebrows when used indiscriminately by visitors. For more than eighty per cent of all visitors to the GDR East Berlin is the only city they ever see. The Ulbricht regime has therefore tried to make it into the showplace of the nation. To some extent he has succeeded. The name "East Berlin" is also taboo. To East Germans the name of their capital is simply "Berlin, GDR". (West Berlin is called Berlin-West sector or sometimes in an amusing allusion to West German language habits — the "US occupied part of Berlin".) East Berlin consists of the southeastern, northern and central sections of the former capital. The central section contains some world-famous landmarks: the Brandenburg Gate near the border, it's westernmost point; Unter den Linden from which the Wilhelmstrasse (now renamed Otto Grothewohlstrasse) branches off near the wall; the Alexanderplatz, affectionately known to East and West Berliners alike as "Alex". East Berlin's second largest district is Pankow. (Because Walter Ulbricht used to live there his government is frequently called "the Pankow regime" by West German newspapers.) East Berlin's suburbs have always been drab working-class areas. They still are. Much of the war damage has been repaired; housing space is still at a premium. While apartments are hard to come by, they cost very little once they are occupied. All rents are controlled at the 1944 price level.

Berlin's central area was always the most beautiful part of town. The Ulbricht government has tried to rebuild it in good taste and — wherever possible — with glamour. In this respect its success has been limited. The Alexanderplatz and the Frankfurter Allee (between 1945 and 1956 it used to be known as Stalin-allee — in 1956 it was renamed Karl Marx Allee) are the landmarks of a newly emerging socialist metropolis. The huge buildings of the Karl Marx Allee look impressive, but hardly artistic. The style reminds the sightseer of efficiently built anthills. The buildings tend to overwhelm, but they lack charm. The dislike of the Karl Marx Allee is shared alike by tourists and old-time Berliners. The Alexanderplatz boasts a huge skyscraper, the "House of the Teacher". It is educational headquarters for East Berlin. Next to this huge structure which looks like a somewhat smaller replica of the United Nations Building in New York stands a round building which could be a big planetarium. Actually it is "Congress Hall". It houses an auditorium for concerts and theatrical performances. It also serves as a temporary meeting place for the GDR's parliament, the *Volkskammer*. The inside furnishings and decorations of this huge hall resemble Montreal's Place des Arts; this similarity is so striking (it even extends to the arrangement of lighting fixtures) that I enquired whether the two buildings were designed by the same architects. They weren't. The similarity is pure coincidence.

The entire sixth floor of the "House of the Teacher" is surrounded by a giant mural giving it a non-European appearance. The city's central sector, once the home of the Kaiser and the very heart of the Kingdom of Prussia, has become almost Asiatic in appearance, for East Berlin's architecture is strongly influenced by Russian artistic expression. This influence is limited to the newly built public structures. It does not extend to the older parts of town.

The Brandenburg Gate did not suffer serious war damage. Unter den Linden was completely smashed. It has been rebuilt. The stately old linden trees which gave the street its name were chopped down during the war. New trees were planted ten years ago. They reach the third stories of some buildings. "In about a hundred years it will all look like it used to", an East Berlin taxi driver quipped.

The State Opera is under reconstruction. The Prinzessinen-palais (Palace of the Imperial princesses) now houses a pretty sidewalk cafe and restaurant. It also sports one of East Berlin's night-clubs. Any devotee of American or Canadian night clubs would feel right at home. At first glance there is but scant difference

between the night life of the two countries — except for one thing —
East Berlin night clubs are never crowded. Compared to everyday
staples, which are cheap, East Berlin's night club rates are sky-
high.

The *Alte Wache,* once one of the shrines of Prussia's military
cult, now serves as a monument to Germany's victims of Fascism.
An honour guard stands watch day and night. In former days
the Linden led directly through the Brandenburg Gate to the
Kurfürstendamm of Berlin-Charlottenburg. Now the wall separa-
tes these two landmarks. Near the Brandenburg Gate the wall
looks forbidding. No one may cross there — and none of the different checkpoints is situated within walking distance of the
Brandenburg Gate. Hotel rooms are one of East Berlin's most
painful shortages. A substantial slice of the country's building
budget has been diverted to hotel construction. The Government
built a huge, modernistic skyscraper hotel, the Interhotel Berolina,
one block from the Karl Marx Allee. Its appearance indicates that
the architect meant to copy the style of America's Hilton chain.
To some extent he succeeded — there is some faint similarity between the Berolina and some of the better-known Hilton hotels,
an affinity like the one existing between an original painting and
a clever copy. The Berolina lobby is glass-encased. Its velvet-
covered benches sparkle in a weird assortment of deep colours.
They look pretty — but when a tired guest wants to sit down, they
feel unpleasantly hard. The dining room could almost be called
majestic — huge candelabra hang from expensively finished ceil-
ings and impeccably-clad waiters serve the public — but a long
line of waiting guests queues up outside its doors; it is always
overcrowded and service is poor. There is a great shortage of waiters, one of the consequences of the migration of manpower to the
West before the wall was built. The rooms — I was finally checked
in after a two-day waiting period — look impressive but the beds
are functional, the furniture uncomfortable and it is sometimes
difficult for guests to reach their rooms unless they are booked
on one of the lower floors. For the hotel's pride, its Soviet-built
elevators, are very unusual machines. They are always overcrowded. Sometimes a hotel employee runs them, more often they operate on a "self-service" basis. I am used to self-service elevators in
almost all parts of the world. But the Berolina elevators completely
frustrated me. They rise quickly, then suddenly stop somewhere
between floors and will not budge. When they finally reach the

proper floor, they often overshoot it — sometimes the passengers
are able to climb out, at other times they remain in the elevator.
After I had been imprisoned in one of them for twenty minutes,
I decided to use the stairs in the future — a tiresome procedure
since my room was on the tenth floor. Soviet science has created
the Sputnik and aims for the moon; but it has not yet succeeded
in exporting a serviceable elevator. Nevertheless, the Berolina
is impressive and its assortment of guests interesting. During my
stay I met several North Vietnamese delegations, the Foreign Minister of Bulgaria, an assortment of African visitors in their flow-
ing robes (East Berlin is crowded with visitors from newly created
African States), and several mainland Chinese. The relations between the GDR and China are somewhat strained — the East German Government is a staunch ally of the Soviet Union. But Chinese visitors are many and they are treated with cordiality. Oddly
enough they are the only foreign visitors who use English as their
lingua franca. I noticed one Chinese delegate reading the latest
issue of *Pravda*. When a hotel employee addressed him in impecca-
ble Russian, he answered in equally perfect English. I approached
him, showed my Canadian newspaper credentials and asked "Don't
you like to speak Russian?" *Answer:* "No, why should I? I studied
in San Francisco." *Question:* "Don't you think your refusal to answer in Russian might cause some raised eyebrows?" *Answer:* "I
couldn't care less!" The conversation soon turned to Canadian-
Chinese wheat sales. "Wonderful country, your Canada", said the
Chinese delegate. "I hope to visit it soon. I am a member of an
agricultural delegation and am trying to be on the next negotiat-
ing team for Canadian wheat. Maybe I will be able to visit the
United States. Who knows?"

The *Neue Heimat* had reserved a room for me at the Berolina.
On arrival the hotel turned me away. Room clerks are among the
GDR's most powerful figures. An embarrassed *Neue Heimat* official started to hunt rooms for me all over East Berlin. Eventually
he placed me in a second-rate hotel, the Sofia. Its elevators did
not function either — apparently one of the trademarks of East
Berlin hotels. The next morning at eight o'clock I received a telephone call from the Foreign Ministry. "We regret the mixup.
Tonight you move to the Johannishof until we get space for you
at the Berolina." The Johannishof, one short block away from the
Sofia, proved an interesting contrast. It only had suites, and for
one night I was allowed to occupy the Royal suite (this name has

somehow stuck in the vocabulary of Socialist East Germany)
usually reserved for top government guests. This suite has one
huge bedroom, two living rooms and bath — all magnificently
furnished. It has a stereo record player, a television set with built-
in bar, and a sofa which adjusted to every possible position. "This
suite was used by the Soviet Prime Minister Kosygin during the
May 8 celebration", I was told. I can assure the world that Mr.
Kosygin's stay in East Berlin must have been very comfortable.
I would have liked to remain in the Johannishof. Unfortunately
this kind of VIP treatment was reserved for highly placed "East
block" statesmen. The next morning I was transferred to the
Berolina.

My first morning in East Berlin was used for sightseeing. At
eight AM (the Germans start their day rather early) a Russian-
built Volga car picked me up; its driver, a middle-aged government chauffeur named Kadenbach and travel guide Wolfgang
Wolf remained with me for the entire length of my East German
trip. The Volga is a medium-sized car resembling a 1955 Buick.
The car runs well — when it feels like it — that's the best way to
describe it. Our particular Volga disliked hills and mountains. It
would run flawlessly on a level road, then stop in its tracks in the
middle of a hill. Most of the time Kadenbach could start it again.
I asked Kadenbach to take me to the old Imperial Palace, the
residence of the Kaiser and once one of Berlin's best known landmarks. He drove to a huge vacant square and shrugged his shoulders. "It used to be right here; it was destroyed during the war
and never rebuilt. It is now called the Marx-Engelsplatz. We
use it for big demonstrations."

Two other buildings of old Berlin have survived the war. The
"Red City Hall" still serves as municipal government headquarters. (It is named for its reddish appearance and not for its present
occupants.) East Berlin's Mayor is Friedrich Ebert, son of the Weimar Republic's first President. The main government building,
now Walter Ulbricht's headquarters, still has the famous balcony
from which Karl Liebknecht proclaimed the end of the Monarchy
and the birth of the Republic, November 9, 1918. Liebknecht, who
together with Rosa Luxemburg headed the left wing of the Social
Democrats, was murdered January 15, 1919; after his death the
Social Democrats veered to the right. East Germany considers him
one of socialism's two important martyrs. Ernst Thaelmann is the
other.

I was treated to a close inspection of the Brandenburg Gate. Traffic barriers are drawn across the Linden some 500 feet from the wall. This is as far as the East German public may go. The Brandenburg Gate itself is forbidden territory for GDR citizens. I was guided through the barrier and received by the commander of the army detail guarding the wall behind the gate, a young lieutenant of the *Volkswehr* (the people's army). He invited me to the guardhouse's upper floor. I entered a small, but well-equipped movie projection room. A row of wooden benches, a huge screen and a projector. The lieutenant patiently explained the "dangers which surround East Berlin". A short motion picture acquainted me with "several Western spies who had been caught red-handed", and with a young arsonist who had "set fire to his place of business because the Americans had promised him money and a safe job in West Berlin if he succeeded". But he had failed and was arrested. This sounded like an interesting news story. I tried to run it down during the next few days, but failed. No one I met had known the young arsonist, no one could name the factory he had set ablaze and none could identify the American officers who had bribed him. Was it a true story or an invention? I can't say.

Te lieutenant told me of his life and work routine. He had once been a brewery employee — the days of the aristocratic Prussian officer are gone. The lieutenant sounded sincere — I am certain that he believed in the justice of his cause and in the truth of every single accusation he hurled against the "Western imperialists".

My visit to the Brandenburg Gate ended with a memorable occasion. I was allowed to walk up the lone stand five feet east of the wall. As I stood there, I suddenly faced many people standing on the huge platform west of the wall. Only one day earlier I myself had stood on that western platform looking at the eastern stand, which at that time had been empty. "Only iron curtain big shots ever get up there", my West German guide had confided to me. Now I stood on that very platform. I could see that my appearance caused a sensation on the other side. Some fifty cameras were trained on me from the western side and clicked. A newsreel truck raced up the western side of the Linden extension, called Avenue of June 17, and trained its lenses on me. I pitied the poor newsreel people. How disappointed they would be when they found out that they had not filmed a Warsaw Pact big shot but an average Canadian newspaper man! ("How could you do it?" my editor-in-chief scolded me later. "Don't you know that even Jugoslav President Tito refused to walk up that platform?")

East Berlin is a Mecca for theatre goers. It houses the world-famous Bert Brecht Ensemble run efficiently by Brecht's widow Helene Weigel. Brecht was probably the most brilliant and prolific German playright of the twentieth century. But to East Germans he is more than a great writer; he is their national poet. Together with Johannes Becher, Brecht created poetry glorifying East German society. Despite his political views Brecht became equally famous in the West. His *Dreigroschenoper* (Three Penny *Opera*) had a Broadway run of several years. In the GDR the *Dreigroschenoper* is not the most popular piece of the Brecht repertoire but it is performed quite frequently. Other Brecht plays performed by the ensemble during my stay were *The Avoidable Rise of Arturo Ui, The Days of the Commune,* and *Coriolan.* Another play shown by the ensemble was *The Case of J. Robert Oppenheimer.* The Brecht group had just completed a tour of the United Kingdom where audiences treated it to thunderous applause. Brecht was a convincing writer and the actors are excellent. At the end of most performances Brecht's message is accepted by the average listener. The audience of *Arturo Ui,* the play I attended, was mixed. Several hundred West German, American and other allied tourists had come from West Berlin on one-day permits to watch the performance. The Soviet Ambassador to West Germany was present. So was Frau Ulbricht, the wife of the head of state (Ulbricht himself was absent). The Brecht Ensemble is by no means East Berlin's only theatrical group. I attended a performance of a young East German writer's latest play *Nine P.M. at the Roller Coaster* in the Maxim Gorky theatre. The play was supposedly non-political — but there were political overtones. Love of peace, friendship among the nations — the evil Nazis of West Germany — East German writers seem to experience difficulty detaching themselves completely from these political slogans. The spectators applauded warmly and I joined in the applause. The play had been interesting — the performance excellent.

East Berlin's movies surprised me. The largest theatre on the Karl Marx Allee played — of all things — *Boccaccio '70.* A smaller theatre had a rerun of John Steinbeck's *Grapes of Wrath.* All other films shown were crime thrillers (in East Germany they are advertised as "detective stories") and ordinary "boy meets girl" yarns. East Berlin is the home of DEWA, the country's largest film studio (before the war it was known as UFA). German films have always been competent since the days in 1930 when a "sleeper" called *Mädchen in Uniform* (Girls in Uniform) broke all box-office records. The GDR has a super star, who is as well known and well-loved in Eastern countries as Sofia Loren or Elizabeth Taylor in the West. Her name is Anne-Katrin Buerger; she bears a slight resemblance to West Germany's Romy Schneider.

East Berlin's political cabaret is called *Die Distel* (the thistle). Carefully edited jokes and occasional barbs are directed against the GDR government and its leaders. The criticism never becomes too harsh — it remains "good-natured". The actors poke occasional fun at Ulbricht's Saxon dialect — some East Germans experience difficulty in understanding their leader. One skit showed a store which had nothing to sell (such themes are taboo to GDR newspapers or the legitimate stage). One joke about Soviet-Canadian relations: two Soviet politicians meet. *Question:* Will Canada eventually go Socialist? *Answer:* Of course! But when they do who the hell will sell us our wheat?

No jokes are directed against the West German Government. The performance's satirical skits are interrupted by deadly serious acts hurling accusations of war crimes against the German General Staff — completely out of tune with the rest of the program. The rancour and bitterness which I had experienced in West Berlin's *Stachelschweine* two days before were repeated in East Berlin's *Distel*.

During the second day of my stay in East Berlin I visited the Humboldt University, formerly the Friedrich Wilhelm University. I found a great number of African and Eastern European students. Its law faculty is the best known of the Socialist states. I had been told of racial tension between African students and the population. But I could not find any evidence of discrimination of the type which arises occasionally in the Slavic countries (Czechoslovakia and Bulgaria).

East Germany's book publishing centre is Leipzig. Only a few publishers make East Berlin their headquarters. I visited the largest of them, *Volk und Welt*. This visit had its amusing aspects. For this publishing house does not print any communist authors. It specializes in the production of the very things frowned upon by East German officialdom — love stories, tales of "cops and robbers" and other popular books. Its present best-seller is *The Bandit's Revenge*. Price: 35 pfennig (9 cents). "No, we do not print gangster stories. Our books are about old-fashioned highwaymen and bandits. There is a definite market for this type of literature. On a per capita basis, we produce only half as many popular books as Western countries." Mr. Czollek, head of the publishing firm, explained his editorial policy to me. "We also translate and print quite a few Anglo-Saxon authors. Presently we are preparing an edition of James Joyce's *Ulysses*. We have printed some of Arthur Miller's and Faulkner's stories and plays. Canadian authors? The only one we ever printed was Dyson Carter. Our firm has to make money on its overall production. The Government does not subsidize us — we do not receive a penny from them! So we specialize in books the public will buy and read. Karl Marx? If he sells, we'll print him. At the moment he is not on our author's list."

Herr Czollek smiled. He told me of his adventures between 1935 and '45. As a Jew, he was forced to leave the country and spent most of the Hitler years in Shanghai. Czollek had personally known Boris Pasternak and knew the inside story of the *Dr. Zhivago* controversy. Pasternak had entrusted the manuscript to a friend to spirit it out of the country. At the last moment he changed his mind and requested the return of the manuscript. A meeting was arranged between Pasternak and his friend, the latter never showed up — and the manuscript suddenly appeared on the Italian market. Pasternak panicked. "Actually he had never been anti-Soviet. I received a few postcards from him after the incident. "I do not wish to lose my Soviet citizenship", he wrote me. "Why, oh why have I been so stupid?" According to Czollek, Pasternak would have given his last ruble to buy back the publication rights of what he called his ill-fated *Dr. Zhivago*.

Is there any interference by the Government with the freedom of East-German writers? Czollek denied it. "Take the case of Professor Havemann, he lectured on philosophy. His philosophy did not coincide with that of the Government. They asked him to stop his lectures. He refused and continued to teach his own brand of philosophy. What happened to him? Nothing!"

The next day I tried to interview the professor. He refused the interview. "The professor rarely sees foreign newspaper men", I was told. It seemed to me that Professor Havemann's activities had been somewhat curtailed after all, and that the Government sometimes exercises gentle pressure on individual writers whenever such action is deemed to be in the public interest.

East Berlin has a Press Club — a convenient country-club type of building where newspapermen meet, eat and talk. The lounges are comfortable, the food is excellent. Here I met Werner Micke, editor of the *Berliner Zeitung,* East Berlin's largest non-political paper — "non-political" by East German standards. Actually, all papers are political, but the *Berliner Zeitung* and its subsidiary, the *BZ am Abend,* try to entertain, not educate. The *Berliner Zeitung* has Berlin's second largest circulation. The Party newspaper *Neues Deutschland* takes first place. An item of interest about East Berlin's newstands: all their papers come from the GDR or Warsaw Pact countries. You can buy *Pravda* at a few New York newsstands. Don't expect to find the *New York Times* in East Berlin!

There are some East German newspapers printed exclusively for the outside world. One of these is the *Union Presse,* a monthly published by East Germany's CDU Party. The paper represents the GDR's religious groups — and almost the entire output is mailed to West German citizens. A part of the issue is returned by West German postal authorities stamped "refused by addressee". But the better part of the unsolicited papers reach their destination. At first glance the paper does not seem to originate in a communist country. Church news is prominently displayed, and more priests, ministers and rabbis appear in them than in most Western magazines. Its editor-in-chief is Otto Hartmut Fuchs, a scholarly gentleman who used to be a member of West Germany's CDU (Adenauer-Erhard) Party. "We are not members of any Communist Party affiliate", he explained to me in a lengthy interview. "We accept socialism as the basis of East German life. We cooperate with the Government. But our politics are our own."

In many ways the *Union Presse* is one of the most unusual publications I found in the GDR. If its motives are genuine, it would prove that a laissez-faire policy is followed toward at least some people whose political views differ from those of the Government. If it is a cleverly-screened Government-controlled enterprise, then the Ulbricht regime would seem to have truly brilliant psychologists in their propaganda department.

East Germany has the world's largest zoo — to the surprise of most outside visitors who have never heard of it. The famous West Berlin Zoo was the capital's only animal shelter. After the town was divided, East Berlin wanted a zoo of its own. The *Tierpark* (animal park) was started by professor Dahte, an internationally known zoologist. It is fabulous — no other expression fits! As in Hamburg's Hagenbeck Park, the animals appear to live in freedom. The East Berlin *Tierpark* emphasizes this impression to the point where a casual visitor may became frightened. I froze in my tracks when I was suddenly charged by a herd of North American buffaloes. No fence or ditch separated me from the attacking animals. Had I accidentally strayed into the buffalo cage? The stampede came to a sudden halt fifteen feet away from me. A wide water-filled moat had stopped it. Its clever camouflage had made it all but invisible.

The *Tierpark's* planners did not save money. The very number of animals staggers the imagination. There are fifteen lions, twelve tigers; camels, buffaloes and elephants come in herds. The building housing the big cats is called the "Alfred Brehm House" (after Germany's most famous zoologist). Two items merit attention: an oversized cage housing the birds of prey — more than 80 feet high — its ground dimensions are 200 by 300 feet. Eagles and condors fly inside the giant cage, the only place where I ever saw an eagle fly in captivity. The tropical bird-house is a big glass-encased building heated to 90 degrees. Trees and tropical plants grow in it. The visitor enters the building and walks in it — he has become part of a huge tropical forest. Humming birds fly about. Large vampire bats hang from trees. The tourist crosses an artificial river over a high wooden bridge. Below him crocodiles bask in the light of sun lamps. The construction of this crocodile-infested river appears dangerous. Small children could jump or fall into it. "It never happens" was my guide's laconic statement. "Well, it might happen some time", I replied.

I spent the last day of my Berlin stay visiting Potsdam. This former seat of Prussian militarism lies twenty miles outside Berlin. To reach it East Berliners must travel around West Berlin, covering 80 miles. It lies directly on West Berlin's western border. I had last seen Potsdam in 1933. Since that time the town has changed completely. The streets are the same, but the spirit of Prussian militarism is gone. Frederik the Great's castle at Sans Souci, where he exchanged barbed pleasantries with France's Voltaire, still stands. To enter it visitors put on huge felt slippers. It takes a few minutes to get accustomed to them. The Sans Souci park is still filled with naughty nude statues. Its creeks and lakes remain feeding grounds for swans and ducks. The Ulbricht government has not excommunicated Frederic's memory. "He was a great old man — a militarist; but he also helped build the nation", explained our guide. The Russians show the same approach to their Peter the Great.

Potsdam is headquarters for the American, French and British military missions. The existence of these missions on East German soil surprised me. The amenities due them are rigidly maintained. American and other allied staff officers ride through East Germany unhindered — a courtesy not always extended to the Soviets in the Federal Republic. Potsdam also is headquarters to the Soviet military mission. Crowds of Soviet soldiers mill around the town square and buy lemonade at odd Soviet-owned candy stands. Most of them speak German and their relations with the local population seem good.

Not far from the heart of town stands Cäcilienhof Castle, the place where the Potsdam Conference decided the fate of post-war Germany. It was built for Germany's last Crown Princess. It looks like a British country mansion. Gardeners have planted flowers forming a huge red star in front of the main entrance. Inside the house tourists are shown the conference rooms where Germany's fate was sealed. The chairs occupied by the different allied leaders are on view. A resourceful American journalist took a small piece of wood from the chair occupied by Marshall Stalin, brought it to the United States and sold it for several thousand dollars. This success gave him courage. He manufactured another splinter and sold it all over again. They say he became quite wealthy. Today the chair is guarded by two East German police-men.

The Potsdam Agreement was the psychological basis for the East German State. The GDR's political leaders pay it frequent lip service. They believe that West Germany's failure to adhere to the conditions of the agreement caused the irreparable split between the two states. West German leaders on the other hand scoff at the Potsdam Agreement. They consider Potsdam to have been the peak of Western gullibility and the cause of communism's victorious sweep across the middle of Europe. What was the blueprint of Potsdam? The creation of the four occupation zones, the forerunners of the two German states of today; the destruction of the Nazy Party; the trial of war criminals; the cession of the Reich's Eastern Provinces to Poland and the Soviet Union.

East Germany claims the Federal Republic has not wiped out Nazism; she permits former war criminals in her civil service; has never recognized the cession of the Eastern Provinces and hopes to absorb East Germany into a United Germany. "Only the GDR is the true Germany; only we have accepted the principles of Potsdam; only we stand for peace and justice; never must another war be unleashed from German soil", are the constant accusations against West Germany. "Here at Potsdam the seeds of our problem were sown. The conference of 1945 was one of history's most fateful meetings.

We returned to East Berlin by driving a huge semi-circle around West Berlin. This made it possible for me to visit the Soviet's giant East Berlin war memorial, one of the most unusual monuments I have ever seen. All identifiable bodies of Soviet soldiers killed in the battle of Berlin have been buried in five huge mass graves. Two long roads flank the graves. Every fifty feet a stone marker depicts a scene of the Second World War. Excerpts of Marshall Stalin's speeches are chiselled beneath each scene in Russian and in German.

The Avenue of the Soviet Heroes — as the road is called — is the only place in Europe (barring Albania) where Stalin's name and words are still prominently displayed. The Soviet Government had decided it unwise to erase the Stalin legend from the war memorial. At the end of the avenue stands a round building. The names of all Soviet soldiers buried in the five huge graves are listed here. A statue of a Soviet soldier towers over the building — symbol of Soviet victory. He holds a wounded child in his arms; at his feet lies a shattered swastika. — The war memorial is overpowering and impressive. It lacks charm but conveys sincerity. Its construction is typically Russian. It does not fit into the Berlin of the past; but it may become a landmark of the Berlin of the future.

CHAPTER II

THE STRUCTURE OF EAST GERMAN SOCIETY

I have visited many Communist nations. East Germany is unlike any other. Her political and social structure are the results of German history; the twelve years of Nazi rule, a short period of time when measured against the long history of the German people, have had more influence in shaping the GDR than the preceding five hundred years.

Journalists who try to analyse the GDR must give up some preconceived notions. Most Westerners think of East Germany as a one-party dictatorship. Actually several parties exist in the GDR: the SED, or Socialist Union (an amalgamation of the Communists and the Social Democrats); the CDU (Christian Socialists, the East German offshoot of West Germany's Adenauer-Erhard party); a Farmer's party; a National Liberal group, and a Free Democratic party. Few outsiders are aware that these parties exist. Their functions differ from those of political parties as we understand them. In a parliamentary democracy political parties go before the voters and fight it out in an election campaign. In East Germany they put up a common list of candidates who cooperate with each other. The purpose of these GDR parties is to give representation to different social and professional groups. The SED — by far the largest and most powerful of the groups — claims to represent the interest of the workers. The Farmer's party those of the farmers; the CDU is the spiritual home of the Catholic and Protestant clergy and their devout followers; the Liberals and Free Democrats represent the vanishing bourgeoisie, including former Nazi Party members; former Wehrmacht officers and the residue of Prussian aristocrats are also organized in these groups.

An East-German election is a cut-and-dried affair. All parties are consulted when the list of candidates is drawn up; the list exceeds the posts to be filled by some 30 per cent. The electors have the right to strike off the ballot any candidate they do not like. This rather limited freedom of choice makes it possible for the voters to rid themselves of particularly unpopular persons, but it ensures the victory of the present regime in any event. East German elections cannot change the form or policies of the country's government. They merely serve as a safety valve by which the population can exercise a minimum of choice. "Could Walter Ulbricht be removed from office by this procedure?" was one of my first somewhat naive questions. I learned that he could — provided most voters in his home district should strike off his name at the party's primary. I was also assured that voting takes place in the privacy of a booth and that the ballots are completely secret. Since anti-Communist election campaigns are not allowed, the problem of Ulbricht's removal by popular will remains wholly academic.

It would be wrong to consider these political parties nothing but government rubber stamps. They do serve the purpose of representing different group interests. This does not take place on a Western parliamentary level. The inter-party differences are adjusted at government and party conferences — talks not usually witnessed by the public. I was present during such a conference in which CDU officials requested better treatment and additional financial support for the reconstructed St. Hedwig Cathedral in East Berlin. It took considerable wrangling, and voices were raised on both sides. Eventually the CDU request was granted.

In Western nations the government's powers stem from the entire population through a system of elections. According to East German standards, the basic source of governmental power is the working class. But this is just lip service for the benefit of socialist theoreticians — the working class as a group remains largely an abstract entity. East German sociologists maintain the present existence of two social classes and one social stratum. Workers and farmers are considered classes, while the intelligentsia is deemed a stratum — a group of people defying exact classification. This view is reflected in the great seal of the East German State. It embodies a hammer (representing the workers), a wreath of corn (the farmers) and a drawing compass (intelligentsia). This seal, when superimposed on the West German flag of

black, red and gold, designates the standard of the German
Democratic Republic.

The country's legislative power is vested in the *Volkskammer*,
an assembly of 500 members elected by the voters. Only 434 of
these members — the elected representatives of the country outside
Berlin proper — have the right to pass legislation. East Berlin
itself elects 66 *Volkskammer* members. They sit in the *Kammer*
as observers but do not vote on legislation (a similar arrangement
ties West Berlin to the Federal Republic). The *Volkskammer* elects
the so-called *Staatsrat* (State council) which actually governs East
Germany. The *Staatsrat* has 24 members: one presiding officer, six
vice presidents, one secretary, and 16 ordinary members. For all
practical purposes the large *Volkskammer* is a body comparable
to the Supreme Soviet of the USSR. All real power is vested in
the *Staatsrat;* its presiding officer, of course, is Walter Ulbricht,
who actually exercises two functions. He heads the *Staatsrat* and
is thus considered head of the State. And he also serves as Secretary-
General of the SED, the Socialist Union Party. The second in
command is a man rarely mentioned in the Western Press, Willy
Stoph, President of the Council of Ministers. (Stoph is Walter Ulbricht's personal choice as his successor.) The third powerful man
of the GDR, Professor Albert Norden, is not a member of the
Staatsrat. He is a member of the SED *Politbureau* and ranks as
the Government's top propaganda spokesman. All information
given to GDR citizens about the outside world, has been channelled
through his office. No Western newspapers are sold on East
German newsstands; the East German Information Ministry however cannot stop its citizens from tuning in on West German radio
or TV programs. Generally speaking, the average GDR citizen
accepts most information stemming from the Norden office as
gospel truth. Western opinion about large-scale dissatisfaction in
East Germany is mostly wishful thinking.

The distant ideal of a classless society prevails in East Germany
as it does in all socialist countries. Some lip service is paid to this
ideal. But class distinctions have not been abolished in the GDR.
Officially the Junker and East-Elbian landowners have ceased to
exist. Their huge landholdings were nationalized during the first
year of the State's existence. I was therefore surprised to find a
number of former Junkers in East Germany. They are generally respected and often hold senior civil service positions. I met one
member of this group in a top Government position where he is able

to influence legislation. These men still carry the word "von" — trademark of German nobility — as part of their name. "The German aristocracy and Junker class is dead", explained a senior official of the Information Ministry. "But we permit former members of this group to serve the public as individuals. We judge them on their personal merit or demerit. The word "von" harms nobody. We consider it to be part of their family name." In this respect the GDR differs from other more orthodox Communist societies. During the first years of the Soviet State, the old Russian aristocracy had either been driven out of the country, or been liquidated. "They suffered several years of protracted civil war and we didn't. We could afford to be more lenient", was the Information Ministry spokesman's explanation. The actual reason is somewhat different. A small group of disenchanted Nazi Wehrmacht officers who changed sides after their capture at Stalingrad and formed the "Free German Committee" were among the GDR's founders. Some key members of this group were aristocrats. They helped the Ulbricht regime to organize the efficient East German army, the *Volkswehr*. I interviewed two of these top officers. "We were trained to serve Germany; the GDR is the true Germany", they explained. I did not have the opportunity to check their sympathies too thoroughly.

Most Western observers when asked about the main difference between East and West German society, would answer that the West has a free enterprise system; the others are communists. This is true. But after travelling in both German states, I found that an equally fundamental cleavage between the competing governments lies in their approach to Nazism. The Nazi empire collapsed in the midst of blood, fire and complete demoralization. Its spectre haunts both Germanies. The memory of Nazism is a powerful catalytic agent in both states. The GDR's way of handling the residual problem of neo-Nazism differs greatly from Bonn's aproach. It is the discrepancy of methods of controlling rightist extremists which explains much of the hatred between the two governments. It may well be the uppermost reason for West Germany's attempt to isolate East Germany diplomatically, militarily and culturally. The basis of West Germany's Hallstein doctrine is not only Bonn's wish to reestablish the German territory of pre-Hitler days. Its true basis is one of fear. Fear lest the East German approach should expose the Nazi past of important West German Government leaders. Fear that the East

German Government, if it ever had a say in West German affairs, would insist on the complete elimination of the residue of Nazism in the Federal Republic. Hitler, the man, is dead. His memory lingers on, and remains the single most important fact of public life in both German states.

When the three Western occupation zones were fused into the Federal Republic, a constitution proclaimed the new country to be a parliamentary democracy. The *Grundgesetz* (basic constitutional law) of West Germany is a curious mixture. Ingredients of the Weimar Constitution which governed the country between the two world wars alternate with the Anglo-Saxon emphasis on electoral constituencies. * When Hitler's Reich collapsed, the occupation authorities took over all governmental functions. Eventually they turned their powers over to German government leaders who had never been officially part of the Nazi government, but who were at the same time opposed to communism. During the Third Reich there had been three basic types of Germans: the followers of the Hitler regime; a small group of devoted anti-Nazis who actively opposed the dictatorship (members of this group either emigrated or were arrested and put into concentration camps, the few who remained completely undetected usually worked against Nazism in whatever way they could); and a third group whose members did not openly oppose Hitler, but who were politically neutral. Because it was "too dangerous" to work actively against Hitler, they remained entirely passive. The Third Reich, therefore, had Nazis, anti-Nazis and non-Nazis. United States policy and to a lesser extent British and French policy makers were suspicious of the anti-Nazis as early as 1945-1948. Therefore the Western occupation authorities turned the reins of the new Federal Republic over to the non-Nazis. This large group included some members of the upper middle class, and industrialists, who had never been active Nazis. Their approach to the Nazi problem was basically pragmatic. Whenever it seemed difficult for them to run an important government service without the know-how of former Nazi Party members, the governing group of the Federal Republic allowed some lesser (and a small number of major) Nazis to remain in office. This applied particularly to the army, the diplomatic service, the courts and the administration

---

* Proportional representation was a feature of the Weimar Constitution in contrast to the principle of one representative for each electoral district as in Canada, England, or the USA.

of justice. It became most pronounced in the teaching profession. Approximately 85 per cent of all teachers had been Nazis in 1945. West Germany dismissed some 20 per cent of her teachers for political reasons — the most fanatical Nazis were usually banned from the teaching profession. But the bulk of grade-school and high-school teachers remained doubtful. The swastikas smeared on the walls of cities like Bamberg and Würzburg, the Jewish cemeteries desecrated in a large number of West German towns are the direct result of this pragmatic policy. Actually the West German Government was not and is not pro-Nazi. The Government's policy is determined by their belief that Nazism, if left alone, will slowly die out. This policy counts heavily on the "economic miracle" and the effect of the passage of time on any hope for renewal of a Nazi regime.

The closely knit little group of devoted anti-Nazis, shunned by the Western occupation authorities, moved into the Soviet occupation zone. When this zone constituted itself the German Democratic Republic, they seized power. Their approach to the Nazi problem was pretty dogmatic. To them Nazism was a basic evil which had to be eradicated. One of the first acts of the East German Government was the summary dismissal of every teacher with a Nazi past. Six months after the founding of the East German Government the nation's schools opened with a skeleton staff of teachers. Only 20 per cent of the vacant posts were filled. By 1952, 80 per cent of all teaching positions were occupied and in 1955 the GDR had succeeded in creating a teaching profession completely untouched by the Nazi virus. This is probably the greatest single achievement of the GDR. The State also eliminated all former Nazis from the courts and the administration of justice. Ex-Nazis were allowed to remain in most other professions provided that they had not been involved in war crimes and were truly repentant of their Nazi past.

Most of the bitterness between the two German states today can be traced back to their methods of handling the Nazi problem. West Germans are pragmatic, East Germans dogmatic where ex-Nazis are concerned. Actually the leaders of the West German Government are by no means pro-Nazi. But because they made compromises as a matter of convenience and permitted former Nazis to remain in office, the average East German firmly and sincerely believes the entire West German State to be Nazi-infested. Dr. Hans Globke, West German Secretary of State under Adenauer,

is a prime example. Globke had been a member of Hitler's civil
service and in this capacity had drawn up the commentaries to
the Nuremberg anti-Semitic laws. Eventually these laws were used
to prepare for the expulsion and murder of the Jews. The presence
of Dr. Globke as a high West German official became proof
positive of the Nazi nature of the West German State to the
average East German citizen. Globke's position was in turn protected by Dr. Adenauer who certainly had no personal liking for
Nazism. But Adenauer felt that Globke was one of the best trained
and best informed civil servants in post-war Germany — an error
based on convenience which backfired and severely damaged the
international image of the Federal Republic.

The fear of living next door to what they believe to be an
unreconstructed neo-Nazi state is the basic motivation for many
East German political actions. From the standpoint of calm
detachment this fear is manifestly absurd. The remaining former
Nazis in the West German civil and governmental services are
mostly elderly people anxious to remain in office long enough
to qualify for their monthly pensions. None holds a high office
where he could actively influence West German policy. Most of
them are desperately anxious to sweep their past under the rug
and keep it well hidden. But the average East German is not
open to logical reasoning. He sees the few ex-Nazis, tame remnants
of a once arrogant and truculent dictatorship, and his emotions
get the better of him. The Berlin wall was built for economic
reasons — but the underlying fear that ex-Nazis might slip into
East Berlin to undermine the GDR government gave strong psychological impetus to the wall's construction. The barbed wire
entanglements, the tank traps, the trained dogs, the wide strip of
no-man's land which mark the entire length of the border between
the GDR and the Federal Republic are not only built to keep
the East German population at home; they are built for the
specific purpose of keeping West German Nazis out.

Because East Germany assumes that Nazis run West Germany,
they expect Bonn to commit acts normally ascribed to the Third
Reich. The Ulbricht government is certain that West Germany
will try to attack, invade and conquer the GDR and that such an
attack is now in the process of being prepared. This belief exploded
into sudden fear with the discovery of what was purported to be a
detailed plan of attack by the West German army against East
Germany. The incident, unknown in most Western countries, took

place in May 1961 — and may have been one of the main reasons for the construction of the Berlin wall (August 13, 1961).

A highly placed West German army officer fled to East Germany and turned a map over to East German officials which showed the alleged plan of a West German attack against the GDR as part of a concerted West German invasion of several Warsaw Pact countries. This map, originally listed as top secret, has recently been shown to foreign journalists. I was the first Western reporter to see it. It shows a strong West German attack based on a line linking Bayreuth and Nuremberg to Munich. From this base two major prongs develop. One, based on Nuremberg, against Prague, Czechoslovakia — from there to Dresden and Berlin. And a southern prong against Budapest based on Munich, later extended into a northerly direction toward Warsaw. The map also indicates a number of secondary attacks, from Braunschweig and Hanover against Berlin, from Hamburg and Kiel against Rostock.

Could this map be a hoax? The West German army is an integrated part of the NATO forces. But the plan seemed wholly West German. The original had listed the GDR territory as "Zone". The prepared translation substituted the initials "GDR". Otherwise it contained only German words and names. After interviewing several East German officials who had investigated the events leading to the map's discovery, I came to the conclusion that the map was technically genuine, but not as dangerous as the GDR had concluded. All defence departments constantly work on theoretical plans to attack and invade other countries without really planning to do so. In some corner of the Pentagon a junior officer may be working on the problem of how American Marines might best invade and defeat Uruguay. A minor Italian staff officer may well draw up a potential Italian naval attack against Iceland. The "plan to attack East Germany" undoubtedly falls into the same category. For any West German government which — twenty years after Hitler — could seriously consider invading Austria, Czechoslovakia, Hungary, Poland and East Germany (a better way to ensure mankind's final nuclear demise could hardly be imagined), would be more than slightly insane. But to the East German resistance fighters who endured the cruel treatment of Hitler's camps for many years, a map of the type discovered in May 1961 is very real. And this makes the map a very explosive document. The alleged attack may indeed never occur; but to a people who expect aggression the incident served as confirmation of their worst fears.

The GDR's policy of military alliances is based on the assumption that West Germany seeks nuclear arms to conquer East Germany. East Berlin fears and suspects Franz Joseph Strauss more than any other Bonn politician, because Strauss has been identified with West Germany's wish for atomic weapons. The project of a multi-lateral nuclear naval force in which the Bonn government would take part, is one of East Berlin's worst nightmares. The fact that nuclear weapons have been in the hands of West German generals, even though actual control of the devices remained with US authorities, has frightened the entire East German population. The East German Government's concern about West German nuclear arms is shared by almost every citizen of the GDR and finds expression in polemic speeches by every local politician. This fear deepens East German hatred and contempt for Prussia's wars and past history. The "old watch" in East Berlin serves as a shrine to the memory of the "victims of Fascism". (The East Germans rarely use the word "Nazi"; they usually call them "Fascists".) Two East German soldiers stand guard outside the gate. Every four hours (it is a 24-hour watch) the soldiers are relieved. The changing of the guards takes place with all the military pomp of ancient Prussia. It reminded me of a similar show at Buckingham Palace. During the change the East German soldiers goose-step — it was the only time during my trip that I encountered this old Prussian *Parademarsch*.

While East Germans are defensively militant against West Germany they propagate *Völkerfreundschaft* — friendship among nations — as part of their governmental philosophy. Children are trained to believe in international solidarity and the basic equality of man at an early age. It has helped to create East Germany's idealistic youth. The existence of a clean-cut young generation who sincerely believe in pacifism and friendship among the world's peoples was the greatest surprise I experienced during my East German trip. This training starts at kindergarten level. The school system has been completely overhauled. Not only have all teachers with a Nazi past been removed, but their replacements had to undergo a rigorous study and indoctrination period. The result of this effort was the creation of a new type of teacher. The East Germans call him the *Neulehrer* (new teacher). Teachers of this type were unknown in prewar Germany and do not exist in the

Federal Republic of today. The *Neulehrer* tries to be a friend rather than a person of authority. There is a distant similarity between these East German teachers and their American and Canadian counterparts. Corporal punishment is outlawed in East German schools. Text books and teachers (all school books have been completely revised and all nationalistic thoughts have been eliminated) constantly hammer the basic principles of anti-Nazism into the children's minds. I was invited to visit East Germany's Education Ministry. It stands a stone's throw from the Brandenburg Gate under the Linden. It was the only East German building I ever visited where I was asked to check my cameras before entering. Even during my later interviews with Ulbricht and my visit to the Ministry of Defence I was allowed to retain my photographic equipment — but not in the Ministery of Education. ("It is our nation's most important ministry", was my guide's explanation.) I interviewed two senior officials, Dr. Reimann and Dr. Habrecht. I entered several school rooms where my appearance caused a minimum of disturbance. I read the textbooks used by the children to study recent German history. I was thus able to reconfirm a previous impression. The main ideology of East Germany is not communism but active anti-Nazism. The constantly recurring thought: Prussian militarism was the forerunner of Nazism. It caused endless wars and suffering for the German people and for mankind. Never must another war be unleashed from German soil! — West German schooling has not changed much since the fall of Hitler. The textbooks used by the Federal Republic still contain nationalistic ideas. When compared to textbooks used during the Nazi period today's West German textbooks are tame; but they still manage to implant a considerable amount of German nationalism into the children's minds. The Nazi period is not mentioned too often — West Germany tries to forget it ever happened. In East Germany the spotlight of public scorn is never turned away from Nazi crimes. The basic difference between the young West German and East German generation is a direct result of the GDR's school reform. This changeover, called the "Anti-fascist-Democratic Reform", overhauled the entire grade system. Before 1945 Germans first went to an elementary school (grades 1-4) and a high school (obligatory high school grades 5-10 and three voluntary grades 11-13). After grade 13, the so called *Prima,* German students took their final examination (the *Abitur*) which allowed them to go on to college. Under this system, only children of the well-to-do could afford to stay in high school to their nineteenth year and attend university for another three to five years. The new East German school system established an elementary school of eight grades — obligatory for all students alike. At the end of the eighth grade children who will go on to university have to pass two additional high school grades. During this total of ten years East German students cover the same amount of material which thirteen years of the old system had implanted. A group of teachers suggest which students they consider gifted enough to go to college. Any student selected for higher studies will then be supported by the State until his studies are completed.

The subjects taught differ from our Canadian and American systems. The Russian language is mandatory, and starts in grade five. English, a voluntary subject, may become mandatory for sixth graders if a proposal presently before the Ministry is accepted. Astronomy is a mandatory subject. The most interesting difference between East German and North American schools is that technology is a mandatory East German school subject. All schools have workshops where students build, dismantle and repair complicated machinery. While some western schools have similar shops, they are nearly always run on a voluntary basis and the work done in them is classified as a useful hobby. In East Germany it becomes a subject of serious study and one of the school system's most vital activities. Students who show particular aptitude for any given technological task are given additional training and their future profession is cut out for them during their later school years.

Children are not separated according to their religion (which is still customary in some parts of West Germany), but are allowed to take religious classes. These lessons are considered a voluntary school subject — students taking them receive marks in their reports. The schools maintain a physical fitness program which is mandatory (a holdover from the old Germany). Swimming has also become mandatory for all students. All East German students can swim — the only country where I have ever encountered this phenomenon. East German children are organized into youth groups. This organization covers all children from the age of six to twenty. Age groups six to fourteen are called "Thaelmann Pioneers". (Ernst Thaelmann, head of the pre-war German Communist Party, was murdered in Buchenwald.) Age groups fourteen to twenty are called *Freie Deutsche Jugend* (Free German Youth) — better known by their alphabethical abbreviation "FDJ".

When I remarked that this arrangement reminded me somewhat of the former Hitler youth organization, I realized too late that I had committed a serious faux pas. The educators rose to their feet and showed their anger in unmistakable terms. "There is no similarity with the Hitler Youth Movement at all. Our children are taught to believe in the friendship of all nations and the fellowship of man. They are shown the evils of war and mankind's need for lasting peace. Our children neither march nor receive military training. They hike. They organize dances. There is no political indoctrination. As a point of fact, our FDJ organization can be compared to your boy scouts and camp fire girls — not with the cursed Hitler Youth of Facist days!" I joined an FDJ hike the next day and wrote a belated apology to my hosts of the Education Ministry. The similarity between the FDJ and the HJ (Hitler Youth) is superficial.

The Government is anxious to keep all moral contamination away from children. East Germany is a nation without girlie magazines and crime comics. The import of this type of literature is strictly forbidden. Anyone carrying such material risks a jail sentence. The education department is convinced that crime comics are basically evil and will contaminate young readers' minds. In the view of East German officials anyone reading such mainstays of American children as the adventures of the Addams family must of necessity become a sex deviate in later life; devotees of vampire stories may end up as dangerous killers and anyone enjoying a gangster movie could easily grow up to be a gangster. To the East German a great many Americans are gangsters and have started their life of crime because they were exposed to the "evil filth of crime comics" during their adolescence. In this respect there exists a certain affinity between East German educators and the Puritans of early American history. Press stories dealing with the problem of juvenile delinquency in American cities are reprinted out of all proportion and are invariably blamed on the American economic system. Actually, all revolutionary societies clamouring for high ideals share these Puritan traits, and East German society is no exception to this rule.

The same philosophy is reflected in East German sexual morality. Divorce is possible but generally frowned upon. The sexual revolution of the West is considered a result of "bourgeois degeneracy". Nudism as such is not practised and the American girlie magazines are believed to exert a basically corrupt and evil influence. Nudity as a sex stimulant comes in for much criticism — occasional nudity in sports is accepted. Western magazines showing scantily-clad girls are banned, but I have seen a number of East German photographic magazines sporting nudes. "This is different. Our pictures are artistic; the Western photos are degenerate", was the explanation given. Both types of photo looked equally nude to me.

Western jazz is tolerated and has made considerable inroads with GDR teenagers. Discotheque dances have somehow managed to penetrate the iron curtain. The "Frug", the "Watusi" and similar fads are occasionally practised by young East Germans. But the relationship between young people on the dance floor remains strictly formal.

A considerable percentage of East German women work — very often at menial jobs. I met two college-educated girls who operated a huge crane near Halle. My question why they did not look for a less arduous job, considering their university training, surprised them. "Why not? It gives us practical knowledge as well. We hope to live to a ripe old age. Lots of time left for desk jobs!" The relationship between men and women in factories and shops is similar to what we're familiar with. But people will help and assist each other more than we do. I once tried to cross an intersection on a red light. Two pedestrians rushed up and held me back by force. "For heaven's sake, man, you might have been killed!" was the explanation for their unsolicited assistance. I have seen four pedestrians help an old lady across the street — an activity allegedly reserved for the boy scouts of Western society. The words "human being" and "humanitarian act" are among the GDR's most frequently used expressions. Most people who use them are deadly serious.

I have found less atheism in East Germany than in any other "East block" country, barring Poland. The country is almost solidly Lutheran. But there are a few Catholics, and considerable assistance is given to all religious organizations. As indicated, the East German CDU Party represents the political interests of East German churches and the former CDU chief Otto Nuschke, now dead, has become one of East Germany's political heroes. The *Union Presse,* which as I mentioned previously, is mailed to West German readers, devotes the major part of its contents to religious matters. Most churches destroyed by the war have been rebuilt at Government expense and returned to their congregations. "No one is forced to be religious and everyone's right to be a non-believer is granted by our Constitution; but we do not encourage atheism and we do help the churches." Later during my trip I learned that this policy also applies to the few remaining members of the Jewish community. The generation who were young impressionable children during the declining years of Hitler's abortive "Thousand Year Empire" has become the backbone of the new regime. They are now in their late twenties or early thirties and comprise the largest proportion of the young idealistic functionaries who run East Germany today. Walter Ulbricht and most of his ministers are old men. The civil service operating the GDR is amazingly young. Unpleasant as this fact may be to Western readers, these young people brought up in the "anti-Nazi spirit" are completely devoted to their ideals. When talking to Westerners who do not share their beliefs, they do not become angry or argumentative. They become sad. "Have we not suffered enough under Nazism", they tend to ask. "The last war cost mankind fifty million dead. No war must ever again start on German soil. The evil designs of West Germany must be quashed!" The assumption that West Germany is basically evil and aims at the destruction of East Germany is deeply ingrained in the minds of most young functionaries.

Relations between East Germany's younger generation and the Soviet Union reflect gratefulness and admiration. It took me some days to realize that many East Germans actually thank the Soviet Union for invading Germany and defeating the Wehrmacht. "We could never have freed ourselves from the Nazi oppressors", is their stock remark. This point of view surprises most visitors for it differs completely from the feelings of most West Germans. While the average West German looks back to 1945 with a feeling of frustration and anger, GDR citizens do not consider the capitulation a defeat, but a victory of the German people over Fascism. May 8, the anniversary of the collapse, is the GDR's most important holiday and is celebrated by young and old alike. In West Germany the day is ignored. Are there exceptions? I spoke to many East Germans who showed no particular liking for the Soviets. They told me sad stories of the war's closing days. Without exception these people belonged to the older generation not trained in the present school system. All East German children learn Russian and quite a few speak this difficult language fluently. The basic relationship between East

Germans and Russians compares to that of West Germans and Americans. The underlying reasons are the same.

Of all Communist countries the GDR is the one least communist. When I pointed this fact out to my hosts, it was hotly denied. But it is nevertheless true. East Germany did not nationalize her soil. Small farmers still own their land — even though most of them have combined into large cooperatives. The big landowners and all absentee landlords have lost their holdings — they were distributed among the small farmers.

Private enterprise still flourishes. Very large companies have usually been nationalized. (There are some exceptions — a few of them are still privately owned.) These nationalized firms are called "V.E." (German abbreviation for "owned by the people"). They account for the larger part of East German production. In sheer numbers, however, more firms are owned by individuals than by the State. "The tradition of private ownership of the soil is deeply rooted in the German people. Therefore we respect this tradition" — a statement by Chief of State Walter Ulbricht — certainly the most unusual statement ever made by a Communist statesman!

The GDR contains a number of private apartment house owners. This discovery was one of the strangest I made during my trip. Most of the modern recently-built units are publicly owned, but a large portion of the prewar multiple-dwelling units still belong to their original owners. "We have expropriated the following groups of people: Nazis, large concerns — the type we socialists call "monopoly capitalists" — people who abused their position and exploited others. Whenever a person did not fall into any of these classifications we did not expropriate him", my guide explained. I interviewed two of these communist landlords. Their fate is not a happy one — from a financial standpoint. All rents are frozen at the 1944 level. Like everywhere else, tradesmen are hard to get and they charge high fees. (Many of the tradesmen are also still self-employed!) In Western countries this situation would immediately lead to a quick deterioration of all older real estate, since no landlord would undertake repairs under these conditions. But in East Germany the landlord is forced by law to arrange for repairs. If he fails to tackle them the Government will do the work and collect from the owner by charging him the expense incurred in form of a forced loan. These "loans" become mortgages on the property ahead of all existing mortgages. Their interest cost is minimal — but I have seen buildings with their original mortgage and several forced loans which took the place of second, third and fourth mortgages. The Government states that it never forecloses on these loans — and they may well be right. For the landlord has become the Government's unpaid janitor — his existence suddenly becomes useful to the State. Thus the fate of East German landlords is indeed not a happy one — their properties have become millstones around their collective necks. They often end up by voluntarily turning their holdings over to the State.

On the other hand I met successful businessmen with six-figure incomes, who operate plants employing as many as 50 employees. I met one man, a former Canadian citizen who had returned to East Germany, the land of his birth. He had had sufficient forethought to change his Canadian dollars into gold bullion before returning. The East German Government holds a monopoly in gold, similar to that of the United States or the United Kingdom. But it pays a special premium of 500 per cent for any gold imported into the GDR. In practice the returning Canadian exchanged his Canadian savings at five times the normal rate — today he leads the life of a wealthy retired gentleman — another anomaly in a Communist nation. The State-owned bank pays him a fair percentage on his savings — a practice frowned upon by both Karl Marx and Lenin.

Much has been said about the 2,000,000 East Germans who moved to the West before the great Berlin wall was built. Little has been said about those moving back to East Germany. The number of returning refugees is staggering — and the existence of this problem is virtually unknown outside Germany. Some 2,000 to 3,000 people reach the East German border from the West every month — the migration has taken on such proportions that the East German Government had to create a number of refugee camps where the *Rückwanderer* are processed. The largest element consists of former refugees who had gone to West Germany and became disenchanted. Others were lonely for the loved ones they had left behind. A considerable group are West Germans who believe in communism (the Communist Party being banned in the Federal Republic) or who are discouraged by signs of neo-Nazi activity in certains sections of West Germany. Finally there are a few opportunists — men who wish to escape their creditors, husbands who wish to desert their wives and families, or criminals hoping for a life of safety behind the iron curtain. East German authorities maintain that these opportunists are refused entry and are returned to West Germany.

The most painful reality of life for the average East German is the fact that West Germany refuses to recognize the GDR. The aim of the Hallstein doctrine to isolate East Germany diplomatically, politically and spiritually, has had a certain amount of success. West German application of this doctrine reaches the point of absurdity. East German hockey and soccer teams can rarely hope to play in Western games; since they carry passports of a "non-existent state" they are refused entry at the border. West German authorities use constant pressure on the allied travel board in West Berlin, the agency having jurisdiction over clearance for all East German visa applications to NATO countries. Officially West Germany denies that such pressure is used. But I have seen it in operation myself a number of times. When Johannes Gnad, a Leipzig book publisher, attempted to obtain a visitor's visa from Canada where he wanted to organize an exhibition of East German non-political books, his request was bluntly denied. The applicant never found out why. Through sources which I cannot reveal here I learned beyond doubt that the West German Press Department had successfully blocked the visa.

The average East German who finds himself unable to travel westward because of the invisible wall erected by West Germany assumes that "the Nazi state fears the influx of anti-Nazis". Actually the Federal Republic does fear the influx of East Germans, but for other more pertinent reasons. West Germany wishes to boycott and isolate East Germany because the West German Government wishes to remain the sole agency representing Germany in the rest of the world. The reason for this policy is the hope for eventual reunification of both states on West German economic and political terms. This would never be possible as long as another German state with a different social and political order exists. Therefore the Hallstein doctrine tries to create the image of an "oppressed Soviet-occupied zone", whose people were never consulted about their political future. This image would evaporate if large numbers of West Germans could travel to the GDR, or if GDR citizens were able to travel freely to the West. The fact that East Germany, with all her faults and shortcomings, is a state founded on the acceptance of the overwhelming majority of her citizens would become known. Consequently, any large movement of East German travellers (other than refugees who are basically dissatisfied with conditions in the first place) would be against the Federal Republic's interests. This fear of "adulteration" of West Germany's sole right to represent the interests of all Germans becomes so overwhelming that Bonn makes a great effort to isolate East Germany from having cultural relations abroad. I have personally experienced this open hostility in places where I had never suspected its existence.

While I was preparing a series of articles on my impressions of East Germany, many West Germans reached me, genuinely upset. They insisted that "the East Germans are an unhappy people since they were never consulted about the form of government under which they have to live". Considerable pressure was used on my newspaper when the series started to appear. A regular campaign was organized against the *Nachrichten* to force the withdrawal of these articles. Large German-Canadian firms withdrew their advertising. The "offending" articles were entirely non-political. But they described my trip through East Germany in condensed form. "We believe the GDR to be an evil country; you describe the GDR as almost human...", a letter accompanying a cancellation of subscription stated. It speaks for the fairness of our Editor-in-Chief that the *Montrealer Nachrichten* continued publication. In most instances the protests came from West German citizens or naturalized Canadians who had emigrated from Germany after 1945. "Oldtimers" who had been in Canada for more than 20 years accepted our reports with interest.

This constant rejection by West Germany has made GDR citizens very touchy. They sometimes appear to carry a chip on their shoulder. They react badly when made to feel unwelcome. They feel isolated. They resent not being able to travel freely. "Why aren't our passports accepted by your government?" an East German visitor to Canada attending a Congress in Montreal asked. (He had finally received a visitor's visa after the greatest effort and the intervention of the Soviet Embassy.) The visa was given him on a separate sheet of paper — the Department of Immigration refused to stamp it into his passport. "You accept Polish, Czech, Rumanian, Soviet passports. All these nations are Socialist — more so than we are. Why this discrimination against our country?" The man expressed the basic complaint of the GDR officials and public.

Germans are basically a dogmatic people. They fought a bloody war which lasted thirty years to decide whether the country should go Protestant or remain Catholic. When the war finally ended, the borders between the two contesting religions were almost the same as the day it had started. The strongest wish of West German policy is eventual reunification of the two states. But two different societies have sprung up on German soil. At a time when ideological conflicts across the world have started to subside, when the Soviet Union attempts to coexist with free enterprise, when the ecumenical spirit has made inroads into most major religions, the ideological conflict between West German non-Nazis and East German anti-Nazis continues without let-up. German history suggests that neither party will withdraw its basic demands. Consequently, the chances for German reunification appear dim.

CHAPTER III

AGRICULTURAL EXPERIMENT
IN CAPITALISTIC SOCIALISM

"Our agricultural cooperatives are an outstanding success." Walter Ulbricht made this statement during his last May Day speech. I had decided to inspect several communes and to interview as many farmers as possible. In the Soviet Union the Kolkhoz system had failed — today's Soviet leaders have admitted it. Mao had established agricultural communes in China — and Chinese agricultural production promptly nosedived.

"We have not copied the Soviet and Chinese systems", explained Franz Mueller, head of a planning commission in the Ministry of Agriculture. "We realized their many shortcomings. We have organized the small farmers into production cooperatives instead. Most of our farm products are grown by these cooperatives. We have three types: LPG (German abbreviation for agricultural cooperatives) number one, whose farmers combine to till the soil but retain individual ownership of their farm animals; LPG number three, where both soil and animals are managed collectively, and LPG number two, where some animals are retained in private ownership while others are held in common. LPG number three are the most common and the most successful!"

I requested permission to inspect such a cooperative — with two provisos: I wanted to select the LPG to be visited myself. And I asked to be permitted to speak to whomever I wanted, without supervision. Both requests were granted.

I picked an LPG called *Neues Leben* (New Life) near the village of Wittbrietzen in the district of Potsdam. My arrangement with the Government called for my visit to remain unannounced — and the Government kept its word. For I not only arrived without previous advice, but I was promptly arrested as a trespasser. They brought me to the village jail, a locked room behind a row of offices, where I spent a pleasant if somewhat lonely morning. After my identity had been checked, I was released and brought to the community manager, a young bull-necked farmer. After an apology, the manager described life on an East German cooperative.

The commune blankets the village of Wittbrietzen. All 200 villagers except two have become members and share in the 1,000 hectare cooperative (a hectare equals approximately two and one half acres). Wittbrietzen is a type three LPG. Farm animals are kept in common, but each farmer may retain for his own use one cow, one hog and four piglets. The great surprise of my visit was the capitalist organization of this allegedly socialist community. Farmers forming the cooperative retain private ownership of their farmhouse and land. The soil is worked by the community — and the management pays "land rent" to the individual owners. Thus the farmers share in the profit of the LPG in two different ways: they receive rent for their land, which means that the income of the farmers who hold much land is disproportionately larger than that of farmers with meagre holdings; they are also paid for whatever labour they perform. Wages are calculated by a complicated system. Its basis is the "work unit", approximately an average day's work. All farm employees receive exact payment for their work at the end of each year; meanwhile they draw monthly paychecks which serve as an advance against their final payment. In our Western society it would be called a "drawing account". At the age of sixty-five farmers may retire. They receive a pension based on a historical average of their earnings. The land rent continues without decrease after retirement. When a farmer dies, he may dispose of his land and buildings through testament — and his heirs become members of the community.

"Very interesting", I remarked to the manager. "Would you please tell me whether a farmer may sell his share of the community on the open market and whether the buyer would automatically become a member of the community?" "I cannot remember such a case ever coming up", he replied. "But we have no law that would forbid it. The community would have to vote whether to admit the buyer as a member; therefore the farmer could only sell to someone acceptable to us. The same would apply if an owner should will his land to someone other than a child or next of kin. This has actually happened. But we accepted the heirs as members."

This LPG's administration is handled by the assembly of all its members. This assembly, which corresponds to a Western shareholders' meeting, makes the laws. Every two years it elects the executive management handling the affairs of the community.

"Are all farmers forced to join the community? May individual farmers remain aloof, if they wish?" "No one is forced to join. But most of them do. We are more efficient than individual owners. Two farmers have not joined our group. They are not ostracized. In fact, one of them is my father-in-law. They will join eventually, because right now they are losing money."

During the next two hours I inspected the extensive farm and stables. Where previously the land had been subdivided into many small plots causing an alleged loss of farming efficiency, the LPG's had been divided into huge districts, specializing in the same most adaptable crop for each area. Ordinary soil for clover, the richest soil for wheat. "We have Government crop insurance. If we suffer storm damage, they compensate us for our losses." All farm animals previously kept in small individual stables are now kept in huge barns served by the most modern farming equipment. I saw one building which housed 220 cows. The pigsty contained more than 400 pigs and piglets. "Our stock increased some 400 per cent since the cooperative was founded. Our increased efficiency is the reason. The average income of our farmers has tripled. They used to earn between 3,000 and 5,000 marks per year as individual owners. Now the lowest income for any of our members approximates 6,500 marks and the highest can go to 15,000. What do you think of our socialist community now?"

"I think it is great", I replied. "You have applied Western economic principles with excellent results. Your LPG is neither socialist nor is it a commune. It is an efficient joint-stock company run almost entirely by standards acceptable to any Western businessman. Naturally it is efficient!" The manager looked at me with an air of astonishment. "What are you saying? We exploit nobody. We are a socialist enterprise!" "I did not say you were exploiting anybody. On the contrary. But you have organized many individual owners into a more efficient cooperative organization. This enables you to make better use of existing facilities. Because your individual owners have pooled resources you have become more successful. My compliments, sir! Your farmers will

probably be happy. They still own their land and their income
has risen — thanks to your adaptation of our systems of combines
and trusts. Your socialist commune *Neues Leben* is a miniature
joint-stock company based on the West's proven methods of rais-
ing production." "I won't even answer this absolute nonsense!"
My host withdrew into silence. But I sensed that my remarks had
not entirely missed their mark.

Actually, East Germany's agricultural policy combines methods
of western efficiency with some of the basic concepts of communism.
The Potsdam district, where Wittbrietzen is situated, was once
the home of the Prussian Junkers. The Junkers and large landowners have been expropriated. A few of them chose to remain in
East Germany and took well-paid government jobs. In some
ministries, particularly the Ministry of Defence, former Junkers
and aristocrats hold key positions. After the expropriation of the
large landowners the soil was redistributed among smaller owners.
For a few years they were permitted to till their soil without
outside interference; then the LPG's were founded but it did not
become obligatory for all farmers to join. This system of voluntary
cooperatives showed fairly good results. There is a basic economic
reason behind the combines' success. The sandy soil of Prussia
does not lend itself to individual ownership. Small farmers can
hardly be successul. This fact had been the reason for the rise of
the Junker class in the first place. Now the Junkers have been
replaced by the so-called communes, which are not communes at
all, but a continuation of the old system under new management,
with better distribution among the small farmers. The men who
conceived the present East German agricultural system were
brilliant, and they succeeded. Fortunately for the West it has been
limited to East Germany. If China or the USSR had originally in-
stituded the LPG system of the Ulbricht government, the large
Canadian wheat sales to these nations might never have been
necessary.

Before leaving Wittbrietzen I decided to visit one of the remaining "independent farmers". I was brought to an elderly
gentleman sitting on his front lawn. His house looked no different
from the other farmhouses of the commune.

"What made you decide to remain on your own?" I asked.
"Are you against the present Government? Do you dislike communism?" "That's all hogwash", the old man answered. "I know
nothing about politics. I don't care a hoot about communism one

way or the other. Ulbricht? He is some guy in Berlin. Hitler was in Berlin too. So was Hindenburg, and the Kaiser before him. Yes, I remember the Kaiser. I served under him in the First World War. I was quite young then.

"Why did I not sell out? Because I have always owned my land and run my affairs, that's why. Ulbricht? He is a nice fellow. In any event, I wouldn't know. I never met him. But he is not going to run my land. The LPG is not going to run my land. I am going to run my land. Yes sir! That's why I did not sell out. I know! I could keep my land and get rent for it. But who wants to get rent? I want to work my own land with my own hands. That's what I want.

"Where do you come from, anyway? You talk with a South-German accent. Bavarian, hey? Of course you are! Well, you are welcome here anyway —

"Yes, you are right! I am not doing too well on my own. How could I? They sell at a lower price. And to whom can I sell? To the Government stores, of course. So far, they have bought my goods. But what would stop them from refusing to buy my goods in the future? Just one single change in the purchasing policy decreed by Berlin, and we remaining individual farmers will be on ice. We exist only because Berlin allows us to exist. How long? Just as long as it suits the Government. If they refuse to buy from me, I will have to join the LPG. So maybe there is a bit of Government pressure after all. But I don't worry. Meanwhile I sit here and enjoy my independence. They allow me to remain by myself. And when I sell out? There will be another red cotton transparent with the inscription: 'The village of Wittbrietzen is now entirely *genossenchaftlich* (community owned). Up to now, they haven't pressed me very hard."

East Germany proceeds very slowly against the few remaining individual farmers. The lessons learned in the Soviet Union during the first fifteen years of her existence have not been lost on East Berlin. The Soviets nationalized the soil. All land belongs to the Government. Private dwellings are sold in the USSR to private owners, but the individual obtains only ownership of the building, not the land it stands on. In East Germany this practice has not been followed. The soil remains individually owned, even where LPG's were formed. This fact, more than any other, has helped to create a stable society in the agricultural districts of the country, far more stable than Bonn and the Western powers imagine. The "flight to the West" which occurred before the Berlin wall was built was generally confined to members of the middle class and to skilled labour. East German farmers never took part in large-scale migration to the West.

Statistics tell the rest of the story: 87 per cent of East Germany's agricultural products are grown by LPGs, 13 per cent by individual farmers. Of the former, 69 per cent are of type three in which farm animals are held in common.

"Within five years our entire production will be handled by LPGs of type three", was the final prophecy of the cooperative's manager, as he bid me goodbye.

CHAPTER IV

WEIMAR, CITY OF POETS

We left Wittbrietzen shortly after noon. Our next destination, Weimar. Germany's Stratford-on-Avon lies hidden in a beautiful valley in the heart of Thuringia, the GDR's southernmost province. To reach it, we had to traverse the greater part of the country — demonstrating the East German State's smallness. We covered the entire distance in less than four hours.

The first leg of our trip took us through Brandenburg, fomerly Prussia's keystone province. But Prussia no longer exists; the Allies abolished it in 1945 with a stroke of the pen. The cradle of German militarism was split into several small *Länder*. Yet Prussia somehow survived her demise. Kossen, Luckenwalde and Jueterbog still are typical small Prussian towns. The older people still salute each other with a stiff, formal bow and their mode of dress has scarcely changed since the days of the Second Reich. Twenty years of Communist rule have left few outward signs. Even today titles retain a semblance of importance and horsedrawn carriages are still used for short pleasure rides.

We stopped in Wittenberg. The East German Government has renamed the town "Lutherstadt Wittenberg". It was here that Martin Luther proclaimed his famous ninety-five theses heralding the beginning of the German Reformation. Communism is supposed to be the mortal enemy of all religion. But in Wittenberg I found my East Berlin experiences repeated. The Government carefully protects all religious shrines. The town has changed little since the days of Luther. The war damaged it only superficially, and everything has been fully restored. Unlike the West German towns of Rothenburg and Dinkelsbuehl, Wittenberg does not advertise itself as a medieval tourist attraction. But it could become the centre of a tourist industry. Modern motorcars look strangely out of place on the ancient city's narrow cobblestoned streets. A visitor would hardly be surprised if people in medieval garb suddenly appeared.

The Autobahn begins behind Wittenberg. Adolf Hitler's superhighways have survived the collapse of his Third Reich. They serve both German states — East and West alike. They are the economic lifelines of both countries; while much of Germany's trade is still carried on by the railroads, the overland trucking companies today account for the biggest share of the country's commerce. In East Germany both railways and large trucking companies are state-owned. But a few privately-owned trucking firms operate as well, and they are taking an ever-increasing bite out of East Germany's transportation business.

The Autobahnen compete with the airlines as well. Compared to North America both German states are so small, that it hardly saves a traveller time to drive to the airport, await his flight, disembark at the distant airport and take ground transportation to his final destination. The use of the Autobahnen is simpler and takes scarcely more time than flying.

Weimar is one of the GDR's truly beautiful towns. For several decades of the eighteenth and the beginning of the nineteenth century Weimar was the focal point of German intellectual life. Germany's greatest poet, Johann Wolfgang von Goethe, was Prime Minister of the small Duchy of Sachsen-Weimar-Eisenach, of which Weimar was the capital. Goethe attracted some of the leading personalities of Germany's golden age of poetry. The other great German poet, Friedrich Schiller, moved to Weimar to be near Goethe. Today both poets are buried in huge brass coffins standing side by side. Their burial vault survived two world wars, but Goethe's famous town house on the Frauenplan received a full hit during the last year of the Second World War. The GDR Government has carefully restored it; the rear of the building which housed the poet's 6,000 volume library was not damaged. Goethe's garden house, a small square structure resembling a British country cottage — completely untypical of Germany — also escaped major war damage.

During its most glorious days Weimar's population never exceeded 5,000. It has grown, but its basic character remains unchanged. Of all the towns in the GDR, it is the one most unusual for East Germany. Its mayor is a member of the National Liberal

Party, one of the political groups accepting former Nazi Party members. The mayor was never a Nazi, but his sympathies are hardly pro-Ulbricht. During my visit to Weimar I saw none of the red-coloured propaganda transparents so common in other East German cities.

Goethe and Schiller have been dead for more than 135 years, but they are still part of the Weimar atmosphere. The average German considers Goethe one of the greatest poets of all time — perhaps the very greatest. He compares him to men like Shakespeare, Dante and Homer — an assumption with which the average non-German would hardly agree. But to the Germans the pre-eminence of Goethe is real. Actually he was a man of many talents like Leonardo da Vinci. He was first of all a poet and a scientist. His theory of colours has become one of the classics in this field. Even today his biological works dealing with animal and human bone structure are often quoted. His great literary work, Faust, is believed by most Germans to be the greatest tragedy ever written. The thesis of the "Faustian man", the human mind reaching from the lower depths to the stars, is equated by many Germans with the destiny of the German nation. In this sense Faust has done much psychological damage which Goethe could hardly have foreseen. For in his everyday life he was a normal, sociable if somewhat conceited man, who knew no racial or nationalist prejudices. He did not always practise what he preached. The strangely ambivalent character of the man can best be described by the following anecdote. In his tragedy Faust Goethe pleads for Gretchen, a young girl who had killed her new-born child. But when a young child murderess was once brought before Prime Minister Goethe, he summarily convicted her.

The Faust tragedy consists of two parts. The second part contains many difficult and confused passages; very few people fully understand the poet's meaning. Paradoxically, this very fact has helped to endear Faust and its creator to the German people.

Goethe's lyrical poems are beautiful and have earned him the title of Germany's greatest lyrical poet. Heinrich Heine's lyrics probably surpass Goethe's as far as sheer beauty is concerned. One of Weimar's anecdotes deals with Heine's visit. The young aspiring poet wanted to pay homage to Germany's great man of letters. Goethe condescendingly received him and asked the young man about his latest literary project. Heine committed a classical error. He answered: "I am working on a modern poem about Faust".

Goethe, who had devoted much of his life to the creation of the
Faust tragedy, dismissed the young caller in icy silence. Years later
Heine repaid Goethe with a short poem in which he sketched the
great man as an "ancient cold-hearted man" *(kalter Kunstgreis)*.
Goethe often misjudged other artists. E.T.A. Hoffmann, the great
romanticist and writer on the supernatural (his works inspired
America's Edgar Allan Poe) was called a "miserable scribbler scar-
ing little children". Goethe never appreciated Beethoven's music.
"No one should compose such music — what would happen to
mankind if Beethoven's revolutionary technique should prevail?"

Germany's other great poet, Friedrich Schiller, is harder to
assess than Goethe. As a young man Schiller, a native of Württemberg, became an ardent fighter for human rights. The ruling Arch-
duke of Württemberg feared the young man's revolutionary impact
and banished him from the state. But later in life Schiller's fervour
cooled considerably. In his great balled *The Bell* he lampooned
the French Revolution. Schiller became the best known German
playwright. He often changed his political theories for the purposes
of dramatic effect. In one drama *(Don Carlos)* he defended freedom
of thought. In the fragment of another *(Demetrius)* he attacked
the principles of democracy which he had lauded in all his previous
works. When Hitler seized power, he used the lines of *Demetrius*
in all school text books:

> What is majority? Majority is nonsense
> Only a few do have the gift of knowledge.
> All votes ought to be weighed and not counted.
> A state ruled by majority must perish
> Sooner or later — since idiots rule the land.

Most of Schiller's tragedies were well written; yet many Germans
dislike them — and their reason is not necessarily political. For
many decades German elementary and high-school pupils were
forced to learn long Schiller passages by heart. *The Maid of
Orleans* is one such drama literally stuffed down the unwilling
throat of millions of German students. After forty years I still
remember much of the *Maid* by heart and I despise the tragedy —
yet by unbiased standards it is a beautiful drama. Most Germans
tend to agree with me on this point.

The lives and works of Goethe and Schiller retain a command-
ing influence on the thinking processes of today's Germany. The
East German Government recognizes this and has established a

seat of learning in Weimar called the "National Shrine of German Poets". This Shrine is located in an annex of Goethe's town house on the Frauenplan. Ten huge rooms added to the original building serve the Shrine's research scientists as headquarters. These men are engaged in classifying material and conducting a never-ending search into the poets' life histories. It is hard to believe that a century and a half after Germany's golden literary age came to an end facts hitherto unknown still await discovery. But it is true. I interviewed a research scientist who was studying Goethe's extensive correspondence with a government coal supplier. The poet, as prime minister, carefully instructed coal miners to look for unusual mineral formations to be brought to him personally. Other scientists are gathering copies of all recent translations of the poets' works into modern African languages. None of these research men are avowed communists. East German Government employees are often selected for their political reliability. These standards are discarded in the hiring of the Shrine's staff. Devotion to the cause of German literature and exact studies in this field are the only essentials asked of the men selected. I asked the chief research man a question which would have drawn a stereotyped answer from most government employees: "Do you believe Goethe and Schiller would have approved of modern East German Socialism?" "Shall I be honest?" he answered. "I believe that Goethe would not have approved. He was a product of bourgeois society and the Prime Minister of a feudal princeling. Yet he helped to form the German mind and to prepare for the world in which we live today. Who can rightfully judge? And Schiller? Which Schiller do you mean? The young revolutionary firebrand who wrote *The Robbers?* He would have approved wholeheartedly. The slightly older Schiller, who wrote *The Bell?* He might have approved — somewhat hesitatingly, perhaps. And the dying Schiller who wrote *Demetrius?* Emphatically not!" The researcher smiled. "If you quote me, do me one favour: Don't use my name!"

"Schiller was a literary opportunist. Aren't we all opportunists in one way or another? During the past fifty years we followed a Kaiser, a Führer and a People's Republic. We all cried Hosannah. When things got uncomfortable, we changed our minds. There were no monarchists left after 1918. Show me one single person who officially endorsed Nazism after May 1945. Today we all laud the Ulbricht government. We all like socialism. Do you think I am an exception? I am not crazy! You want to know what Schiller would have thought of our present-day government? Leaf through his works and take your pick!"

The Shrine has reserved some of its time and effort for Germany's most unusual poet, Heinrich Heine. Heine never lived in Weimar and visited it only once. He left his native Düsseldorf as a young man and moved to Paris, where he lived most of his life, and where he died. In his day he became the enfant terrible of German letters and the most brilliant critic of emerging German nationalism. At other times he wrote the most sensitive lyrical poems ever written. His *Wintermärchen* ("Winter's Fairy Tale") is a lengthy ballad in which Heine describes a visit to his native Germany after living in Paris for several decades. The *Wintermärchen*, probably Heine's most famous work, clearly foresees the Nazi movement in all its details. The amazing fact about this literary prophecy is that it was written ninety years before the advent of Nazism.

Unlike Goethe and Schiller, Heine would almost certainly have approved of modern East German Socialism. Heine is greatly honoured by the Ulbricht government and often ignored by the West Germans — regrettably so, for he is undoubtedly the third of Germany's major poets.

Goethe's town house still contains most of the poet's original furniture. Other parts of the spacious mansion serve as a museum. The rear rooms, where the Shrine has its headquarters, are not open to the public. The town house was one of the most spacious and luxurious homes of its day. But to a modern visitor it appears uncomfortable and somewhat primitive. Goethe apparently liked to stand in front of his desk while writing. Many of his works were dictated in staccato sentences to his secretary, Eckermann, who found it difficult to follow the thoughts of the quick thinking poet at a time when shorthand and typewriters were still things of the future. Goethe's library is still usable and interesting to us now. German spelling has not changed appreciably during the past two hundred years and most of the books in the library may be enjoyed by a modern reader.

Goethe's garden house stands in the centre of a large park. It is warm, more intimate than the rambling town house. From the standpoint of comfort it would not satisfy the humblest homeowner of our time. Even though built some 200 years later it compares to Shakespeare's home in Stratford-on-Avon.

Weimar exerts a strange influence on most visitors. I had come to East Germany to study political and social conditions; but Weimar as a city has little to offer in that respect. Socialism exists there, as it does everywhere in East Germany. But the casual visitor gains the impression that a moratorium has been extended to all temporal things. The town's atmosphere is almost unreal, as if the eighteenth century had come to engulf the present. Versailles, Potsdam, Stratford and Nuremberg all are communities whose glory lies in the past. But the visitor never achieves the complete feeling of detachment from the present which permeates the Weimar sights. It is a strange world, a world that was and can never live again. A world of greatness and sadness. It is understandable that Weimar has never adjusted to present political realities. The influence of the past is far too strong.

A movie performance in the Shrine's main hall ended the unusual day. It was the life history of Christiane Vulpius, Goethe's young wife. The aging genius was attracted to the young girl — a simple person of average intelligence — a poor match for Goethe as far as learning and upbringing were concerned. But the poet saw Christiane in a different light; primitive beauty and complete trust. Goethe described his young wife in one his most famous poems, the *Rose of the Heather.*

> Boy once saw a rosebud rare,
> rosebud in the heather.
> Fresh as morning's glow and fair
> near he ran to see her there,
> saw the rose with pleasure.
> Rosebud, little rosebud red,
> rosebud in the heather.

> "I will pick you, rose" said he
> "rosebud in the heather."
> "I will prick you, boy" said she
> "that you'll always think of me,
> I'll not grant you pleasure."
> Rosebud, little rosebud red,
> rosebud in the heather.

> **And the rash boy broke the rose,**
> **rosebud in the heather.**

With her thorns she dared oppose
useless all her ahs and ohs
had to grant him pleasure.
Rosebud, little rosebud red,
rosebud in the heather.

This beautiful song, set to music by two of Germany's great
composers, Schubert and Mendelssohn, remains one of the most
famous classical songs of the country. It is sung by young lovers
and old art devotees alike. It was also the favourite poem of Ilse
Koch, the witch of Buchenwald, who used to hum it while watch-
ing the execution of her victims.

CHAPTER V

BUCHENWALD — A MONUMENT TO HORROR

The Ettersberg is a lovely tree-covered mountain near Weimar, For many centuries it had been one of the town's favourite excursion spots. Its woods were the meeting place of generations of local lovers; its meadows served as Weimar's most convenient picnic grounds. Goethe and Schiller spent many hours there discussing mankind's lofty ideals. Goethe's favourite spot was a beech forest near the mountain top which he called "one of nature's beauty spots". Little did Goethe know that within 115 years the beech forest on the Ettersberg would become one of Germany's most infamous places.

After the Nazis had seized power in 1933 they organized their first concentration camps to imprison and torture their political enemies. In one of history's supreme ironies the beech forest on the Ettersberg became a Nazi camp. The place was simply called "beech forest" — *Buchenwald* in German. Buchenwald was a comparatively "good" camp if I may use the word in this connection. It contained no gas chambers and no large-scale extermination program was planned. Later during the war mass killings were conducted at Buchenwald; these killings did not exceed 50,000, a modest figure by Nazi standards. The crematoria had originally been installed at the camp to cremate inmates who had died of natural causes. After 1943 a number of Soviet war prisoners, mostly members of the Communist Party or army officers, were killed here; they were despatched by a shot in the neck and cremated in the six-chamber crematorium. The most prominent local murder victim was Ernst Thaelmann, head of the outlawed German Communist Party. Today Buchenwald has been preserved as a national shrine. It looks exactly as it did during the closing days of the war, with two exceptions. A large monument, probably the most impressive structure erected on the grounds of a former Nazi camp, has been built by the East German Government; a huge belltower with an elaborate memorial chapel, and a monument of a group of resistance fighters guards the tower's entrance. Again, the barracks which once housed the prisoners have been removed and memorial plates indicate the spots where they stood.

Many former Nazi camps have been preserved in both East and West Germany. Both States maintain them as memorial places, with a clear difference in objective. West Germany dedicates the spots to the memory of the anonymous murder victims; East Germany to the memory of the political and communist prisoners who perished there and to venerate the resistance fighters who survived. This is understandable; for West Germany's society differs from that of the GDR. Both states were formed after the collapse of the Nazi dictatorship. Both governments formally oppose Nazism. But the strength of the West's reaction to the past does not compare to that of the East.

During their twelve years of power the Nazis arrested their active enemies. Those not immediately killed were imprisoned in concentration camps. There remained a huge number of people at large — a group not sufficiently interested in politics to fight the Nazis actively. Very often this neutral group cooperated with the Nazi Government without actually endorsing its acts. During the first few years most of the politically neutral folk had screamed "Heil Hitler" and had followed their seemingly invincible leader. Later when the fortunes of war had begun to change, they turned from him. But their opposition remained entirely passive. There existed a closely-knit group of active anti-Nazis, and a large apathetic mass of loosely defined non-Nazis. When the West German State was created, members of the "non-Nazi" group seized power. To these people all radicals became equally suspect. The "Nazis" and the "Communists" were equally detestable to them. And since the West German Government was reluctant to admit that communist prisoners were better than their Nazi jailers, their presence in the camps was played down. The West German Government dedicated the memorials to the anonymous concentration camp victims.

In East Germany the active anti-Nazi group having seized power, the camp's former political prisoners, the active communists who had run the underground resistance became the governing elite of the new East German State. Most leading figures of the GDR Government had spent the Hitler years either in exile outside the Third Reich or else had survived one of Hitler's camps. Therefore the East Germans see the concentration camps as the birthplace of the GDR — horrible places of trial and suffering from which today's leaders graduated; the hell camps in which today's heroes lived their finest hour. Therefore the East Germans emphasize the fate of the resistance fighters who survived and the memory of the political prisoners who died. Broadly, West German visitors see the camps as places of utter horror; East Germans visit them as historic monuments of yesterday's trials and today's greatness.

I arrived at Buchenwald on a misty Sunday morning. The visit became a ghastly experience which will forever remain in my memory. As a journalist I had read much of the literature written about the Nazi camps. I had interviewed hundreds of survivors. I had visited most of West Germany's camps. But I had never seen anything resembling the unparallelled horror of Buchenwald.

My travelling guide, Wolf, excused himself. "Sorry — I cannot take Buchenwald!" he confided. "Dont be offended. I saw it once. I don't wish to see it again." Wolf remained at the Weimar railway station. My driver Kadenbach — an old Communist Party member — was less squeamish. "If the prisoners could stand it, I should be able to stand visiting the place. After all, the Nazis are gone", was his comment. The Ettersberg was covered by heavy fog — a freak of nature creating a fitting background for my Buchenwald visit. Near the foot of the mountain a winding road of a few kilometres begins. "It's called blood alley", Kadenbach remarked casually. "The prisoners were driven uphill by the whips of the local SS detachment. If they couldn't run fast enough, they were shot. Some 800 prisoners died on this road."

I had always thought of Buchenwald as a small confined space where people were tortured behind barbed wire. Actually Buchenwald is a large area of seventy-five acres. The better part of the beech forest which had given its name to the camp had been cut down to make the space needed by the SS. The guards' barracks were outside the camp proper. Ilse Koch's villa still stands. The commander's offices now serve as a cafeteria and restaurant for the many visitors the camp attracts. It is a strange sight to see hundreds of people order and consume excellent meals in a place which saw so much suffering. "Why not? Would you want the visitors to starve?" was Kadenbach's answer to my surprised question.

I too ate a good meal in the camp cafeteria before entering, and looking back at the experience which awaited me, the meal was a good idea. After the visit I was unable to eat for the rest of the day.

Former Buchenwald political prisoners serve as guides. Our guide, an old Communist Party member named Richard Kucharczyk, had been arrested during the first two weeks of the Nazi regime. He arrived at Buchenwald while the camp was still under construction and left it when the first American armoured units appeared eleven years later. To men like Kucharczyk, Buchenwald has become a home unlike any other home. These former prisoners live in the past and their hatred of Nazism remains a burning reality. He remembered most of the other inmates by name, an unusual feat since as many as 50,000 were imprisoned at one time. Kucharczyk had served as member of a work gang which had to carry the bodies of murdered Soviet war prisoners from their place of execution to the crematorium. He was also detailed to cut off prisoners hanged on makeshift gallows for minor infractions of camp rules. Finally, he was one of the few prisoners who witnessed at least in part the most important execution ever conducted at Buchenwald, the shooting of Ernst Thaelmann, head of the German Communist Party and East Germany's best known martyr.

Outside the camp gates stands a small movie theatre. Its appointments are luxurious; it is adorned with soft lights, comfortable seats and even usherettes. But the films presented here are unlike any other films anywhere on earth. They are documentaries of Buchenwald's days of horror. Unlike Western movies dealing with the same theme, East German movies do not appeal to sensationalism. They tell a story. First they show the Ettersberg as it looked before the camp was established. Then they record the work battalions building the camp. Later the first prisoners arrive. None of the shots are staged — the Government has used old newsreels and films the Nazis took of their own crimes. One of the discoveries I made during my Buchenwald visit is the fact that many high-ranking Nazis liked to be filmed committing sadistic crimes, and that they carefully guarded these films in a manner reminiscent of followers of modern sex cults. The visitor sees these films before he enters the camp itself. The performance serves as an introduction to the horrors of Buchenwald.

Even today the camp remains a world apart. It has retained a ghastly life of its own, an air of utter unreality. Visitors enter through a huge forged iron gate bearing the fitting inscription: "To each his own" *(Jedem das Seine)*. Sometimes prisoners were shackled to this door. Inmates who did not work fast enough or when called did not run fast enough would be handcuffed to the gate with both arms stretched over their heads. After an hour the circulation would stop. Prisoners often remained shackled for several days. Without further injury many died after two days. There is a record of four Polish war prisoners who became insane after two nights and one day. When they were untied, they tore one SS-man to pieces with their bare hands. The four Poles were nailed to a wooden post and left to die. Twenty-five other Polish war prisoners were hanged in reprisal.

The worst attraction of the camp is the crematorium and the "cellar of gallows". This cellar actually is the ante-room of the crematorium itself. It is a large chamber. Along its walls two vertical bars are attached near the ceiling. Some thirty butchers' hooks are nailed to the bars; the hooks served as gallows. Usually a batch of thirty prisoners would be brought to this room and hanged. After twenty minutes (the executions took a long time, since no trap doors were provided and the victims died of slow suffocation), the prisoners' work battalion cut off the bodies and brought them to the crematorium next door.

Another grisly structure is a barn in which prisoners, mostly Soviet soldiers, were shot. To the other inmates the building was screened as a hospital. In the first room the prisoners undressed. They were brought single file into a small room, where an SS-man dressed in white would receive them. This alleged "doctor" talked in a friendly confidence-inspiring manner. He asked the prisoner to step on a scale. His weight was carefully recorded. A wooden measuring rod was gently put on his head. At this moment another SS-man hidden behind the wall would discharge a pistol into the victim's neck. "When the execution chamber worked full blast, they could kill one man every ten seconds", explained our guide.

I learned that several Canadian prisoners of war had been executed in Buchenwald. During 1944, in a fit of anger against allied air raids, Hitler ordered all pilots who had baled out imprisoned in concentration camps. Several Canadian pilots suffered this fate. Shortly after the great air raid against Dresden (February 13, 1945) Hitler ordered the "execution of all British air raid criminals". The order was never fully complied with; at the time it had already become apparent even to the most fanatical Nazis that Germany had lost the war. A few pilots however were killed. The Nazis never drew a distinct line between British and Canadian nationals. Consequently, several Canadians were executed. Their exact number is not known; our guide believed it to be four. Several brass memorial plates bear the names of allied soldiers executed near the Buchenwald crematoria.

Prisoners guilty of minor camp infractions were either executed or imprisoned in the camp barracks. The SS official in charge of these barracks was SS *Scharführer* Sommer. This man personally killed 187 prisoners by beating them to death; in some instances he choked them with his bare hands. Often he would enter the cells, pick a prisoner at random, take him to his room, kill him, push him under his bed and then retire to sleep for the rest of the night. In the morning the prisoners' work detail had to pull the bodies from under his bed to the crematorium. Sommer, a sex deviate, fled to West Germany after the war. He was sentenced to life imprisonment, West Germany's maximum punishment. (The Federal Republic has abolished the death penalty.)

There remain other places of Buchenwald horror — trees from which prisoners were hanged by their wrists, tables to which they were tied while receiving brutal beatings. But all these places and stories were overshadowed by a phenomenon which can be rightfully called the "Buchenwald Legend", the formation of a well-functioning underground guerilla group among the prisoners.

How could these helpless unarmed prisoners form an underground combat unit? It seems incredible; yet, it's true. The nucleus of the resistance were Communist Party members of Barrack number thirty-eight. Toward the end of the war an assortment of knives and pistols had been carefully hoarded and kept hidden from the SS. On April 11, 1945 the underground seized power, killed a number of SS-men, forced the others into flight and set up a camp government. Buchenwald is the only Nazi concentration camp which freed itself. When American troops arrived several days later, the camp had already liberated itself.

The Buchenwald resistance unit achieved many notable victories. One of the minor ones was the survival of a small four-year old Jewish boy, who had been smuggled into camp in a large handbag by a Jewish deportee. The SS knew that the child was somewhere in the camp, but the prisoners succeeded in keeping it hidden until the end of the war. Today the boy, whose life was so miraculously saved, studies at a Belgian university. The East German author Bruno Apitz wrote one of his country's best-loved novels, *Naked among the Wolves,* dealing with this event. It is a moving story and conveys much of the horror that was Buchenwald.

Ernst Thaelmann's execution also became part of the Buchenwald legend. During the spring of 1944 Thaelmann was brought to the camp, shot and cremated. This was one of the few murders the Nazis tried to hide. All prisoners were herded out of the crematorium and the Nazis did the cremating themselves. But two prisoners watched the execution and advised their friends. The next event appears completely unbelievable, but five survivors bear witness to it. The leaders of the camp resistance group met in a cellar near the crematorium the following night and conducted a regular memorial service for Thaelmann. Members of the camp orchestra played one of Tschaikovsky's funeral marches; two others made speeches. Fifteen minutes later they returned to their bunks without being discovered.

The surviving witnesses reproduced the entire memorial service after the war and put it on tape. Our guide led us into the cellar where the original service had been held. It was left exactly as it had been during the Nazi period. It was so effective that the visitor left feeling as if he had witnessed one of history's most secret martyrdoms. The spot of Thaelmann's execution is covered with wreaths and flowers, and serves East Germany's youth as a place of pilgrimage.

The last building we entered was a museum — one of the world's most unbelievable museums. It showed instruments of torture, human hair shorn from people before their execution and manufactured into hairy rugs. One such rug — used by Ilse Koch, the camp commander's wife — is the core of this eery display. Ilse Koch's notorious lampshades, made of human skin taken from tattooed prisoners executed at Ilse Koch's command, can also be seen. Another exhibit is a collection of human skulls reduced to the size of a fist — an "art" originally practised by a few savage tribes in remote regions, and borrowed by the Nazis for their personal gratification.

Finally we came to a display of statistics. "These show the annual profits of the giant I.G. Farben combine", our guide explained. "I.G. Farben had built a plant near the camp and exploited the

prisoners' labour. In fact, originally Buchenwald had been built
at the specific request of I.G. Farben. This combine was the
greatest of all Nazi criminals. Compared to the Farben crimes, the
acts of *Scharführer* Sommer appear puny indeed!"

The figures shown are impressive. If they are true, I.G. Farben
would appear as the war's greatest profiteer. The Allies dissolved
the giant combine after the war, but today several successor firms
in West Germany exceed the size of their dissolved parent company.
This fact has created anger and resentment in East Germany
where hatred of huge combines (Krupp, Flick, Thyssen, I.G. Farben, etc.), is a pronounced national thought pattern. The I.G.
Farben profits were listed as follows: *

1932 — 48 million marks
1937 — 231   "   "
1939 — 363   "   "
1943 — 822   "   "

Two leading Farben directors, Dr. Otto Ambros and Dr. Fritz
Ter Meer, were convicted of war crimes in one of Nuremberg's
lesser trials. Ter Meer is still an active planner of one of the
Farben's successor firms.

"What I consider unforgivable in the present situation is
the fact that West Germany forgets too easily and forgives too
many of them", our guide stated angrily. "Let me give you a few
examples. . . ."

My Buchenwald visit had taken only three hours. But I felt
that I had been in the camp for several days. When I walked
past the iron gate with its ironical inscription I felt that I had
escaped a living nightmare. "Let's get going", said Kadenbach.
"We are late. Our travel companion Wolf awaits us at the station."
I asked him to give me a few extra minutes. "Have you forgotten
something? Is there anything you want to do while we wait?"
"Yes", I replied, "I want to do something I could not do inside.
I just want to breathe — deeply!" I sat down on a tree stump and
relaxed. I felt I had never needed a rest so much as just then.
After five minutes had passed, I said, "Let's go and pick up Mr.
Wolf — on to Dresden!"

As the car descended "blood alley" toward Weimar, we passed
the Buchenwald monument and the Bell Tower. On the tower the
famous Buchenwald oath was inscribed, the article of faith which

---

* One mark is equivalent to approximately one quarter of a dollar.

every German school child must learn by heart and recite as his life's pledge:

We swear never to forget the victims of Nazi terror!

We swear that no death camps shall ever exist again and that no mass killings will ever happen again!

We swear that the executioners, their masters and their financiers will never be rearmed!

We swear to be true to the ideals of unity against fascism, friendship among the nations of the world, peace, independence and freedom!

CHAPTER VI

THE TRUTH ABOUT DRESDEN

On March 12, 1945, Dresden, the capital of Saxony, was one of Europe's truly beautiful cities. It was the second-largest city of the *Land* with a peacetime population of 650,000. Saxony's kings had wanted to erect a dream city, a Germanic Versailles, and they had succeeded. *Elbflorenz* (Florence on the Elbe) as it was popularly called, became Germany's art centre. The Dresden art gallery in the Zwinger (literally, enclosure) contained well known paintings: Rafael's Sistine Madonna, Rembrandt's most famous self-portrait and other art treasures. The fury of World War II had almost bypassed the city. For more than five years Dresden had not been hit by a single bomb. During January and February 1945 a stream of refugees had inundated Dresden; its population grew to more than 1,100,100. Living space was at a premium. But Hamburg and Cologne newspapers still called Dresden the *Insel der Seligen* — island of the blessed.

This peace was shattered by the war's heaviest air-raid on February 13, 1945. It was mardi gras, the last day of the *Fasching*, the German carnival, still celebrated in the stricken Third Reich. In the night between mardi gras and Ash Wednesday, a fiery witches' Sabbath gripped the unprepared city. The raid began at 10.05 P.M., when RAF contingents dropped more than 400,000 incendiary and high explosive bombs. A second wave attacked at 1.30 A.M. Ash Wednesday. A third wave at noon on February 14 gave the dying city the coup de grâce. When the raids had ended, the Altstadt, venerable heart of Dresden, had ceased to exist. Untold thousands of civilians lay dead in the smouldering ruins. Parts of human bodies defied identification. Many lay buried under the rubble. Hundreds had drowned in the Elbe River — they had jumped in to escape the fire storm which consumed the city.

The fierceness of the attack caused a traumatic shock in most survivors. There had been many cities which suffered major air raids during the war. The havoc wrought on Hamburg, Cologne and Berlin was as complete as the destruction of Dresden. But many raids, stretched over several years, had caused the desolation of the other cities. Dresden's agony was concentrated into fourteen short hours.

The people of Dresden have never forgotten the night of February 13, 1945. Citizens of other German cities describe the war years like a distant memory of a long forgotten misfortune. But in Dresden the raid's memory lingers on. Emotionally, the town has never recovered. I have visited Hiroshima and Nagasaki, whose people seem to be less impressed by their misfortune than the people of Dresden. Because the city is still stricken, the average Dresdener views foreigners with suspicion and ill-concealed resentment. These feelings are shown particularly to Britishers and Americans. The British RAF mounted the attack, but the average Dresdener's anger vents itself with equal fury against the United States.

Many stories have been written about the raid. Much of the material published is contradictory. The first major work on this tragedy was written by German author Juergen Thorwald (*Flight in Winter*, Pantheon, New York 1951). Thorwald listed the number of casualties at 40,000. The work on the Dresden raid most widely read in the West is that of British author David Irving who gives a casualty figure of 150,000. Other estimates vary from 50,000 (A. Haenecke) to 85,000 (Otto Ernst).

To foreign correspondents Dresden is almost a forbidden city. Few journalists have received an entry permit; even fewer were allowed to conduct large-scale investigations. I decided to get all the information possible on the raid and its after-effects, the history of Dresden's reconstruction and — most important — an explanation for the strange discrepancy of loss figures reported by the different authors.

I entered Dresden on a misty Sunday evening on the Autobahn Weimar-Dresden. My head was still heavy from my afternoon visit to Buchenwald. The ride brought me back to life. An improbable number of cars and motor cycles created a regular Western-style traffic jam. Most cars were driven by East Germans returning from week-end excursions. The Autobahn starts west of Weimar, by-passes Leipzig, Saxony's largest city, and ends five miles east of

Dresden. During the last few miles we had bumper-to-bumper traffic. There were no traffic cops, few lights and a great number of "Sunday drivers" who acted very much like those familiar to us in the West. Most people were well dressed and — like Sunday drivers in almost any country — polite in private life and tough behind the wheel. But I noticed more observance of traffic rules than among any corresponding Canadian or American group.

We entered Dresden without really noticing it. For Dresden's centre has been rebuilt in a haphazard way. The former "Old Town", which consisted mostly of wooden buildings before the raid, now contains a number of tall, very modern apartment and office structures. Between these buildings — nothing! The rubble of destruction was removed, only a few ruins remain. But the wild grass and unkempt vegetation of the bombed-out spaces remain and create a weird picture in the heart of a modern city — multiple dwellings, ultra-modern in style, surrounded by nothingness.

Dresden's best hotel stands opposite the old railway station — one of the raid's main targets. But somehow the RAF missed the station. It remained virtually intact. The hotel was rebuilt after the war, a beautiful structure — modern yet comfortable. Sunday night a well-dressed crowd of citizens jammed its large restaurant. Dresden's teenagers who at first glance are no different from the Canadian variety danced in two dance halls lit by crystal chandeliers. The music could have been played in any North American discotheque. The atmosphere was hectic. While registering I noticed the cold hostility of the room clerk. I had shown my Canadian passport which his untried eye had not immediately identified. "You are British?" he asked, a slight hiss in his voice. "No, Canadian", I replied in English. "But Canada is British!" he countered. "Not exactly", I answered. "Incidentally, I speak German!" I had decided to end the English part of our conversation — which brought an almost audible sigh of relief from the clerk.

This type of reaction is uncommon in East Germany. Westerners who receive visas to enter the GDR are usually well received and well treated. Xenophobic behaviour is typical of Dresden, not of the country as a whole. It is one of the after-effects of history's largest non-nuclear air raid. The English language is popular in East Germany — the cold war has not changed that. But in Dresden it is definitely unpopular. Monday morning I strolled through the streets of Dresden before my first appointment. I noticed something which I had not observed the day before — Sunday when no work went on. Reconstruction crews were active almost everywhere. But when I tried to snap pictures, two irate workmen rushed toward me with a forbiding *"Photographieren verboten!"* For the rest of my Dresden stay, I learned to "snap from the hip" without attracting attention. Again I learned that this reaction is typical only of Dresden. The Government does not forbid the taking of pictures. The official government guide who accompanied me was embarrassed by the reaction of the two workers. It took him a full hour to explain that this type of "Citizen's discourtesy" is actually discouraged by the Government.

At 10 A.M. on an extended car ride through the entire city, I discovered one of the raid's anomalies. Only the heart of the old town and the so-called Johannisstadt had been razed. The rest of Dresden was barely touched. The beautiful villas across the river Elbe remained intact. In the very centre of destruction the old river bridge across the Elbe was unharmed. Its original colour had been a light blue. Today Dresdeners call their bridge, which was miraculously spared, *Blaues Wunder* (blue wonder).

The guide pointed out a yellow villa. "From this house an American spy guided the approaching bombers with light signals." Several former anti-aircraft gunners repeated the story. It had never become public knowledge because the alleged spy had himself become one of the air raid's victims. Another large villa, also unharmed, had belonged to the Nazi Gauleiter (governor), Martin Mutschmann. Mutschmann is supposed to have had advance warning of the raid. He and his entire family left Dresden one day before it was attacked. So did most of the other Nazi bigwigs. Mutschmann died shortly after the war's end. His wife escaped to West Germany and is still alive. — The suburban area across the river was hardly damaged. We passed the residence of Manfred von Ardenne, East Germany's best known scientist. Ardenne granted me a brief interview. He is not a Marxist. But like most of his countrymen he feels that after twelve years of Nazi rule and history's most costly war the present East German Government does pretty well. He explained: "My lab belongs to me personally. It is not nationalized. I am allowed to retain the profits of my work." This discriminating East German approach to the problems of nationalization exists throughout the country. Some establishments are in private hands, others belong to the State. In the case of Ardenne the reason was obvious — to keep the famous scientist happy and contented. Ardenne had received many offers to emigrate to the West and had refused them all. "I have visited West Germany several times. If I had wanted to, I could simply have stayed there. But I didn't. Why? Let's put it this way, I like it better here. It's my home. No, I am not a socialist. But I admit it seems to work for our country. But let's not bother with politics. I am a scientist, not a politician."

Ardenne became the first lead in my search for the truth about the great air raid. He gave me the address of two friends: Herr and Frau von Ameln, members of the former German aristocracy. Today both of them are members of the National Liberal Party, the aforesaid East German group which accepts former Nazi Party members. Frau von Ameln lived through the raid and survived. And she is a personal acquaintance of the most important link to the truth about Dresden, a man who during the past decade has been rarely interviewed by Western correspondents, former Lord Mayor Weidauer, now living in seclusion in a small villa near Dresden.

When I returned to my hotel Herr and Frau von Ameln were waiting for me. They both looked like fugitives from a Hollywood war film. Von Ameln had several sabre cuts across his face — memories of his college days. Around his left eye there was a red mark, sign that he used to wear a monocle, once the trademark of the "arrogant Prussian officer". Frau von Ameln was a fine, aristocratic-looking woman. Obviously not communists, they had somehow adjusted to the present political system. They criticized quite openly. Herr von Ameln in particular talked in a loud voice that carried. People at neighbouring tables were able to hear him; clearly this did not seem to disturb my guests. My observation in other East German towns repeated itself. There is more freedom of expression in the GDR than Western newspaper readers are led to believe.

"We have become accustomed to conditions here — no, we would not emigrate to the West. We were born here, we are Dresdeners and we want to live out our lives in our home town." Herr von Ameln had been a prisoner of war in North Africa at the time of the Dresden air raid. He first learned of the attack on his home town by accidentally reading a report on the desk of a British air force general whose orderly he had become. He gave me a few details of the report which I could not find stated anywhere else: "Eight of the pilots were negroes; one of the pilots was a woman; one pilot died of a heart attack while the raid was on, and his command was taken over by his co-pilot; one of the bombardiers fell through the open bomb raft into the burning city."

Frau von Ameln had lived through the raid. "It had been a rather quiet night; my children had attended a mardi gras party and were returning home, when the alarm sounded at 9.30 P.M. There had been many alarms before — none of them was ever followed by a real raid. So we did not take the alarm too seriously. But when the "Christmas trees" — illuminating light flares dropped by parachutes — began lighting up the night, we knew we were in for it this time. Hell started to descend seconds later. I rushed upstairs because some of the children were still there. I had no chance to go to the shelter. By some miracle the house remained intact during the first attack. One of the walls collapsed and crushed my brother to death.

"A minor miracle during the first raid was that the electricity did not fail. Our radio kept on blaring — a speech by Goebbels announcing new super weapons which would turn the fortunes of war. An infernal paradox; our world was collapsing around us but Goebbels' voice remained with us. A nightmare dreamed up by some medieval hell-fire preacher.

"The all-clear soueded around 12.20 A.M. By that time electricity and other services had failed. We had no water or gas. Nazi Party whips forced us into the streets to help fight the fires. It was hopeless from the start. But we worked furiously until the second alarm sounded around 1.00 A.M. This time we reached a public shelter. And inside this cellar we remained for three days — never-ending days! Fortunately there must have remained a small opening to the outside — for we had enough air to breathe or we could not have survived. When we were dug out during the morning hours of February 17, we were starved and crazed by thirst. More than fifty occupants had died — killed by the heat. I was alive. The picture that greeted us outside defies description. But the destruction around us was not the worst part of our fate. During the next three months the Nazis conducted a reign of terror to stop any potential revolt in its tracks. More than five hundred people were hanged from lanterns, fences and walls for "defeatism". Only on May 8, the day of capitulation, did Soviet forces occupy the city. During the early morning hours of May 8, the Nazis still executed a number of people."

Mrs. von Ameln admitted her Nazi Party membership. "Yes, we were Party members. During the war we changed our views. After Stalingrad almost all my friends realized that we had followed a madman. We did not know about the extermination of the Jews. Many Soviet prisoners worked in Dresden and I met quite a few of them. Our family treated them well. Elsewhere? I am afraid they sometimes were handled roughly. I once saw a Nazi block leader whip an old Russian woman till she collapsed."

I learned of many tragic events during the Dresden holocaust. A well known local doctor named Fletscher had wanted to avoid needless bloodshed during the closing hours of the war. He raised a white flag and marched toward the Soviet lines. A group of SS-men fleeing in the opposite direction met and shot him. He was the last victim of the Nazi dictatorship. Today one of Dresden's best known thoroughfares is named after him.

I was told how Dresden's landmark, the "blue wonder" bridge, was saved from destruction. May 7, 1945 the Nazis attached dynamite to the structure to blow it up. An anti-Nazi soldier cut the electric wire secretly and saved the bridge. — During my conversation with Mrs. von Ameln one name came up again and again, "Weidauer". This remarkable man had been Dresden's Lord Mayor from 1945 to 1958. He started to manage the affairs of the stricken city when the Nazis left. He presided over the first few years of difficult reconstruction. He had assembled a complete card-index file, which contains exact figures on Dresden's air raid losses. "It is understandable that our misfortune was exaggerated", Frau von Ameln explained. "Sensational stories always sell well. Journalists know that. Our losses were tremendous — but exaggeration never helps the victims. It only aggravates their fate. Actually 36,000 people died that night — but one of the best known works dealing with the raid, David Irving's book, alleges a death toll four times as high!"

After my conversation with the Ameln couple I talked to many highly placed city officials. I asked for permission to inspect the "Weidauer files". I hoped that I could find in them the answer to the Dresden riddle. How much damage did the raid actually cause? How many people really lost their lives? Why was Dresden singled out for such a devastating raid at a time when the issue of victory was no longer in doubt?

All my queries about inspection of the files met with icy

silence. "These files are confidential; they are closed to the public." Attempts to locate Weidauer met with similar failure. The man who held the answer to one of the last war's most puzzling riddles lived somewhere in or near Dresden. His name appeared in no telephone book or directory. The travel agency in Dresden which looks after foreign visitors did not know how to contact him. I decided not to leave Dresden until I had interviewed Weidauer.

During the afternoon I visited the devastated area near the river Elbe. The Bruehl Terrace, an elevated road along the river, has been rebuilt. The Royal Castle still lies in ruins. The Church of St. Sophie remains untouched since the raid. Most of the buildings surrounding the castle are burnt-out hulls. But the most important of Dresden buildings, the Zwinger, has been completely restored. I had seen it before the war and can attest to the fact that its reconstruction is perfect — a piece of architectural wizardry. The Zwinger is a huge baroque building complex surrounding one of Europe's lovely fountain-dotted gardens. These unique fountains give the entire area an aspect of enchantment. The collection of paintings had been shipped to the Soviet Union immediately after the war. A few of the more famous paintings had been damaged by moisture and mildew. The Soviets had restored them and returned them to East Germany some years later. Now they hang once again in the original Zwinger Gallery — four rooms which contain some of mankind's most priceless art. Europe has five such places, the Zwinger is one of them. The others are the Louvre in Paris, the Prado in Madrid, the Vatican Museum in Rome, and the Rijksmuseum in Amsterdam. Thousands of art students and tourists thronged the four Zwinger rooms. I found it difficult to enter. When I had finally fought my way to the Sistine Madonna, it became one of the highlights of my trip. — The Zwinger's reconstruction was the life work of several art professors who insisted on an exact reproduction of the original building. The Government had planned to change its appearance — to make it less expensive to rebuild and to underline the functional. Fortunately the professors were able to overrule the Government planners. A high price was paid for this traditionalist gesture. It cost more than 40 million marks (10 million dollars) to rebuild the Zwinger — a lot of money for East Germany. The restoration of the Dresden Opera and the Royal Palace are now in the planning stages. They will be completed in 1975 —

thirty years after the raid that destroyed them. The projected cost is about 75 million marks.

The space opposite the Zwinger between the river and the Bruehl Terrace is occupied by one of Dresden's best restaurants. For six marks ($1.50) menus luxurious even by American standards are served to all comers. Understandably, long lines of prospective patrons form far outside the restaurant. I failed to get in, and finally had to use influence to get a table. The restaurant has four dining rooms and an open-air terrace. On the terrace a band played for Dresden's younger generation. How do young Communists behave on a dance floor? The night before I had had a glimpse. Now I decided to watch closely.

The band played lively music. Jazz is definitely popular on the other side of the curtain. I noticed couples dancing a reasonable facsimile of North American discotheque dances. Others danced more sedately. One behaviour pattern reminded me that I was still in Germany. After each dance the boy would politely and formally bow to his girl and accompany her back to her seat. Then another formal bow, before returning to his own table.

The waiter brought me a folded sheet of paper. Its contents electrified me. "I have found Weidauer; he expects you in half an hour" — signed Kadenbach. My chauffeur had succeeded where all the local bigwigs had failed and he had done it simply by calling his Berlin office. The travel bureau had called the Foreign Ministry; they in turn had contacted Weidauer and arranged for the appointment. The method was roundabout, but it had sidestepped the Dresden barricades surrounding its most important citizen. Even more important Berlin had cleared me to inspect the Weidauer files.

Former Lord Mayor Weidauer lives in a small luxurious villa in a fashionable hilly suburb — the existence of fashionable suburbs in a Communist country was a surprise to me. We crossed the "blue wonder" bridge and travelled through a district which reminded me of Westmount. Twenty minutes later I met the man who more than any other could rightfully be called "Mr. Dresden". Weidauer headed the city government during the most difficult post-war period. He chaired the planning commission which drew up the blueprints for the Zwinger's reconstruction. He negotiated the return of the art treasures with the Soviet Union. His most important achievement was the assembly of a detailed card-index file of the air-raid damage. He became Dresden's official historian — the chronicler of its destruction.

Weidauer is well into his sixties. He is stout and bears a slight resemblance to British Columbia's Premier Bennett. He is witty, polite, attentive and converses well. He is the author of several articles dealing with the Dresden debacle but none was ever published in the West. At present, he is working on a full-length book. — Weidauer opened the interview with an amazing statement about his conviction that Dresden had not been bombed before February 13, 1945, because the United States General Staff had earmarked it as the first American nuclear target. "Our city would have been very suitable for this grisly experiment", he remarked. "Dresden lies in a valley surrounded by mountains on all sides, and it consisted mainly of wooden structures. A nuclear device dropped on Dresden would have been effective. We were spared conventional bombing raids because we were the Pentagon's atomic guinea pig; Washington wanted to observe the maximum effect of its new secret weapon.

"When the Soviet offensive of January 1945 broke the back of Nazi resistance, the European war drew to a close much sooner than the strategists had foreseen. They had counted on Germany staying in the war until late 1945. Their first bomb was not yet operative. So they gave the green light to the RAF to hit us with all their conventional might. I asked Weidauer to prove his theory. "First of all, let me refer you to the work of US General Leslie Groves", he replied. "According to Groves, President Roosevelt proposed as early as January 1945 that a nuclear device should be dropped on Germany, and that Dresden was the logical target.* Why? Because the American General Staff knew that Hitler's scientists were working feverishly on a new secret weapon. Late in 1943 Germany had banned the export of uranium. Most of Germany's uranium is mined in the Erzgebirge (iron ore mountains), and Dresden is the main shipping centre for that region. The United States military planners concluded

---

* I could not find any reference to Dresden in General Groves' book. What he actually wrote on this point is the following: "It was at this same conference (before his departure for Yalta) that Mr. Roosevelt informed me that if the European war was not over before we had our first bombs he wanted us to be ready to drop them on Germany." See *Now It Can Be Told: The Story of the Manhattan Project*, Harper & Bros., N.Y., 1962, p. 184.

that Hitler was working on a nuclear bomb and that he had it almost completed. The American decision to use their first atom bomb on Dresden appears logical.

"How many casualties would a nuclear attack have cost us? I think at least 300,000. (When the RAF finally hit us with conventional weapons, we lost 35,000 people — you will find the exact number when you check our files tomorrow. Most Dresdeners know this.) This explains our bitterness against the Americans. They are actually less popular than their British allies, even though the British and not the Americans mounted the destructive Dresden air raid."

"Would you say", I interrupted, " that under the circumstances the conventional RAF raid was a blessing in disguise? The nuclear attack would have been far more destructive." "Not really", answered my host. "It still was the war's biggest non-nuclear raid. No one who did not live through it can possibly know the horror it brought down on Dresden." Weidauer went to his desk and returned with a stack of documents. "I will give you a brief resumé of some of the facts. We suffered between 35,600 and 35,700 casualties. 85,000 were injured. We had 205,000 dwelling units before the raid; 96,312 were completely destroyed. The number of bombs dropped? Approximately 8,000 blockbusters, 5,000 liquid fire bombs, 500,000 small incendiaries. Forty-four hospitals were destroyed; forty-two schools; twenty-one churches and sixty-eight cultural centres were obliterated. Twelve million cubic yards of rubble had to be cleared away. It took us twelve years to do it.

"Why is so much wrong information given about the raid? I will tell you. Take the book by British author David Irving. He claims 135,000 casualties.* As I pointed out, we had only 35,600. Why this exaggeration? Mr. Irving came to Dresden and interviewed me. I gave him the facts. He did not inspect our files. Instead he wrote that all records had been "fed to the pigs" by Soviet military authorities.** Complete nonsense! Irving relied heavily on information supplied by former Dresden residents

---

* See David Irving, *The Destruction of Dresden*, p. 210.

** Irving's actual statement on this head was as follows: "The army had taken over the former offices of the *"Abteilung Tote"* ... and had turned loose a score of pigs in the school housing the clothing cards which were the last hope of identifying some 11,000 more victims. A few days later the cards were burnt, because of their offensive smell."

who fled to West Germany. One of them was a former city employee named Hanns Voigt. Voigt was originally a high-school teacher put in charge of a municipal department by Hitler in 1944. Five years later I fired him for pro-Nazi statements. Voigt fled to West Germany and became one of Irving's key witnesses — and the information supplied by him was all wrong. Only the pro-Nazis are jubilant. Because they can point to the book and compare the Dresden raid with their own crime of genocide. But this comparison which would excuse and minimize the Nazi crimes, does not hold water. That is why such false information is so dangerous. My Government would like you to inspect the files and figures of the raid tomorrow. Take all the time you wish. Then tell the world the truth about Dresden."

After this hard-hitting interview, I spent three days in research. I examined the tabulated detail of one of mankind's grisliest body of statistics. The first document I checked was a police report addressed by the Gauleiter's office to Hitler, dated March 2, 1945. Estimated dead: 35,000. (This figure proved to be amazingly correct in the light of later more exacting tabulations.) Under the date of March 18, 1945, the Reich Chancellery demanded a minute search for all corpses not yet identified and buried, and exact details about every single feature of the raid — for use by Goebbels' Propaganda Ministry. This resulted in the "search of the rubble" as the police called it at the time. A large number of air-raid wardens and assistants combed through every ruined building street after street and listed their findings. Parts of bodies which were otherwise not identifiable were listed separately — and added to the number of the dead buried or cremated shortly after the raid. The results were not complete at the time the Third Reich collapsed. Weidauer had ordered a continuation of the search. Toward the end of October 1945 temporary results were in: known dead, 35,642. The great search was not limited to human beings. It covered all life lost. I learned the number of dogs destroyed by the raid, 8,340. Police horses killed, forty-five. Other horses killed, sixty-seven. Cattle lost, 452. (A considerable number of cattle was kept in the city of Dresden at the time.)

As in the practice of double-entry bookkeeping, Weidauer used a second means to arrive at the approximate number of dead. The number of ration cards issued on February 1, 1945 was 1,185,-543. This means that that many people lived in Dresden at the time. After the surrender new cards were printed on May 23, 1945. The number issued was 1,148,200. The difference between the two sets of figures is 40,343. According to the *Einwohnermeldeamt* (citizens registration office) some 4,000 people had left Dresden between March 1 and May 8, 1945. This leaves 36,343 cards unaccounted for — the approximate number of people killed in the raid. I had found the true figure of losses. It had not been difficult to get the information. Why had these figures precipitated one of the great controversies of our time? Why the exaggerations? Were they simply caused by the wish of a few authors to write sensational stories? Were they the result of honest differences of opinion? Or were they part of a carefully laid neo-Nazi plot to justify Nazi war crimes by creating the image of equally serious Allied crimes? The Dresden officials were certain that the last-mentioned purpose was the reason for the exaggeration of losses. It's an interesting point of view!

I left the Dresden archives late that night. It was a beautiful clear evening. As I walked toward my hotel along the Bruehl Terrace, the full moon was reflected in the calm waters of the Elbe River. In the distance a young couple walked arm-in-arm singing an old German folksong. Then they suddenly started to sing in high-school English — a folksong made famous by American radio and television.

A song sung in English in the middle of the Dresden night — this surprised me. Perhaps some hidden points of contact are left between the two sides of the tattered curtain — a trace of the force which young Germans call *Völkerfreundschaft* — friendship among the world's nations. It spans the gulf between two countries which have no diplomatic ties, do not recognize each other's existence and are separated by a cleavage of social and political convictions. But can the world's youth really be divided? The cold war of our times is not the first wall created between the nations who share our planet. There have been many similar divisions before: the crusades and later the Turkish wars — between Christianity and Islam; the Thirty Years' War — between Protestants and Catholics. None of these wars ever decided a religious or philosophical issue. When the storms of devastation had swept across the world, millions lay dead, whole countries were decimated — but the boundaries between Christianity and Islam, between Catholics and Protestants had not changed appreciably. If there should ever be a third world war, ninety per cent of mankind would perish. But on the ruins of the world as we knew it, the remaining ten per cent would probably still believe in free enterprise or socialism, as they had done before Armaggedon.

CHAPTER VII

EAST GERMANY'S
MOST REMARKABLE WOMAN

Dresden is the GDR's art centre. The East German Academy of Arts is situated in a building near the Bruehl Terrace. The Academy's best known teacher and artist is a middle-aged woman named Lea Grundig. Considered the greatest living graphic artist, her name has become a household word not only in East Germany but in most other Socialist countries as well. Her own countrymen treat her with a veneration usually reserved for leading statesmen. I had seen some of her works in an East Berlin art gallery. They had fascinated me. I had requested a short interview with her. To my surprise my request had been firmly turned down. While I had little difficulty meeting Walter Ulbricht and other Government leaders, Lea Grundig's was the first interview flatly refused me. "Mrs. Grundig is a great artist. Her time is so valuable that we cannot let her waste it on newspaper interviews", was the answer given me. My first reaction was that the Government simply did not care to make Mrs. Grundig's views public. Later I found that this assumption had been wrong. Strange as it seems, the excuse given me had been the truth — at least as far as the collective mind of the East German Government was concerned. I had given up hope of meeting this interesting woman, when I casually told former Lord Mayor Weidauer of my disappointment. "I might be of some help", he said. "At least, let me try."

Weidauer went to his telephone and dialed a number. "Mrs. Grundig? Weidauer speaking. I have a Canadian journalist here. He speaks excellent German. I think you would like to meet him. He certainly wants to meet you. Fine — I will give him your message. Tomorrow at ten? Excellent!"

I had not counted on this stroke of luck. The next morning at ten I stood outside East Germany's most remarkable artist's studio. Situated on the ground floor of the Academy building at the end of a long corridor, its rooms are crowded with many paintings, sculptures and desks. I have rarely seen a more inspiring state of utter disorder. But after I had been in the room for several minutes the disorder seemed unimportant. For the woman who had invited me to enter filled the room with her presence.

Lea Grundig is a short, black-haired woman in her late fifties. Jewish by birth, she grew up in Dresden and married Hans Grundig one of Germany's best known painters. Both Hans and Lea were members of the pre-war Communist Party. Hans Grundig, a gentile, was put in a concentration camp where he managed to survive the war. Lea fled to Palestine entering it as an illegal immigrant. Later she legalized her status and became an Israeli citizen at that State's inception in 1948. She is one of the very few Jews (the only one I ever met) who voluntarily left Israel to return to a Communist nation.

She was reunited with her husband in Dresden and continued to live there. Hans Grundig died six years ago. Both Hans and Lea created many masterpieces during their later years. They were also writers. Lea's book, *Faces and History,* is brilliantly written and made the best-seller list not only in her own country but in several other European nations as well. Her husband's autobiography *Between Mardi Gras and Ash Wednesday* is an interesting document of the years preceding Hitler's rise to power and of his experiences under Nazi rule.

After we had settled down to coffee and the inevitable cookies (which are offered in like appearance, quality and size to every visiting journalist in both East and West Germany), Mrs. Grundig made the following statement: "I was only nineteen years old when I was fortunate enough to be admitted to the Communist Party". The statement surprised me, for it was made with complete sincerity and conviction. It was the first time that someone had used these words to describe Communist Party membership. The attitude of most Party members I had interviewed ran the gamut from tolerance to wholehearted acceptance. But at no time had anyone ever told me that his Party affiliation had caused him great happiness. Was Lea Grundig an opportunist anxious to heighten her influence and status by pointing out her early conversion to the philosophy which now ruled the country? Was she serious? I decided to find out.

During the following hour I learned much about the history
of German communism during the two wars. Lea Grundig had
meant every word she said. She considered her conversion to communism the most important event of her life. Her reaction differed
from other people in high places. She ignored most of communism's
political implications and concentrated on the human and philosophical aspects. "My most important job is not artistic creation
alone, but to teach people who do not understand art to learn
to appreciate it. We must bring art to the people — into their
homes and places of work. Any kind-hearted person can understand art. It is not true that people need to be intellectuals or
highly educated to accept great art. To make them understand art
is my life's work."

Mrs. Grundig then explained a movement which she called
the *"Bitterfelder Weg"* (the road to Bitterfeld). Bitterfeld is the
name of an industrial town not far from Dresden where she had
conducted a series of experiments. Artists were brought into industrial plants. They worked there as common labourers side by
side with the regular workers and after hours painted what they
had seen. When this experiment had been labelled "successful"
by the Government, several writers tried the same routine and
wrote about their experiences. Alternately they read their works
to the workers and emended their writing according to suggestions
made by them. "It was a great experiment — bringing artists and
workers together", Lea Grundig explained. "Artists should not
be a privileged group. Once they lose contact with the rest of
society, their art will degenerate and their achievements will
suffer."

I indicated that I had some misgivings about the Bitterfeld
experiment. "Would such contacts not make the artist dependant
on the will of the public?" was my main objection. "Should a
writer not have the right to work without being subjected to
pressure about what he should write?"

"No pressure whatever is used on our writers or artists. They
may write as they wish and they may draw what they like. We
simply want to maintain a live contact between the artist and his
public. This is what the *Bitterfelder Weg* tried to do. I know
that Western writers have often done the same thing. Is it not
true that Jack London deliberately lived in the surroundings
which he later described in his writings? Or Faulkner and Steinbeck?"

We discussed censorship. "We have none", she assured me. "Anyone may write what he likes."

"What would happen if one criticized socialism?" I asked.

"Nothing would happen. In fact, we have had such cases. Let me put it this way, what would happen to an American writer who wrote against the free enterprise system? He probably would not sell many books. This is the worst that could happen to one of our writers who wrote something contrary to the feelings of a large number of GDR citizens."

Our conversation turned to her years in Palestine, and her story was fascinating. She had spent the most significant years of her life there — at the time of the country's turmoil. At first she had worked wholeheartedly with the Jewish groups, as long as a state of latent revolution had existed against the imperial power of Britain. But after Israel had declared her independence and the Arab war had started, she could no longer see eye to eye with the Jewish majority. She not only criticized and attacked the nationalist groups of Israel, particularly the *Irgun Zwei Leumi*, which she compared to the Nazis, but she established contact with the small communist groups there.

Some of her best-loved works were produced during her stay in the Near East, and she was helped by some of Israel's leading figures. I was interested to hear the story of her friendship with the present Israeli President Salman Shazar (at the time he was still known by his original name Zalman Rubashov). "Rubashov was editor of the newspaper *Dawar* and one of the most interesting and gifted members of the *Mapai*", she explained. Rubashov belonged to the elite of the immigration — he rejected communism. Oddly enough his sister was a convinced communist living in the Soviet Union. But his nationalism blinded him. He forgot his real friends. He ended by making compromises with the right. Today he is Israel's President. Ben Gurion and all the other founding members of the State belong to the same group.

"You asked why I left Israel to return to Dresden", she continued. "Mostly because I could not watch my fellow Jews who had just undergone history's worst wave of persecution at the hands of Fascism turn fascist themselves. I am still fond of Zalman Rubashov or as he now calls himself, Salman Shazar. He gave me much help when I needed it. But by right Israel should be on our side of the cold war, not on that of the West."

This statement started a friendly dispute between Lea Grundig and myself. "I see you are somewhat of a pro-Israel nationalist", she finally stated with a broad smile. "That's your privilege. I do not share your opinions. But let's discuss it anyway!"

This gave me the opportunity to test a prominent East German Jewess' reaction to the close relations between the Ulbricht regime and Nasser's Egypt.

"I do not object", was Lea Grundig's answer. "First of all, I am a citizen of the GDR. I am also a human being. My ethnic background is not important. Would it interest you to see the project on which I am working now?" she asked. "You will be the first foreigner to see it." She brought a folder from her desk and took out eleven huge graphic drawings. They showed concentration camp prisoners with emaciated faces and terror in their eyes in the hands of their torturers. There were masses of children about to be driven into gas chambers. The horror of the camps had found its ultimate expression — in a manner surpassing the art of Doré or Breughel. In the background of every single drawing lurked an evil, grinning, bespectacled face — a caricature of Dr. Hans Globke, author of the commentaries to the Nuremberg racial laws and until 1963 Secretary of State in Dr. Adenauer's Cabinet.

"I call these drawings the Globke series, because they depict the mass murders abetted by this vicious Nazi. Instead of getting his just deserts, he was given a high government post in the Adenauer Cabinet. Perhaps you will understand now why we are fighting and what we are fighting against."

I looked at the drawings very carefully. Some of them were half completed, others were finished. The figures of the victims drew my attention. There was a strong similarity between their faces and emaciated figures and those of early Christian martyrs drawn by the painters of the Middle Ages. While Mrs. Grundig's style is faintly reminiscent of that of George Grosz, her martyrs' faces are similar to those drawn by the German medieval artist Albrecht Dürer. I had suddenly discovered the intent and meaning of Lea Grundig's work. Communism to her is not a social and political movement, but a religion. She is neither a convinced nor a fanatical communist; she is more than that. She is a devout communist!

Lea Grundig can be classed with a group of people who were quite common in Germany during the early days of the communist movement of the nineteenth century. They were called *Edel-kommunisten* (communists by conviction — literally, noble communists). They did not engage in political power plays. Instead they tried to convert the common people to their cause. They behaved in almost every way as Christian missionaries might have behaved in hostile surroundings. Their aim was to help people and make the world a better place to live in. There are few such people left in the East European Communist parties of our time.

"I came back from Israel to help my people here in Dresden. I came back to bring joy and fulfilment to the citizens of this Republic", were her parting words as the interview ended.

CHAPTER VIII

AN ISLAND OF TRANQUILITY

Saxony is the GDR's key area. It contains much of her industry and commerce. Leipzig, the Republic's second largest city, is the country's publishing and marketing core. Its annual spring fair attracts thousands of visitors from both East and West.

Strictly speaking Saxony no longer exists. East Germany has done away with the Federal system which dominated the German national scene for many centuries and still characterizes the present West German State. The country was split up into fifteen districts. Saxony accounts for three — Leipzig, Dresden and Karl-Marxstadt (formerly Chemnitz). But the Government's political planners were unsuccessful in extinguishing the national characteristics of the Saxons, and Saxony still remains one of East Germany's political realities.

The Saxon dialect sounds amusing to most Germans. Saxons can be clearly identified by their accent, but the peoples' character belies their accent. The average Saxon is a hard-working and determined person trying to succeed at his trade as well as in his personal and political life.

East Germany has a "Saxon problem". Many of the State's leaders come from this part of the country. Walter Ulbricht, Chief of the State and of its most powerful political party, was born in Leipzig. Many other key Government positions are filled by Saxons. To many Berliners members of this easily identified group remain "foreigners". To some extent they are unpopular. These facts have created a regional jealousy in Saxony. Berliners are often denied a hearty welcome. A tourist has little chance of noticing these facts. They remain however a strong undercurrent of everyday life. Because of the great importance of the three Saxon districts in any sound evaluation of the GDR, I decided to spend a few days in the vicinity of Dresden. In the process I discovered a district which in sheer beauty outdoes many of the better advertised tourist attractions of the Western world.

According to our original travel plans we were to proceed from Dresden to Halle. Instead I requested permission to travel through the mountainous area southeast of Dresden, commonly known as "Saxony's Switzerland". This beautiful region stretches from the Dresden outskirts to the Czech border. It combines a well-developed industrial district, built around the town of Pirna, with East Germany's uranium-producing area. If Dresden seems difficult to reach for Western tourists, the Pirna area is completely closed to visitors from NATO countries. "Highly classified industry — you will never get a permit to enter Pirna", I was told by my driver Kadenbach whose prophecies had always come true in the past. "Don't even bother to ask. As far as the uranium mines are concerned, forget that they exist!"

I agreed with Kadenbach's reasoning to some extent. If no foreigners had been admitted before, the chance that I would be allowed to travel there seemed slim. But I was more interested in the mountain beauty spots than in any industrial plants — and I feared that my wish to visit them would be vetoed by Berlin. "Would you take a chance with me — would you simply start out and drive me there without government clearance? If we don't ask them, they can't say no."

Such a request was unheard of. To the average German, government orders still are law. This thought pattern has not changed during two world wars and three political upheavals. At first Kadenbach was not receptive. Finally he made a suggestion: "If you cut out the industrial plants of Pirna and aren't inclined to explore the uranium mines, I will take a chance and simply drive you through "Saxony's Switzerland". Let's also keep away from the Czech border. They check border crossers very carefully these days."

We had an appointment for the next day with the head of the Jewish community in Dresden, Helmut Aris. I advanced the appointment to the end of the week. We left Dresden in our Soviet-made Volga car and headed for Pirna. "Wonderful engineers, the Russians", Kadenbach said. "They make the world's best cars. Not too much is known about their auto industry, but Soviet cars are ever so much better than American cars — a bit more expensive perhaps. But it's well worth the difference."

Unfortunately Kadenbach's opinion of Soviet automotive ingenuity was somewhat premature. On a steep hill halfway between Dresden and Pirna the Volga stopped and refused to move further. We signalled several drivers who passed us without stopping to give assistance. Finally a farmer hitched two draft horses to Russia's challenge to Detroit and pulled us into Pirna where the car was repaired. The fuel pump had broken down.

Pirna is a small industrial town without the slums usually associated with such urban areas. Most workers own their tiny homes. The streets are lined by long rows of beech trees and the small front lawns reminded me of small midwestern towns. Pirna is called the "gate to Saxony's Switzerland". The beautiful mountain area starts a few kilometres outside the town.

While they repaired the car we hired a local taxi and visited Pillnitz Castle, the summer residence of Saxony's former kings. Built by the most famous of all castle builders, August the Strong, Prince Elector of Saxony and King of Poland, the castle escaped without major war damage. August, an amazing man credited with fifty mistresses and some 200 illegitimate children, also built Dresden's Zwinger. But Pillnitz is his most famous work. August never tried to create pale imitations of Versailles (one of the weaknesses of Frederik the Great of Prussia). Instead he built fairyland castles after his own taste in simple, impressive, almost modern architecture. I believe August would have liked the huge buildings of modern New York or Montreal.

The extensive gardens of Pillnitz are filled with wondrous creations which do not seem to have any direct connection with castles or rococo gardens. In the middle of a lawn a huge wooden boat is propped up — obviously more than 200 years old but well preserved. August had ordered the boat built to his specifications. When the construction was completed, it proved unseaworthy. "I have not spent all this money for nothing", raged August. "Put it in the garden so that I can at least look at it from time to time." Other statues placed at odd intervals in the Royal gardens represent horses, dogs, cattle, cats and other animals. I did not see any monument to humans. Apparently August was something of a misanthrope. The Pillnitz gardens now serve as a public park. Crowds walk and play on the lawns once reserved for Saxon Royalty. Never-ending streams of tourists visit the castle itself.

Some forty kilometres southeast of Pirna lies a medieval castle called Koenigstein. Modern know-how blasted a well-paved highway into the rocks. How the medieval knights and their fair ladies ever reached the mountain top I could not say. The Koenigstein commands a breathtaking view of the Elbe River which at this point resembles the panoramic section of the river Rhine. The Koenigstein has an interesting history. It served as prison for a famous eighteenth century chemist named Boettger. A native Prussian, Boettger had tried to change lead into gold, and the king of Prussia — in order to bolster his sagging credit — had spread the word that Boettger had succeeded where all others had failed. August the Strong invited the young chemist to come to his kingdom, and when the invitation was refused, had him kidnapped and imprisoned in the Koenigstein. Boettger never succeeded in concocting artificial gold, but he became the first European to copy the Chinese art of making porcelain. (The production process of this porcelain — even today known as "China" — was a carefully guarded trade secret in the possession of the Chinese Imperial family.) Boettger was locked up in a primitive two-room apartment on the Koenigstein and given alchemist's tools. "Produce gold, and you will be freed. Until you do, you will remain in this prison", were August's parting words.

Boettger worked for several years and discovered the secret of porcelain production in the course of his unsuccessful efforts to create gold. August realized that this discovery might become more lucrative than the precious metal he had been asking for. He promptly freed Boettger and asked him to build a plant for the production of "Royal Saxon porcelain" in the little town of Meissen on the Elber River. The world-famous Meissen porcelain is still manufactured there by the original company chartered under August's rule. It provides one of East Germany's most valuable exports.

Behind the Koenigstein the scenery compares to that of the Alps at their best. The mountains are not quite as high but they are very steep. They are miniature Matterhorns, wild rock formations which defy the ability of all but the toughest mountain climbers. East German engineers have connected some of the peaks with hanging bridges. People not accustomed to high places are not advised to cross these bridges. I tried and proceeded some twenty feet. When I had almost reached the other side I committed the grave error of glancing downward — into a thousand feet of nothingness. I completed the rest of the way on my hands and knees.

In the middle of this wild enchanted forest of rocks and hanging bridges a huge restaurant and hotel has been built. The place was crowded. We were unable to get service for almost two hours. Who were the thousands of tourists meeting at this unusual restaurant? Mostly everyday East Germans: students and their girl friends; workers and farmers on their holidays. For the first time since Potsdam I saw comparatively large groups of Soviet soldiers. It seemed strange — but in their attitudes and behaviour Soviet soldiers on holiday in East Germany remind one of American service men. Most of them sport cameras and spend their time snapping pictures or pointing movie cameras. They try to "make time" with local girls and some of them seem to succeed. They make love and joke in public. Sometimes they chew gum! (Something I had thought only Americans or Canadians did, but the habit must have caught on.) A great many of them like popular music and jazz and they dance with their girl friends whenever an opportunity presents itself.

It was in this restaurant that I met one of the most interesting persons of this trip. When I finally got a table, I started to read the *Toronto Globe and Mail* which had been forwarded to me by air from Montreal. Suddenly I heard a young German voice address me in poor English: "You are Canadian?" I confirmed the fact. The voice's owner, a pretty young girl, countered: "You don't look Canadian at all!"

"How are Canadians supposed to look?" I answered, still in English. This question called for a reply for which her English vocabulary was clearly insufficient. "You can talk German to me" I continued in German, dropping the linguistic masquerade. "See, I knew it all the time", she said. "You are German — from West Germany. Right? In fact, you sound as if you came from Nuremberg — I can tell by your accent!" I was flabbergasted. The girl had guessed my birthplace correctly. "I don't see how I still speak with a clearly recognizable Nuremberg accent more than thirty years after I left", I remarked. "In any event, I really am a Canadian, though of the naturalized kind!"

During the next half hour I was subjected to a quick series of questions. "How is it out there? Is it true that they exploit everyone? Have you ever been in contact with the Ku-Klux-Klan? Is it true that there will be a revolution soon? How come they allowed you to come over here? Did you have trouble getting a Canadian exit visa? When you go back home, will they arrest you because you have been in East Germany?"

The girl was twenty, slightly older than East Germany. Her name was Ulla ("a Swedish name — my mother was Swedish"). She was a camp counsellor in a nearby children's camp. She had never been outside East Germany "except once or twice in nearby Czechoslovakia — for a few days". By reason of her age and life history, Ulla was a typical East German girl. I felt that by getting to know her, I might understand the GDR's youth better. I decided to spend a few hours with her and find out what she knew and how she felt about her country's relations with the outside world. The few hours became two days — and my quest for knowledge was well rewarded.

Ulla was a member of the FDJ — Free German Youth Movement, the Government-sponsored youth organization. She believed wholeheartedly in socialism and assured me that 90 per cent of her fellow members felt the same way. Her feeling for the Soviet Union was based on respect and friendship. ("Don't forget that without their help we could not have freed ourselves from fascism", she said and it was obvious that she meant it.) "The Americans? I like the American people. No, I have never met any real live Americans. But I read some American books. Mark Twain, Arthur Miller, John Steinbeck. They are a great people. It is tragic that we are not friends. But our two people could be friends, I believe!"

The average East German's reaction to the United States and her people is not one of hatred or resentment. Most East Germans draw the line between what they call the "imperialist American government" and "the American people". I found that a great number of East Germans and particularly young people talked about Franklin Delano Roosevelt even though most of them were far too young to remember him. President Kennedy also seemed to command the respect of most young East Germans. The name of Eisenhower usually caused unfavourable comment, and Lyndon Johnson seems to be very unpopular — but the American President most resented by Ulla and — as she assured me — by most of her friends was Harry Truman. ("The man who ended the era of understanding and friendship initiated by Franklin Roosevelt", she explained.)

"Is our GDR perfect? Of course not. Nothing is perfect. But

at least we are trying to build a new way of life. A peaceful Germany that will not make war. A Germany without Junkers, steel barons and fascists. Our leaders want to avoid a repetition of the past. Since 1864 Prussian militarists have invaded peaceful nations no less than five times. This must never happen again.

"Is our country a dictatorship? Well, look around and find out for yourself." Ulla laughed. "We have several political parties. I can take my choice. No, I am not a SED (Socialist Union) girl. I think I prefer the CDU. My father is a *Pfarrer,* a Protestant Minister. Socialism? Why not! I don't see any difference between real Christianity as it should be practised and the socialism we have in our country.

"Would I like to travel to the West, if I could? Of course I would, as a tourist, for a vacation. Why not? I like to travel and see distant places. What girl wouldn't? But live there? Never!

"The many people who fled to the West? They did not flee. They emigrated to a place where they got higher wages. Yes, the wages over there are higher. But you also have to live in a competitive society. You have to fight your way to the top. It's a dog-eat-dog life over there. Right? Well, here we live like human beings. What price peace of mind? Of course, not everyone thinks this way. Those who like money more than self-respect went across the demarcation line in Berlin. Good riddance! We didn't lose much when they left!

"I want you to meet some of our young people. Would you come to our children's camp? We have 800 boys and girls there. Age five to twenty. I am the oldest."

I accepted. The following two days were among the most memorable of my trip. The children lived in a tent city, similar to the many camps in which American and Canadian children spend their summers, with one exception: only 70 per cent of the children were East German. The others were guests of the State, from other Eastern nations: Czechoslovakia, Poland, Hungary, Rumania, the USSR, North Vietnam (three North Vietnamese boys, age fifteen to eighteen, explained their side of the Vietnamese war). But there were also a number of children from Western countries: France, West Germany (The presence of West German children in this East German camp could have been called a miracle!), Denmark, Sweden and Finland. The camp's name was *Völkerfreundschaft* — friendship among the nations of the world. "Our most important task is to build up friendships on an international scale", Ulla explained. "The peace of the world will be secure once nations understand each other. Is it not true that two people in love, who wish to stay in love, should work at building their lives together day by day? The same applies to friendship among nations. From knowledge springs respect and respect ripens into friendship. The reward of lasting friendship is peace." Ulla stood before me, her eyes shining, her face flushed. "Let us never forget what happened during the fascist years. Why were six million Jews killed? Because the fascists had created, built up and nourished hatred instead of love, hostility instead of friendship. The result? The Second World War and its fifty million dead. Don't ever forget, Canadians and Americans died in that war too. They should remember their sacrifices and the need for a lasting peace."

Ulla asked me to talk to the children about Canada. "Anything you tell them will be appreciated. How your cities look, what life is like there — the organization of schooling and recreational activities. . ."

That evening after supper I started to prepare a short speech. It was supposed to last fifteen minutes. After five minutes I stopped reading my manuscript and talked. I told the children about Canada's history, about the dialogue between the English and French Canadians, about Canadian politics and personalities, about the Canadian Broadcasting Corporation (CBC), about life's hopes and the tribulations of the average German-Canadian immigrant; and when I had finished and had answered the children's questions, more than three hours had gone by.

The next morning I had to repeat many of the explanations given the night before. Some twenty youngsters had missed my first speech. ("A hike to the Czech border", was Ulla's explanation.)

The children obviously had a wonderful time at the camp. Summer camps are very similar in the East and West. "How much do the children pay for their stay?" I asked Ulla.

"One mark a day, including meals", she replied. This would put the daily tab at 25 cents. "That's unbelievable", I countered. "In Canada they charge close to 500 dollars for a summer season."

"That's way out of line", she replied. "At that rate none of our children could afford camp. We set our rates very low. The Government meets our deficit, of course. But the services of the counsellors are free. The camp site is free. We only have to worry about buying food and sports equipment. I am not certain what the camp deficit amounts to. I would guess the real cost per child is probably around five marks a day. Our children pay one fifth of the real cost. Fair?"

The next morning I received an urgent phone call from Kadenbach. "Berlin wants to know where you are", he advised. "Don't forget, you broke contact with the department planning your trip three days ago. What shall I tell them?" "Tell them that I found an island of tranquility", I answered. "I want my peace for one more day!"

During this last day I made the trip which Kadenbach had assured me was impossible. I went to the Czech border. Not only did I reach the border; I crossed it twice, made a short excursion into Czechoslovakia, and returned. All I did was show my Canadian press card. Far from questioning and harassing me, the border police on both sides were friendly and polite. The Czech - East German border lies several miles southeast of Bad Schandau, a picturesque tourist village hidden in a deep valley between huge rock formations. It is one of the liveliest border points I have ever seen. Except for the long brightly coloured wooden beams which open and close like gates protecting American or Canadian railway crossings, the border reminded me somewhat of the United States-Canadian border at Champlain, New York. The traffic was as heavy as Champlain traffic. Most vehicles crossing the border are long trucks. Much of the East German-Czech commerce seems to move by highway. There are fewer passenger cars, but far more motor bikes and ordinary bicycles than would be found near the Canadian border. The examination of luggage and persons is far less strict than I had expected at "Curtain" border points, even with the thaw in the cold war. Heavy pedestrian traffic also moves in both directions — a phenomenon reserved for Europe where short distances and the comparative lack of motorization make this development possible. Another difference between Canadian and East German border points was a huge sign: *"Photographieren verboten"* — "Do not take pictures!"

It was late at night when I returned from my completely unauthorized border visit. Kadenbach and Wolf awaited me in Bad Schandau with worried faces. Would East Berlin give them a severe tongue-lashing for my unorthodox behaviour? Could they really be held responsible for my wrong-doing, if indeed I had done wrong?

The department in East Berlin which plans journalist' trips chose to overlook my demonstration of rugged individualism. We returned to Dresden and to our original travel schedule at two o'clock the next morning.

CHAPTER IX

EAST GERMANY'S JEWISH COMMUNITY

Helmut Aris, an undersized middle-aged former businessman, heads East Germany's remaining Jewish communities. He runs their affairs from a second-storey office in a residential area of downtown Dresden. I had to cross two back yards to reach it. The building is served by a small prewar elevator of doubtful construction, bearing an oversized "out of order" sign.

The country's Jewish religious communities have 1,642 members. The Dresden chapter boasts a roster of 105, compared to its prewar number of 9,000. Eighteen are children — and everyone under seventeen is classified as a child. Four Jewish babies were born in Dresden last year; this fact merited a headline in the *Nachrichtenblatt,* a small semi-tabloid newspaper serving the small communities every month. East Berlin has the largest Jewish group with 804 members; but not a single birth was recorded in East Berlin's chapter last year.

These left-overs of East German Jewry are organized into eight regional groups. East Berlin (this chapter still calls itself "Jewish community of Greater Berlin"), Halle, Karl-Marxstadt (formerly Chemnitz), Dresden, Schwerin, Leipzig and Magdeburg. The head of the Dresden group serves as chief of all groups. The Berlin chapter is headed by Heinz Schenk, a middle-aged survivor of a Nazi concentration camp and an outspoken anti-fascist. Schenk, in his late fifties, recently suffered a heart attack and during my stay in Berlin his activities were curtailed by doctor's orders. The monthly newspaper lists all births and deaths on its last page. Births, as pointed out, make headlines. Deaths occur with regrettable regularity. For more than 75 per cent of East German Jews are over fifty. In East Berlin the age group fifty-five to ninety reaches an unbelievable 92 per cent.

Are these conditions the result of an anti-Semitic policy of the GDR Government? It had been one of the prime purposes of my trip to find the answer to this riddle. After a thorough investigation of every aspect of Jewish life in East Germany I concluded that the answer to this question is no. The East German Government is not anti-Semitic. On the contrary. It employs every effort to appear pro-Jewish — except in its foreign policy. It anxiously attempts, without much success, to get more former Jewish residents to return to the country. The small Jewish communities are well treated — within the limitations of communist society. These limitations are the cause for the slow eclipse of what remains of East Germany's Jews.

Unlike West Germany, where restitution is paid to the Jewish population, East Germany makes no such payments. Jews are no more reimbursed for their losses of business, personal property and income than non-Jews. A socialist state does not recognize the right of businessmen or capitalists to own capital goods or tools of production. Therefore Jews and non-Jews alike are denied restitution for such losses.

But Jews are considered "victims of fascism" and unlike gentiles who must prove their anti-fascist past to qualify for financial help as "Nazi victims", Jews are automatically classified as persecutees. Each persecutee receives 600 marks per month, when he reaches the age of 60 (55 for women). Because of the inverted age pyramid of East German Jewry, more than fifty-five per cent of all community members are on the Government payroll. Six hundred marks is usually sufficient for most East Germans to live simply — prices of food, rent and necessities are rigidly controlled in the GDR.

The Jewish groups are helped by the Government in various other ways. The State maintains all Jewish cemeteries and pays for their upkeep. The absurdity of figures becomes apparent by the number of Jewish government-sponsored cemeteries. There are 197 of them, containing more than 160,000 graves. For each German Jew alive in the GDR, more than 100 graves are maintained by the State; the Jewish community would be utterly unable to carry this load. The Government took great care to rebuild temples and synagogues wherever the existence of a Jewish group made it feasible. The Dresden Synagogue in the Fiedlerstrasse was rebuilt and turned over to Dresden's microscopic congregation on June 18, 1950. Members of every Government office were present when Lord

Mayor Weidauer turned the keys over to Helmut Aris. The famous
choir of the Protestant Kreuzkirche sang Jewish religious songs. But
the 105 members are hardly sufficient to fill the impressive building. Men and women are not seated separately in this reconstructed
temple. "There simply are not enough people to make such a
separation feasible", explained Aris.

No Jewish religious schools exist in East Germany. I asked
whether these schools were omitted by Government order. "God,
no!", he replied. "They would like us to have such schools. But
we don't need them — unfortunately. We do not have enough
children to fill one single room, let alone a school. Our few
youngsters were taught by the Chief Rabbi once a week. Now the
Rabbi is dead, and a new one has not been named so far."

Last year's death of East Germany's Chief Rabbi, Dr. Riesenburger, struck a body blow to the vanishing East German Jewish
congregations. In West Berlin I had been permitted to browse
through the prosperous West Berlin community's correspondence
files. Since no telephone connection could be established at the
time, East Berlin sent the death notice to the West Berlin chapter
by telegram. This communication reached the West Berlin community in the Fasanenstrasse one day after it had been despatched
— the distance between the Eastern and Western point is less
than two miles. West Berlin's Rabbi and Cantor travelled to the
City's Eastern sector and were present at the funeral. West Berlin
Cantor Nachama has been allowed to conduct services in East
Berlin ever since. West Berlin's Jewish leaders do not appear to
suffer the other West Berliners' inability to cross over to East
Berlin. The GDR Government appears anxious to be cooperative
in all matters relating to the Jews. Since the death of Rabbi
Riesenburger the East German Government has tried to provide
the tiny congregation with another Rabbi. But there was none
in East Germany. Helmut Aris and his Berlin lieutenant Heinz
Schenk actually travelled to Budapest, accompanied by a member
of the GDR Government's Ministry of the Interior, trying to find
a substitute Rabbi. During July of 1965 they received the acceptance of a Budapest Rabbi to serve in the GDR for a two-year
term.

It took me several days to get at the root of the GDR's Jewish
problem. My visit to Lea Grundig had provided my first lead.
Mrs. Grundig had admitted her Jewish background and heritage.
"But I am not a member of the Jewish community", she had

hastened to add. "Why not?" I had asked. "No particular reason, except that I am not religious."

The membership figures of the congregations list only those Jews who profess and exercise their religion. In addition some 2,000 people of Jewish descent in East Germany are not members of these communities. They might be members of the SED Party, the country's most popular political group, highly placed government employees, or convinced Marxists rejecting all religion including that of their fathers, as being "outdated in these modern times". Altogether, East Germany numbers some 3,500 people of Jewish descent (compared to West Germany's 27,000) and of these 3,500 only 1,600 are members of the congregations.

Does the Government deliberately try to discourage Jews in top positions from being members of religious communities? This question will be hotly denied by all prominent Jews. I believe it actually works the opposite way. Only Jews interested in socialism and completely loyal to the regime could hope to reach a high position in public life. Such persons would either be irreligious or even openly anti-religious.

There are some exceptions. The best known religious Jew is Arnold Zweig. Since the death of Bertolt Brecht and Johannes Becher he is probably East Germany's most illustrious writer. Zweig, in his late eighties, almost blind, is a devout Jew and until recently was active in community affairs. Zweig is also one of the best known men in the GDR, one of the few Jews in an exposed position who is openly Jewish. Most others are hyper-assimilated. I have found no evidence that this assimilation was forced on them.

The State's most influential man of Jewish extraction is Professor Albert Norden, a member of the ten-man Politbureau steering East Germany's SED (Communist-Socialist) Party. Norden is East Germany's chief propagandist, a position previously filled by another German Jew, Gerhard Eisler. Eisler, who had lived out the war in the United States, made headlines some fifteen years ago when he fled the United States on a Polish liner while under a United States Federal indictment. I met Eisler during a TV and radio interview. His appearance has hardly changed since the day when his name had been a household word in the Western hemisphere. He lost much of his influence but did not seem to be in the Government's bad graces — for he still holds one of his department's senior jobs.

Albert Norden is an impressive man. The Government makes few decisions without first asking his advice. The *Brown Book,* the GDR's list of all former Nazis allegedly employed by the West German Government, was Norden's brainchild. The book had been published three weeks before my arrival in the GDR and had created a mild sensation. — When I first met Norden in Berlin, one of my first questions had been: "You are of Jewish descent, Professor Norden. Do you still feel friendship and affinity for the Jewish religion? And what do you think of Israel?"

"Yes, I am of Jewish descent", had been his answer. "I often forget this fact because in our State a person's ethnic extraction has lost all importance. We treat all people with equal respect. I am a citizen of this country; that is all I wish to be. I am not a religious man, so I would answer no, I have no particular interest in the Jewish religion. But I feel friendship for all people of Jewish descent, not because of my own background but because I like people."

When I asked him for his late father's profession, Norden replied: "My father was a worker and I am a worker". Actually, Professor Norden's father had been a Rabbi and I can hardly classify Professor Norden as a worker.

My question about Israel drew the same stereotyped set of answers which I had heard from other sources: "a United States dominated country — servants of Imperialism — no, I am not fond of Israel — I am of course fond of her people but not her government". The same line of reasoning is not only followed by East Germany's assimilated Jews in high Government positions, but by members of the religious communities as well. There appears to be no contact and no deep-seated desire for contact between the GDR's Jews and Israel. I had almost concluded that East German Jews were hopelessly anti-zionist, when I finally struck up the following conversation with an elderly Jew: "Israel? I love it. Of course I'd like to go there and finish my days in the Holy Land. But please don't write about it, and if you do, don't give my name." This remark had been overheard by the old gentleman's fifty-year old son, a "youngster" by East German Jewish standards. "Father is right", he confided. "There are a few of us who would like to go to Israel. But how do we ever get there? We cannot even get to West Germany. Don't get me wrong! I like the GDR — if I stay in Europe I'd rather stay here. At least there are no

Nazis left in East Germany. But the fact is we want to go to Israel!"

Correspondence and official contact between the GDR's Jews and the Jewish communities of other countries are almost non-existent. Helmut Aris had travelled to New York a few years ago and complained, "My reception was none too friendly. They took me to be a communist official, while I actually wanted to establish amicable contacts with the Jewish communities there." I was shown a number of polite but coldly efficient letters exchanged between Israeli Government officials and the community centre of Dresden. "If we ask the Israeli Government for favours, we usually do not get them", was the blunt statement of Helmut Aris. Relations between West and East Germany's Jewish groups are almost non-existent, barring the travel permits issued to West Berlin Jewish leaders after the death of Rabbi Riesenburger.

I had decided to submit my findings to the leading German-Jewish newspapers. After I had mailed the description of my Dresden visit to the *Allgemeine,* whose editor-in-chief Herman Lewy happens to be my colleague on the editorial staff of the *Montrealer Nachrichten,* Lewy sent me the following cordial letter:

Dear colleague Lust, I found your report very interesting. But I do not feel that we should print any report about the East German Jewish community. After all, why should we advertise the activities of this group? Please send us reports about Jewish life in Canada instead. We will appreciate this, and print it at once. Kind regards.

"We are left without contacts with the outside world. Our West German brothers have forsaken and forgotten us. They do not wish to remember that an East German Jewish community exists. Why are we being boycotted? Are we considered to be communists by the outside world? Some of us are — others are not. First of all we are Jews. Why have our brothers forgotten us?" These were the parting words of Helmut Aris when I left his Dresden office. Based on my experiences since my homecoming, I had to conclude that Aris was partly right.

The GDR's Jews are divided into two easily distinguishable groups: super-assimilated Jews who either have forgotten or would like to forget their background and origin; and the members of the religious community. Assimilated Jews often hold high Government offices. In fact proportionately they are more prominent than non-Jews and this is understandable. The power of government is exercised by an "elite" forged together in the Nazi concentration camps. Most Jews who had remained in Germany and survived went through the hell of the "KZ". Only a small number of non-Jews were incarcerated, members of the leftist parties and other opposition groups. Approximately 15 per cent of all resistance fighters had been Jewish. When the GDR Government was formed resistance fighters became the new elite.

The Jews of the religious communities are the atrophied remainder of the once teaming German-Jewish group. The silent witnesses of their past are their greatest assets: temples, cemeteries (more properly described as burial museums), literature. The small religious congregations far from being persecuted by the Government, are treated like rare specimens. And rare specimens they are indeed. They are museum pieces, and the GDR Government would like to keep them in existence as long as possible, to prove to the outside world that it is indeed the most anti-Nazi government in Europe; that Jews are being helped and encouraged; and that religion is not being persecuted in East Germany.

CHAPTER X

THE AFFLUENT SOCIETY, EASTERN STYLE

The GDR is in the midst of an economic boom. Construction crews are working everywhere. There is no unemployment. People are well dressed and there is no shortage of spending money. Words like "boom" are never used by East German economists. "Booms and recessions are symptoms of capitalism", they say. "Our constant prosperity is based on economic planning."

In reality the GDR has its booms and recessions too. The symptoms are just not so apparent. Even during bad times people are continually employed — for the Government is the largest employer and can create wage funds at will. Anyone who wants to find out whether a socialist state is having a boom or a depression, should study its international balance of payments, its exports and imports and — finally — the government balance sheet. The latter is rarely published and it takes considerable digging to get at the figures. One of the major disappointments of my East German trip was that I was unable to compile an acceptable GDR balance sheet.

But however one looks at it, an East German boom is certainly underway. The GDR has become the fifth largest industrial producer of Europe. She outranks well-organized industrial States like Belgium, Poland and Czechoslovakia. Before the war Czechoslovakia and even Poland outproduced that part of the Reich which today has constituted itself as the GDR. So did Belgium, Holland, Sweden and a few other smaller States. East Germany's balance of international payments is favourable. Most of her exports go to Warsaw Pact countries where the payments are ultimately credited against imports. The impression of certain West German economists who see in East Germany a Soviet satellite bled white by her masters hardly applies. The days when machinery was dismantled and shipped to the USSR as war reparations are long since gone.* The GDR's industrial advance has been less spectacular than West Germany's Wirtschaftswunder. It also took several years longer; but today East Germany is a country with a buoyant economy, whose citizens appear prosperous.

The lack of unemployment and the increase of the production of consumer goods has created an affluent society. This word, usually reserved for North America, can be applied to broad strata of East German society as well. The GDR's affluence does not reach the levels of West Germany and it develops along slightly different lines. But it exists. The West German worker's prosperity is based on rising wages which in turn are paced by rising prices and a corresponding drop in the Westmark's purchasing power. Whenever wages rise faster than the drop in purchasing power of the Westmark, the West German level of living has improved. The East German worker's prosperity is based on comparatively low, but stable wages and a rigid price control system for finished products and services, which places the East German worker on a living level comparable to that of his West German opposite number. This applies to food, housing and staples. He has some difficulty acquiring large consumer durable goods. Automobiles are hard to come by in East Germany. They are out of the average worker's or farmer's reach. Their places are taken by an ever-increasing fleet of motor bikes. Most families who in Canada would own a car, own a motor bike in the GDR. There are far fewer washing machines and refrigerators available. ("This will eventually come; meanwhile our old-fashioned ice-boxes keep our food just as cool", my guide explained.) Whenever a West German increase in living level is signified by a rise in wages, it is heralded in East Germany by a decrease in the price of a basic commodity with salaries remaining stable. This has resulted in some hard-to-believe figures. A three-room apartment

---

* "There is thus nothing in the record to suggest that the industrial plant was built from nothing. It is true that the Soviet occupation forces thoroughly dismantled most of the plants in their zone between 1945 and 1953. . . . . However, when skilled workers, blueprints and know-how are available, it doesn't take long to reestablish an industry, as experience on this side of the Iron Curtain has shown." (See R.W. Herzer, "Let's Keep West Berlin as an Island", Commentator, Toronto, June 1963.) Herzer also refers in this article to the "very substantial secondary manufacturing and chemical industry" located in the GDR before the war.

in one of East Berlin's most elegant streets rents for one hundred and ten marks ($30.00); a good meal in a choice restaurant will cost approximately eight marks ($2.40); in a simple restaurant the prices run from three to five marks. Food costs are equally low when bought in the old market places which in the GDR have not yet been replaced by Western-style supermarkets.

The relatively satisfactory living conditions are one of the reasons why many East Germans who once fled to the West are returning. Their main reason for defection was the higher West German wages which they accumulated and saved. When they had accumulated enough money they came back to the GDR where in terms of the low controlled prices of consumer goods they had a small fortune. A similar situation existed in the United States during the 19th century. Europeans used to come there, make their small fortune, then return home.

West German prosperity is based on privately-owned business. Large concerns usually are joint-stock companies; in each one a few large shareholders control the firm; many small shareholders have a beneficial interest. West German concerns involve three interested groups: shareholders, management and employees. West German prosperity is based on the mutual interest of all three groups.

In a sense, there is a similar division in East Germany. Large concerns are usually Government owned. They have two of West Germany's participating groups: management and employees. There are obviously no shareholders in the GDR. The State takes the place of this third group. The Government is forever anxious to explain that the citizens as a group are the true owners of the concern. In place of many individual shareholders of large West German concerns, the East German public-at-large shares equally in the ownership of its concerns. At least this is the way the Government explains it and most citizens accept that at face value.

In most West German as well as North American concerns, the management has the decisive power. Frequently members of the board of directors and administration are among the company's large shareholders. In East Germany the management holds similar powers. It is not based on ownership of stock — there isn't any. Management's truly sweeping authority is granted by the Government Planning Commission. There is but scant difference between the duties of a West German and an East German plant manager. I had opportunity to inspect and visit one of the

GDR's largest publicly-owned firms, the *Fotofabrik* in Wolfen, producers of film and photographic equipment. The giant concern, called the "Kodak of East Germany", had once been known under the name of *Agfa*. During the Soviet occupation the military authorities ordered the firm expropriated. After the GDR had been founded, the Soviets turned the firm's control over to the new State. It became a *Volkseigener Betrieb* (People's concern), abbreviated in German as "VEB"; the expropriated *Agfa* owners made their way into West Germany and built a new plant there. There still is an *Agfa* plant in West Germany today, and they do considerable business with the former *Agfa* plant in Wolfen. The position of the *Fotofabrik* managers is typical of the GDR's new managerial class. Most of them are comparatively young. They have become the elite of a new society slowly emerging in East Germany. They get annual salaries between 25,000 and 50,000 marks, which in terms of buying power compares to a Canadian salary of between $12,500 and $25,000. It must also be borne in mind that East Germany has no graduated income tax; since the Government is the largest entrepreneur and the profits of the State-owned concerns form its largest source of revenue, East Germany does not need the complicated graduated income tax structure of the West. These managers live in well-built one-family houses; the housing shortage so typical of countries like the Soviet Union where even today many people have to share their rooms, let alone apartments, does not exist in East Germany. One of the managers owned a small car of East German make, a *Trabant*. This car, made by the DKW works in Zwickau, costs 8,000 marks in the domestic market. Its export price is only 4,000 marks. East Germany sells her cars abroad for half the price charged GDR citizens at home. This is the Socialist State's way of making certain that only very few citizens can afford new cars. "Once our car production has sufficiently expanded we will produce cars for the home market. As soon as this happens, our own people will pay the same price as foreign customers. We have not reached this stage yet," my guide explained. At the official exchange rate, the *Trabant* would cost its German owner more than $2,000. It compares to the West German Volkswagen. The other manager of *Fotofabrik* drove a *Wartburg*, manufactured by the DKW works at Eisenach. The *Wartburg* is East Germany's attempt to enter the market of larger American-type cars. The average citizen could not afford a *Wartburg*. It costs 14,000 marks ($4,000 at the official exchange rate) to domestic users. The manager sighed: "This *Wartburg* car is my great luxury; having bought it I cannot afford vacations for at least three years". He later invited me to his home where his wife served tea. The table was set with an exquisite sterling set and Meissen teacups. The maid serving the tea was impeccably dressed in a white uniform and cap. I rubbed my eyes in amazement. I had not expected this type of living in a communist state, and explained to my host the reasons for my surprise. "You Westerners all have the wrong ideas about socialism", he explained. "Why shouldn't we live well and enjoy the comforts of life? The principal difference between your society and ours is the fact that our large firms are publicly-owned. Yours are privately-owned. But all large firms must be managed, no matter who owns them. I am a manager. Your business firms also employ managers. I receive an excellent salary for the work I do. So do yours. I choose to spend my salary on good living. I could also save it for my old age. I won't. When I am old, the State will take care of me and my family — this is one of the advantages of socialism. There is nothing wrong in having domestic employees. We are not allowed to employ workers and sell the fruits of their labour. That would be exploitation — we consider that to be a grave crime. But the domestic servant produces nothing, except good service. We don't sell that. It stays at home. There is only one thing wrong with maids, there aren't enough of them. Our cook gave us notice last week. She can earn twice the salary we pay her by working in the plant. Can we really blame her for leaving? I know we won't be able to replace her. So we'll have to live without a cook. My wife will have to cook. How she hates the idea!"

The thought struck me that this conversation could well have taken place in North America. I was reminded of this when the manager's wife asked me about the servant situation in Canada. She was visibly relieved when she heard that domestic employees are equally scarce in the West. "We should arrange for an international exchange of domestic workers", she finally suggested. "Apparently neither your system nor ours has ever solved this problem."

The *Fotofabrik* maintains many social services for its employees. It has its own nursery schools and kindergartens for some 1,000 children. This service is not entirely free — it costs one mark forty pfennig per child per day (forty cents) which includes two meals and supervision. The firm also operates a theatre for its employees which seats 800. The plant maintains a milk bar (the German equivalent of the North American coffee shop) and a dance hall. In the evening the dancers' spirits rise and the noise can be heard for several blocks. Most of these services could be found in the West as well — but a company dance hall is something specifically German.

The Wolfen products no longer use the trade name of *Agfa*. They have been renamed *Orwo* (original Wolfen). *Orwo* participates in many trade fairs abroad. In addition to trade fairs in socialist countries, *Orwo* products were exhibited last year in India, Stockholm, Helsinki, Milan, Vienna and Cairo.

Wolfen is a suburb of Halle, one of East Germany's industrial complexes. I managed to inspect the plant and editorial offices of East Germany's largest provincial newspaper, the *Freiheit*. This paper has a paid daily circulation of almost half a million copies and is owned by the ruling political party, the SED. The printing equipment is modern and the plant is run in exemplary fashion. Newsprint used is of Soviet origin — in my opinion of indifferent quality. "Much of our paper actually comes from Finland — some from the USSR. Frankly, I prefer the Finnish paper", was the confidential remark of one of the head printers. The *Freiheit* sells for fifteen pfennig (four cents) per issue. The monthly rate is three marks. This price is standard for East German papers — their cost is slightly lower than that of Western papers. East German newspapers are not owned by the Government or the public at large. They are owned either by the political parties or by trade organizations. The editors do not consider themselves to be public servants. The right of criticism is exercised, but polemics printed in the GDR differ from our Western kind in several important points. No straight criticism is ever directed against socialism or communism, nor do heads of Government come in for critical remarks. The GDR's newspaper ire is directed against business firms who fall behind in their deliveries, public servants who treat the public discourteously, or individuals whose personal lives or views are unpopular. It is a highly embarrassing situation for a large firm to be attacked by a newspaper. Such an attack invariably carries official invitation to reply and — if the need arises — to correct the actions which had been criticised. If no reply is forthcoming the newspaper will publish the fact and eventually the criticised firm or person will be asked by the Government to explain. If on the other hand it should be found that the criticism was not justified, the paper must print a formal retraction. This "right to criticise constructively" within the limitations of the socalist state makes newspaper editors very powerful men in East Germany's affluent society; but this power stems from a different source than that of our Western editors.

One of the *Freiheit* editors had just returned from a trip through the Soviet Union. Another had spent his vacation at Bulgaria's seashore. East Germans are amongst the most travel-minded people of our time. There are lovely spots in their own country: Saxony's Switzerland, where I had just spent a few days; the Baltic sea with its magnificent seacoast — which almost every GDR citizen visits at least once a year — the forests and mountains of Thuringia. All this is for the workers with moderate means. The managerial class and the political functionaries specialize in trips to the Black Sea coast of Bulgaria and Rumania. The more affluent visit the Crimea and its elegant spa at Socchi. Most East German newspapermen can take trips which Western journalists would envy. It took my stay at the offices of the *Freiheit* to realize how large the Communist world had become. One reporter had just returned from a trip to China and the "liberated part of Viet Nam" (meaning North Viet Nam). Another had flown in non-stop from Cuba. I had always thought of Cuba as an island completely isolated from all air travel except two slender links by the Spanish airline *Iberia*, one flight a week to Madrid, another to Mexico City. Actually Cuba is not isolated, as far as air travel to Communist nations is concerned. There is a direct link to East Berlin's airport. Another non-stop flight goes between Havana and Moscow. I learned that most European businessmen wishing to visit Havana shun the use of the Spanish airline *Iberia* which might list them as potential "subversives". Most fly to West Berlin, enter East Berlin on a one-day permit requiring no special visa and then exit from East Berlin within their allotted day via a non-stop flight to Havana. Upon arrival, the Cuban officials issue their visa on a separate sheet of paper without stamping the visitors' passports. The traveller will eventually return to his home town via Berlin; no trace of his Cuban stay remains in his passport. This makes him eligible for eventual later visits to the United States. The touchiness of American immigration officials about travellers with Cuban visas in their passports can be likened to the attitude of Arab officials toward Israeli visas.

After I left the *Freiheit* offices I realized why there is unlikely ever to be a full-fledged revolt against the East German Government. The citizens are far too prosperous. Our Western belief in large-scale hunger and want in the GDR is based on wishful thinking.

CHAPTER XI

THE MEN AROUND ULBRICHT

We had left Halle and the *Freiheit* offices at four PM. Two hours later I had once again checked into East Berlin's Hotel Berolina. My trip was drawing to a close. I had been in the GDR for more than two weeks and had travelled through most of it. My last two days were reserved for interviews with the country's ruling group, the men around Ulbricht. My interview with the Chief of State, Walter Ulbricht, was set for Friday afternoon. Saturday morning I was scheduled to fly back home.

There are actually two ruling groups, the *Staatsrat* or regular government and the "Politbureau" of the SED, the country's most important political party. Walter Ulbricht heads both groups. Professor Albert Norden, chief propagandist and perhaps the most influential man in the Politbureau after Ulbricht, had been interviewed during my previous stay. The *Staatsrat* or State Council, has twenty-three members. The men who count are Willy Stoph, head of the Council of Ministers (the title "Prime Minister", sometimes attributed to this office, is not quite correct); Professor Johannes Dieckmann, Chairman of the *Volkskammer*, the rubber-stamp parliament; Manfred Gerlach; and Friedrich Ebert.

Not all of the GDR's leading men are members of the group which Marxists like to call "the proletariat". More often they have been teachers, university professors or leaders of their own profession. The SED Party is a fusion of the old leftist Social Democrats (under the leadership of Otto Grothewohl) and of the Moscow-oriented Communists under the guidance of Walter Ulbricht. When they fused, Social Democratic influence became secondary. But Grothewohl was number two man in East Germany until his recent death.

East German leaders try to create the impression that the *Staaatsrat* is representative of all the major parties and points of view in the country. Gerald Goetting, one of the Council's members, came from the CDU — the Christian Democratic Union. Manfred Gerlach, founder of the "Free German Youth" movement, has been called the "Baldur von Schirach of the Ulbricht regime". This insult is unjustified. Except that both have founded youth movements, there is little similarity between the Hitler Youth and the Free German Youth. It is of interest that Gerlach became one of the most prominent members of the National Liberal Party, one of the few political groups in East Germany accepting former Nazi Party members. Gerlach, born May 8, 1928, was seventeen years old when the Hitler Reich collapsed. According to available records he had never been a member of the Hitler Youth.

Heinrich Homann, Vice Chairman of the *Staatsrat,* has a notable past. The son of a wealthy shipbuilder of Bremerhaven, he studied law under the Nazi regime. Later he became a Wehrmacht officer and was captured at Stalingrad. He was one of the organizers of the Moscow Committee "Free Germany" in 1943.

Dr. Johannes Dieckmann, Chairman of the East German Parliament, is the son of a Protestant Minister of the Bremen district. One of the observations I made after interviewing many of the Government leaders was that quite a few of them were born in West Germany. Walter Ulbricht himself, born in Leipzig on June 30, 1893, a worker's son, is a notable exception. Professor Dr. Eric Correns is a native of Tübingen, South-West Germany. He became one of the leading chemists and physicists. Friedrich Ebert, son of the Weimar Republic's first President and present Lord Mayor of East Berlin, actually started out as a newspaper editor. Professor Liselott Herforth, a physicist and one of the *Staatsrat's* women members, is the daughter of a well-known writer; her fellow member, Mrs. Else Merke, was born the daughter of a small farmer. The youngest member of the *Staatsrat* is thirty-year old Christel Pappe, daughter of a furniture manufacturer.

Nowhere in the GDR did I find an exact breakdown of the social and geographic origins of the *Staatsrat* members. One evening I converted myself into a miniature gallup poll. Here are my results.

Geographic Origin

13 members were born in present-day GDR territory

8 members were born in West Germany

2 came from Eastern territories lost after the Second World War

—

23 Members

Social Origin

3 hail from the intelligentsia

6 were children of wealthy families

14 belonged to what Marxists call "the workers and farmers" class

—

23 Members

My first scheduled interview was with Dr. Dengler, member of the steering committee of the *Nationalrat* (National Council). This organization expedites cooperation between the various political parties and professional groups of the country. Dr. Dengler can look back on an interesting past. He served as a captain on the staff of the ill-fated General von Paulus, commander of the Stalingrad armies. When during the last four weeks of the epic battle the general had ordered him to organize further resistance, he refused. He bolted and crossed into Soviet lines. He became one of the founding members of the "National Committee Free Germany" and eventually embraced communism. He served as representative of several Eastern newspapers in Bonn. Could I have heard right? I asked him to repeat. "Yes indeed; I have represented the SED Party newspaper *Neues Deutschland*, East Germany's largest communist newspaper, in Bonn." His amazing position lasted for a number of years; eventually the Bonn Government had ordered his expulsion.

Dr. Dengler was the most outspoken critic of West German foreign policy I had ever interviewed. He likes to call a spade a spade. I had heard similar views expressed elsewhere. But never had a high Government official said them so clearly with full permission to quote. "Viet Nam? Bonn just loves this little American war. Why? While the US is busy fighting the Viet Cong and slowly spends herself into an economic recession, the Federal Republic, which is not militarily involved, will go out and corner a few important world markets. The Americans will be defeated militarily; the West German cartels will emerge victorious in the realm of trade and commerce. The Hallstein doctrine? No, it is not idiotic at all! It is highly intelligent. It was created to keep up the fiction of the "one, undivided, indivisible Germany". Will

West Germany eventually attack the East? No! They will do it with more finesse this time. They use the expellee organizations. How? The Federal Government finances them. The expellees advertise their demands and organize their little storm trooper-type columns. One of the most dangerous organizations is the *Witikobund*. Notice the statement made by its leader Bechert: "The expellee organizations will always demand a bit more than what they are really aiming for; this makes it possible for the West German Government to 'tone down the excessive demands' somewhat. The Bonn diplomats will appear reasonable and peaceful if they ask merely for 'the revision of the Oder-Neisse line'. The *Witikobund*, after all, had asked for the return of all the Eastern provinces. This makes the official demand of the West German Government tame by comparison — worthy of discussion!

"Take a classical case: Transport Minister Hans Christian See-bohm — one of the heads of the Sudeten-German expellee organ-ization — officially requested that Czechoslovakia return the Sudeten territory to Germany. This territorial cession had been the original cause of the outbreak of the Second World War. The West German Government immediately replied. 'No, we will not ask for the return of the Sudetenland. We only wish to discuss certain minor border adjustments with the Eastern countries.' Sounds reasonable, doesn't it? Until you take a good look at the basic impertinence of the very people whose antics had prepared Hitler's rise to power and world domination! Erwin Schuele? He was made chief Nazi prosecutor with one aim in mind, to protect the high Nazis still wielding power within the Bonn Government. You say that Schuele did a good job? Indeed he did! He caught a lot of minor concentration camp guards and convicted them. The little fellows who flogged prisoners got long penitentiary terms. The big fellows are still in the Bonn Government. Don't make me laugh!

"I tell you, West Germany's non-recognition of our State is not just stupidity. It is deliberate perfidy. Bonn wishes to main-tain the impression that seventeen million Germans have been deprived of their freedom of choice. We do have full freedom of choice. We have elections. We change our government by popular will. But Bonn deliberately keeps this from the world. Why? Be-cause they wish to seize the GDR first, then march eastward."

I found Dr. Dengler's views interesting. I countered that I had been in West Germany and had interviewed many of the men whose actions and intentions he impugned, and that I couldn't quite agree with his findings. "Well, you don't agree with me now. Twenty years from now you and most other North Americans will remember my words and will agree. Unfortunately it will be too late. You cannot eradicate the *furor facisticus* within a few years. Especially not if you allow Nazi teachers to implant their poison into the minds of the young."

My second appointment was with East Germany's acting Foreign Minister, George Stibi. The cabinet portfolio is actually held by Dr. Winzer. Winzer formulates the policies, Stibi executes them. George Stibi, an elderly, gray-haired, distinguished looking man, is a native of the West German state of Württemberg. His principal task is to break through the invisible fence erected around the GDR by the Hallstein doctrine and establish diplomatic relations with the outside world. My stay in Stibi's office proved very informative.

A wide table, completely devoid of papers or files. Four telephones ringing incessantly. (I learned later that one line was directly connected with the office of Walter Ulbricht.) Before I had travelled to the GDR I had set myself the goal of finding out whether relations between the East German State and the United Arab Republic were potentially dangerous to Israel. Whether the ties were taken seriously, or were only skin deep. Was there any latent anti-Israel feeling in the GDR? In my interview with George Stibi I was less fortunate, however, than in my previous one with Dr. Dengler. Stibi advised me: "Anything I tell you is confidential and may not be quoted". Since I was unable to make notes during the interview, I can only describe my general impressions.

Most GDR leaders believe in the cause they call "anti-fascism". They accept the fact that the Jewish people have suffered most during Nazi rule — far more than any other group. The ties between the GDR and the Arab States were formed mostly to outflank the diplomatic efforts of West Germany. Out of fear of playing into the hands of Bonn the GDR will not undertake any overt act which might antagonize the Arabs. The East German press tends to ignore Israel. Officially, Israel receives much criticism. But very often an East German official would drop a remark like "Confidentially, our State and Israel share an anti-fascist tradition. It's too bad Israel is playing it so close to the USA. The Arabs? Look, we've got to be practical. There are forty million

Arabs and less than three million Israelis. Isn't it too bad? Don't we wish it was the other way around!"

This latent pro-Israeli feeling never reaches the pages of GDR newspapers or the speeches of highly placed officials. It is no more than a strong undercurrent. It will not influence GDR policy. At the time these lines are written, West Germany is officially pro-Israel and East Germany pro-Arab.

Has East Germany delivered arms to Egypt? If she has, no Government member will admit it. "Why should we deliver arms to Egypt?" I was asked. "The Arabs can buy arms far more advantageously in Czechoslovakia or the Soviet Union. We try to deliver machinery to them for their industrial expansion. We have sold them many vitally important products and our trade with them has increased. But we do not sell them arms!"

Stibi explained the tedious road they have to travel to establish contact with the outside world. "Here you may quote me", he said. "This information is available to the public." East Germany does not maintain diplomatic relations with any Western country. Ambassadors and ministers are exchanged with all members of the Communist world. But there are trade missions and consulates in the non-socialist world which assume all the functions normally associated with embassies. When Tanganyika and Zanzibar united into Tanzania, the GDR established a Consulate General in the new State. For all practical purposes it is an embassy. There are GDR trade missions in many African countries. The one in Ghana is the most active. No diplomatic relations exist betwen the United Arab Republic and East Germany. There is however a Consulate General — again I could quote Shakespeare's immortal words: 'What's in a name?' This consulate actually is an embassy."

"Is there any chance of your country ever establishing diplomatic relations with the United States or Canada?" I asked.

"Most people would say, not a ghost of a chance", he replied. "The prospects at the moment look grim. On the other hand, the Federal Republic maintainss diplomatic relations with the Soviet Union. By the same logic, we could maintain diplomatic relations with the United States. Of course we haven't been asked.

"We could improve our status vis-a-vis Canada. A trade mission? No, at the moment we do not have a trade mission in Canada. We would certainly not refuse if the subject were ever broached by Ottawa. We would certainly like to improve our relations with your country."

My interview with Foreign Minister Stibi was to take half an hour. I spent more than two hours in the Ministry. Stibi used the last fifteen minutes of the interview to tell me a story dealing with Canadian-GDR relations which if true, is sensational. I had never heard of it in Canada. The story deals with an alleged kidnapping of an East German sailor in the port of St. John's Newfoundland, in the early fall of 1964.

An East German fishing vessel, the "Peter Nell" was brought to St. John's for emergency repairs. Three young sailors, Hans Burzler, Karl Heinz Peters and Hans Juergen Lipka, went on shore leave and got drunk. When Lipka woke the next day, he found himself at police headquarters where he was told that he had signed a petition asking Canada for political asylum; the request had been granted. Lipka did not remember signing the petition. He claimed to be a patriotic GDR citizen. He asked to be allowed to return to his ship. The request was refused. He was flown to Halifax, Nova Scotia. Often during the following days and weeks he tried to return to the GDR. Instead Canadian authorities put him on the West German freighter "Erich Schroeder". He was brought to the Federal Republic. But Lipka had set his mind on returning to East Germany. He crossed the border October 24, 1964, and returned home. The two other sailors Hans Burzler and Karl Heinz Peters had defected. They had made him drunk and had tried to take him along. Why? Because they had been promised payment for each and every GDR sailor they could bring "over to the West".

The story sounded fantastic. Kidnapping is a serious criminal offence in Canada. Later that same night when I was ready to retire someone knocked at my hotelroom door. Half asleep I opened up. Two men stood outside. "Sorry to disturb you so late! We have an important letter for you from the Foreign Ministry. Please read it at your leisure." They gave me a huge brown envelope, then disappeared. The time was 2:30 A.M. — an ungodly hour for any Foreign Ministry to send documents to a foreign newspaper man!

The envelope contained the January 17, 1965 issue of *Neues Deutschland* where the story of the "kidnapping of GDR sailor Hans Juergen Lipka" was prominently displayed in great detail on page 7B. The newspaper was accompanied by a typewritten letter with the following text:

Mr. Peter Lust

Dear Sir. The matter discussed in the enclosed newspaper story has been brought to the attention of the Canadian Government by the Foreign Ministry of the GDR in a note. The Foreign Ministry of Czechoslovakia transmitted this note on our behalf to the Canadian Embassy in Prague on February 1, 1965.

In our note we advised the Canadian Government of the facts as they appear in the enclosed newspaper article, and we protested the circumstances that Lipka was taken on board a West German boat against his will.

At the same time we advised the Canadian Department of External Affairs that the immigration officials in St. John's, Newfoundland, tolerate the activities of a West German group in that city who habitually try to induce GDR sailors to defect, by offering them financial reward. Not only are the illegal activities of this group tolerated, but very often they are actually helped by Canadian immigration officials in St. John's. A German-Canadian businessman is said to be an active member of this group.

The Canadian Department for External Affairs has never replied to our note.

The letter which accompanied the newspaper was typewritten on blank stationary and was not signed.

Was the Foreign Affairs Ministry afraid to put its name and seal to this serious accusation against the Canadian Government? Or was the letter's anonymity occasioned by the fact that I, as a newspaperman, had no diplomatic status and could not convey messages from one government to another?

The manner in which I obtained the information, the late hour at which the document reached me and the amazing anonymity which covered the transfer reminded me of a cloak-and-dagger movie. I tried to dig up further information. The Foreign Office of Czechoslovakia admitted receiving the GDR note and transmitting it to the Canadian Embassy in Prague. Ottawa answered with icy silence. "There is no record on file of any such GDR demarche", I was told. Eventually I was informed confidentially through sources which I as a newspaperman have no right to reveal: "The Department for External Affairs did receive a note from the East German Government. We did not reply to it since we do not recognize East Germany. We checked on the allegations and believe them to be unfounded."

Is there really a group of kidnappers operating against East German vessels in Canadian ports? I do not know the answer. The next morning, the last day of my trip, was reserved for an interview with the Chairman of the State Council, Walter Ulbricht. "*Der Herr Staatsratvorsitzende* is very busy. He can give you fifteen minutes. Please prepare your questions so that you can use your allotted time to full advantage." This advice had been given me four days before by Wolfgang Wolf, my guide. "Since you speak German I need not be there as an interpreter. It would only complicate things!"

West Germany considers Ulbricht to be the "Soviet-appointed dictator of the Russian occupied zone of Germany". By East German standards he is Head of the State. Thus formalities are stictly observed. Foreign diplomats accredited to the GDR (all Warsaw Pact nations have embassies in East Berlin) present their papers to Ulbricht. His flag is flown wherever he goes. Any East Berlin child can tell at a glance whether Ulbricht is present or absent from his official residence.

Ulbricht is a native of Leipzig. He chose to become a carpenter, but at an early age he became interested in politics. He joined the pre-World War I Social Democratic Party and became an ardent follower of left-wing leader Karl Liebnecht. He served in the Imperial Army during World War I, engaged in pacifist propaganda and was arrested. The revolution of 1918 freed him from a military prison in Belgium. He helped found the "Spartacus Group", forerunner of the Weimar Republic's Communist Party. "Thaelmann — Pieck — Ulbricht"; these names were household words in the Weimar Republic. Thaelmann was killed by the Nazis. Wilhelm Pieck, the second of the Communist triumvirate, was Ulbricht's immediate predecessor. He held the office Ulbricht now holds, when the GDR was first proclaimed. When he died, Ulbricht took over. He is the only one of the Communists' "Big Three" who survived. This is the basis of his popularity in East Germany. Ulbricht lived out the Nazi years in the Soviet Union. This is seldom held against him. "How would you have it? The Nazis would certainly have killed him," seems to sum up the views of the people I asked "Do you disapprove of the fact that Ulbricht fled the country when the Nazis came to power?"

I arrived at Government House half an hour before the appointed time. I was brought into a well-lit anteroom and faced two secretaries. "Do you smoke, sir?" was their first question. I knew what my answer had to be — I had been forewarned that Ulbricht disliked smoking and that all visitors had to extinguish their cigarettes before seeing him. I had remarked to Wolf some days before: "It seems German leaders usually dislike smoking" (alluding to Adolf Hitler). "Yes, I know whom you mean, Adenauer!" Wolf had laughingly answered. It was true. It seems most German leaders of the past two generations disliked smoking — Nazis, Communists and centre group leaders alike. Erhard and his big cigar is the exception to this rule.

Ulbricht likes to rise early. He is an ardent sportsman. Even at his advanced age he is still an excellent swimmer — the rule that all East German children must learn to swim was initiated by him. His motto in one of his early speeches: *Jeder Mann an jedem Ort einmal in der Woche Sport* ... Everyone should engage in some physical activity at least once a week. ...

At the appointed moment — I noticed that even the second hand moved to the mark — I was brought into Walter Ulbricht's presence. During the first few minutes of the interview I had to revise many preconceived notions I had formed about this controversial man.

I had always believed him to be of small stature. Actually he is tall. I had imagined him to be a casual, if not a sloppy dresser. But he dresses immaculately — his appearance could be called elegant. I had expected some difficulty in understanding his Saxon dialect. While he talked with a slight trace of an accent he was very easy to understand. The allegation that his people can not follow his speeches springs from the fertile minds of Western newspapermen. His voice is supposed to be shrill and grating — it is somewhat high but not to a point where it is disagreeable.

My first question had nothing to do with the East-West conflict. "You knew Georgi Dimitrov?' I asked. Dimitrov was the Bulgarian communist who was put on trial by Goering for allegedly setting fire to the *Reichstag* building in 1933 — a crime actually committed by Goering himself. Dimitrov's defence had been so brilliant that the Nazi Government was forced to acquit him. Later he went to the Soviet Union and became one of the organizers of international communism. — "Indeed I did", Ulbricht answered. "He was a brilliant man, and a believer in the cause of socialism." The first few minutes of the interview were used up by Ulbricht's reminiscences of Dimitrov — no waste of time, as far as I was concerned. Dimitrov, one of the most fascinating personalities of our age, preferred to remain in the background of events. He preferred his study to the public limelight others coveted. Not many people met him or knew him intimately. Ulbricht was one of the exceptions.

My second question: "I noticed that May 8, the day of the war's end, is celebrated in the GDR, while it is ignored in West Germany. Do the people of East Germany really consider this date of capitulation a day of victory?"

Ulbricht took off his glasses, cleaned them carefully, then looked at me: "Yes, indeed! It was a day of victory for our people. The imperialists who had started the Second World War, the criminal elements who operated the gas ovens till the last minute, were defeated. I quite agree with you; the forces running the Federal Republic do not celebrate the day. A lost war does not constitute liberation, they say. Of course not! It was their war they lost!"

Next question: "Under what terms would the GDR sign a treaty of friendship with West Germany?"

Answer: "We are ready to meet with West Geman leaders any time, anywhere, on the basis of equality. We do not refuse to recognize them. They refuse to recognize us. They attempt to deal with us through the Soviet Government as if we were — as they so openly call it — a province of the Soviet Union. Well, our Government has never tried to negotiate with Bonn via Washington. We fully realize that West Germany is a sovereign State. We do not like the forces which run that State. But they are sovereign. So are we!"

Question: "We frequently hear about interference on the Autobahnen linking Berlin with West Germany. Is there such interference?" *Answer:* "We never interfere with normal, legitimate traffic. You understand that these Autobahnen traverse our country. They are on our soil. If we find that they are being used for hostile purposes against our State we have the right to act. Actually all we ever did was stop dangerous shipments from crossing our territory. We do not seize them. We merely escort them back to West Germany."

Question: "Will there ever be another embargo against West Berlin?" *Answer:* "You have been misinformed. We never enforced an embargo against West Berlin. If you refer to the so-called Ber-

lin airlift, this was an entirely different matter. We cannot consider
that West Berlin is a part of the West German Republic. We
treat it as a free city. In short, we feel that there are three political
entities on German soil: West Germany, the GDR, and West
Berlin."

Question: "Would your Government ever consider joining the
United Nations? Answer: "You should have asked this question
of the Foreign Minister you met yesterday. We have never been
asked to join. If we were asked and a majority of the UN membership should endorse our candidacy, we certainly would join. But
this is an entirely academic question. As you know, neither of the
two German states is a member — for obvious reasons."

Question: "Do you believe the cold war will eventually subside?" Answer: "We do not wage a cold war; the others do;
should they stop their cold war, we would be very happy indeed.
Our State is built on a basis of peace and friendship for all
nations."

Question: "Would you ever enter into diplomatic relations
with Israel?" Ulbricht did not answer right away. Obviously my
question had caught him by surprise. He had been Nasser's guest
earlier that year. It took him exactly eighteen seconds to formulate
his answer: "The Jewish people have suffered much at the hands
of fascism. We do have a good many friends among the Jews, men
who fought fascism side by side with our underground fighters.
I like the Jewish people. If the Government of Israel should ever
come to the conclusion that its past policies have helped imperialism; if they should make peace with their Arab neighbours; if
they should install a progressive, humanitarian government, their
outstretched hand would not be rejected by us."

I mulled over this answer long after the interview had ended
and came to the conclusion that Ulbricht had elegantly evaded my
question. Next question: "You visited President Nasser of Egypt.
Did you discuss the Israeli situation with him? How did you like
your trip?" Answer: "It was a very pleasant trip. Nasser has done
much for his people. Many vitally important reforms were initiated
by his government. The President's reception was cordial and he
did everything to make our stay memorable and pleasant. We enjoyed the trip tremendously. No, we did not discuss anything
except German-Arab relations with the President."

The last minutes of the interview dealt with the German
quetion. "The problem is one of non-recognition", Ulbricht

explained. "Obviously, two German states exist side by side — let us ignore the city of West Berlin for a moment. We are prepared to accept the existence of West Germany. But they steadfastly refuse to accept our existence. The Hallstein doctrine is only part of the story. Our passports are not accepted by West German officials. Our ice-hockey players cannot go to international meets, if they are held in the West. Representatives of our cultural agencies cannot move freely in West Germany. Some of our press representatives were recently arrested in West Germany — they had travelled there on a peaceful visit. Werner Micke of the *Berliner Zeitung* was one of them.

"How can we effectively deal with a government which claims that we do not exist? Notes we send them are never answered. They are bending over backward trying to ignore us. Do you know that West Germany has never signed a document which was also signed by us? By signing such a paper, they would have to admit by inference that we exist. They refuse to do this. Childish? Yes, if one individual should act that way toward another, I would call it childish. But in international relations? It ceases to be childish. It is outright criminal!

"Tell the world that we exist. Give them your impressions of our State, good or bad. Not everything is perfect here. We know it. We had to build from scratch after history's most devastating war. But build we did. And we do exist. The West says they want our people to have free unhampered elections. We have had them for many years. Did they have free elections? Where is the Communist Party on their election platforms? There is no real freedom in West Germany. Our State is the only true Germany — anti-fascist, peace-loving, defending the peace against the revanchist dreams of West Germany's General Staff." Ulbricht rose and showed me to the door. He had given me thirty-two minutes instead of the fifteen planned originally. Wolf was waiting outside the Chairman's office. "It is the first time that the Chief has given more than five minutes over the allotted time to any visiting foreign journalist", he said. "He must have liked you!"

I drove back to my hotel. I had to file my final report and start packing. The next morning I was to fly back to Canada.

WHERE DO WE GO FROM HERE?

East Germany has an airport of her own. Unlike West Berlin's Tempelhof it is situated well outside the city proper. It is the home base of the GDR's national airline *Interflug*.

In contrast to West Germany's *Lufthansa, Interflug* does not fly to Western countries. Its operations are limited to Warsaw Pact nations. But it is possible for travellers who wish to fly from East Berlin to the West to do so. The Polish airline *Lot* makes a scheduled stop in East Berlin on its Warsaw-Brussels run. I reached the airport rather late — eight minutes before flight time. As a Government guest I received preferential treatment. My bags were not searched. I received a quick exit permit. (Foreigners, like East Germans, require printed exit permits — holders of Western passports usually receive them as a formality.) When I finally reached my airplane two *Vopos* stood there checking passengers for the second time. The only other country where I had observed this practice was Cuba. — They checked me in. The plane warmed its engines and started its run. Eight minutes later we flew over the Berlin wall — plainly visible below us. From above it looked like a toy structure. The barbed wire entanglements on the other side of West Berlin were barely visible. One hour later we had crossed the GDR and were flying over the Federal Republic. How strangely peaceful the two hostile camps looked from ten thousand feet up.

Thirty years ago all this had been one undivided country bent on war and destruction. Now two states had arisen from the ashes of one. Would they survive? West Germany had trained her citizens and her youth to believe that there could be but one indivisible Germany and that the smaller of the two German states had come into being against the will of its people; it would be up to the West to free its enslaved population. East Germany had indoctrinated its youth and had convinced the greater part of their parents that East Germany was the only true and democratic

Germany and that the Federal Republic was an unrepentant neo-Nazi State. As I flew over the divided land, I felt clearly that the schism would last. Different doctrines had remoulded the character of each side. Two political organisms had indeed become two nations. What creates a nation? Common interests, a common philosophy, a common state of mind. Britain and the United States both speak the same language but they became two nations when the British colonials of the New World suddenly discovered a new historic revolutionary philosophy of life. A common language and a common religion do not make nations. Switzerland — home of four different languages and two major religions — is one of the world's most cohesive nations. Germany, land of one language, never was. German unity was built on a series of successful aggressive wars rather late in her history. Bismark forged German unity in 1871. It lasted only seventy-four years. The two German states of our day have lasted the better part of one generation.

When Hitler's Reich collapsed, Germany's political structure evaporated. A new one had to be built. Each occupation zone followed the political philosophy of its new masters. The three Western zones adopted Western democracy. The Russian zone copied the Soviet system. West Germany claims that the GDR's communism is completely un-German. It is. But so is their Western type of democracy. Neither system has ever ruled Germany before. Communism actually is of German origin, developed by Karl Marx and Friedrich Engels. To this extent, East German communism is actually more German than West German democracy. Germany never had real democracy, not even during the Weimar Republic. Both Western democracy and communism are equally new to the Germans; neither is historically rooted in the people. The seeds of the two German states were sown by Adolf Hitler when he attacked the Soviet Union June 22, 1941. This attack forged the grand coalition of the Second World War making the Western democracies allies of the Soviet Union. It took both parts of the alliance to destroy the Nazi State and made both parties partners in the German occupation. This started the division of Germany.

Both West and East Germany are the children of the Grand Alliance of World War II. Their unremitting struggle is merely the continuation of the war mankind had hoped to end forever in 1945. The cold war is equally disastrous for both West and East and will eventually bring back a militant West Germany. Unless the two German states can find a way of living together peacefully all the sacrifices of the Second World War will have been in vain.

As the plane slowly rolled to a stop on the landing strip of the Brussels airport, I decided to report what I had seen, not only to the readers of my newspaper, but to the public at large.

FREQUENTLY USED ABBREVIATIONS

CDU: Christlich-Demokratische Union (Christian Democratic Union)

CSU: Christlich Soziale Union (Christian Social Union)

GDR: German Democratic Republic

LPG: Landwirtschaftliche Produktionsgemeinschaft (Agricutural Production Cooperative)

SED: Sozialistische Einheitspartei Deutschlands (Socialist Unity Party of Germany)

SPD: Sozialdemokratische Partei Deutschlands (Social Democratic Party of Germany)